Talking to the Other

Jacob said to Esau: I have seen your face as if seeing the face of God and you have received me favourably.

(Genesis 33:10)

Talking to the Other

Jewish Interfaith Dialogue with Christians and Muslims

Jonathan Magonet

I.B. TAURIS
LONDON · NEW YORK

The publication of this book was made possible
through a subsidy from the Stone Ashdown Trust

Published in 2003 by I.B.Tauris & Co Ltd
6 Salem Road, London W2 4BU
175 Fifth Avenue, New York NY 10010
www.ibtauris.com

In the United States and Canada distributed by Palgrave Macmillan
a division of St. Martin's Press
175 Fifth Avenue, New York NY 10010

ISBN 1 86064 905 X

A full CIP record for this book is available from the British Library

Typeset in Caslon by Dexter Haven Associates, London
Printed and bound in Great Britain by MPG Books, Bodmin

Contents

Foreword

by Prince Hassan bin Tallal

> Do you not see that God sends down water from the sky, by which We bring forth
> fruits of different colours? – and in the mountains, too, there are white and red tracks
> of different shades, as well as black? And of human beings, beasts and cattle, there are
> also various colours.
>
> Holy Qur'an (35:27–8)

In 1965, Abraham Heschel – the great rabbi, spiritual teacher and professor
at the Jewish Theological Seminary in New York – asked the question: on
what basis do people of different religious commitments meet each other?
He immediately answered himself by speaking of the identical traits that
humans share: a voice, a face, fear, hope, the capacity to trust. But then the
rabbi answered his question again by speaking of the differences through
which religion is revealed: 'Revelation is always an accommodation to the
capacity of man. No two minds are alike, just as no two faces are alike.
The voice of God reaches the spirit of man in a variety of ways, in a
multiplicity of languages. One truth comes to expression in many ways of
understanding.'

It is more than three decades now since I had the pleasure of first
discussing ideas about interfaith dialogue with Professor Rabbi Magonet,
the author of this book. We agreed then, as now, on the importance of
mutual understanding between adherents of the sibling faiths of Judaism,
Christianity and Islam. At that time, merely for such conversations to take
place anywhere in the world was unusual and – to some – even shocking,
in a way which can hardly be imagined today. Rabbi Magonet undertook
a project for interfaith dialogue which developed into the well-known
meetings at Bendorf, now part of a Standing Conference of Jews, Christians
and Muslims in Europe.

Meanwhile I promoted interfaith dialogue between Jews, Christians
and Muslims in a series of encounters in Windsor and Amman. At our
early meetings, we could not imagine what phases of fear and acceptance
we would pass through over the course of 25 years to produce a single page

of principles for Abrahamic dialogue: begin with commonality; emphasise the association between theology and practicality; recognise the political and economic dimensions of interfaith dialogue; take into account the Enlightenment tradition; embrace the principle of no coercion; uphold the right to proclaim one's own religion; reconsider the content of education; ensure a free flow of information; be courageous in looking afresh at, first, our own, and, secondly, each other's texts, heritage and history; accept responsibility for words and actions at all levels; develop a civilised framework for disagreement.

Professor Rabbi Magonet has taken a parallel approach with the essays below: his introduction voices a personal and humane urge to strengthen our commonalities, followed by an opening section dealing with the question of how to put theory into practice. Specific perceptions of each other's characteristics by members of the three monotheistic faiths precede a documentation of interfaith in the Middle Eastern context – where the political and economic dimensions, philosophical traditions and issues of coercion, rights, education, freedom, courage, responsibility and the capacity to disagree peacefully are certainly extremely relevant.

The great religions together recognise today that, if globalisation is to succeed and civilisation benefit all people, shared human imperatives must outweigh economic and political expediencies. The question is how to evoke or instill the common values in the broader community. As a race, we seem to suffer a lack of political and economic will at the same time as thinking that all solutions must be political and economic. Politics and economics provide means for material security, but people cannot live with each other without some security of identity, a sense of dignity and respect for others which is the 'soft security' of self; such security is not innate but learned and experienced.

According to Islam, many values can be invoked in encouraging active altruism: *ukhowwah* – brotherhood promoting the bonds of human fraternity, *adl* – enforcing a system of individual and social obligations, and *ihsan* – beneficence, which supplements *ukhowwah* and *adl* with charitable acts. There are also the more institutionalised systems of *waqf* and *zakat*, which pool financial donations for disbursement to the poor and for the common good.

In the chapter entitled 'The Challenges Facing the Muslim Community', Professor Magonet outlines a number of similarities and differences between Jewish and Muslim historical experiences and religious thought. As he comments, 'We share the conviction that love, compassion, friendship, mercy and pity for a suffering world are at the heart of everything our two faiths stand for, despite the ways in which both of our traditions have been slandered over the centuries as lacking in such values'.

Jewish and Muslim thinkers today continue to emphasise the possibility – or, indeed, inevitability – of peaceful co-existence. As the Jewish scholar Professor Shimon Shamir recently commented during a documentation of such thinking, 'In the life of a movement, sometimes trend is more important than volume … Paradoxically, interest in theories and methods of mutual acceptance grows precisely when extremism looms large.'

Parallels between the Holy Qur'an, the Torah and the Old and New Testaments indicate that an ethic of human solidarity, a sense of responsibility and an impulse towards altruism are supposed to accompany the material charity which is a common theme in our three faiths. If everybody who professed monotheism obeyed the Ten Commandments, universal values would be well within reach. Spiritual altruism – the reaching out to acknowledge, understand and respect each other's dignity and humanity – is the necessary counterpart if altruism is not to degenerate into mere patronage. The spirit of this altruistic love is perhaps not described so well by 'charity' in its modern sense as by the Latin biblical term *caritas*. It is powerfully illustrated in a number of places in the New Testament. One might recall Jesus's words to the crowd who would stone the adultress, 'Let him who is without sin among you cast the first stone' (John 8:3–9); and the famous parable of the Good Samaritan, who set aside the ideological divide between himself and the victim of a robbery in order to help him (Luke 10:25–37).

When we neglect the spirit of human solidarity in our faiths, we abandon the middle ground – which is our shared heritage and should be our most sacred space – to be occupied by hatred, division, exclusion, political infighting and isolationism. Well might Rabbi Tony Bayfield bitterly have lamented the neglect of that common ground, which he described as 'the failure of Jewish, Christian and Muslim leaders alike to denounce fundamentalism and to stand together in affirmation of shared values, in particular values relating to the sanctity of life and the central role of religion to challenge power, not to seize it for coercive purposes'.

As Professor Magonet himself knows well, and as he discusses in the chapter titled 'Risk-taking in Religious Dialogue', the desire to find common ground and common solutions between faiths means taking risks and crossing boundaries. There is no shortage of people ready to criticise those leaders – sadly, especially those religious leaders – who are willing to communicate, to share ideas and promote diversity in the interests of greater knowledge and greater security for all. In the face of such opposition, I agree with Professor Shamir when he says that it may be time to turn our attention from 'the threat projected by the radicals to the promise implied by the liberals.'

It might be added here that these principles apply to intrafaith as well as interfaith dialogue. It should be a matter for concern that there is so little conversation between Sunnis and Shi'ites today, or even between the four schools of orthodox Sunni Islam. It is regrettable that there is not more contact and dialogue between Jewish peace movements in Israel and orthodox Jews in Europe and the US. Baptist Christianity in Florida has little to do with Catholicism in Guadaloupe. People share identities based on their cultures as well as their religions: a Jordanian Sunni may well have more in common with a Jordanian Catholic than with a Moroccan Sufi or an American Shi'ite. It is especially important today to recognise that no religion is inherently a geo-political entity.

Nor do the principles of interfaith dialogue exclude the broad common ground shared with the secular. Rabbi Albert Friedlander reminded religious representatives of the need to cultivate solidarity, not only between and within faiths, but among all people in a world which recognises religion as a major part of the social dimension, but not as its totality: 'As the spokespersons of religion we sometimes forget that all humanity is bound together by social contracts where religion is not given automatic authority: we have to earn it. We do not possess the monopoly of ethical insights.'

Our secular codes – the Universal Declaration of Human Rights and the various declarations based on it – may largely consist of concessions from the law of war, but they provide a legal structure which coincides in important respects with the religious injunctions concerning treatment of other human beings. Hans Küng's important work with the Declaration of Human Responsibilities indicates that a shared code of behaviour for us all is not only possible but already exists in potentia; now, the task is one of dialogue and endorsement, which is why interfaith conversation and publication continues to be one of the most effective tools in promoting understanding and peace between and within cultures.

As part of our various faiths in God it behoves us to have faith in our one humanity, in all its variety, as a creation by the Divine in His image. Those who oppose diversity and difference claim they have the monopoly upon a single truth. There is no such monopoly. The real enemies – those who aim to destroy human civilisation in the name of distorted and perverted ideologies – are acting with great energy against God's creation. We need today not just speakers for human ideals; we need 'moral grandeur and spiritual audacity'. It is urgent that the people of the middle ground in every religion and society seek to outdo the extremists in renewed energy and commitment for humanity's cause.

A Muslim tradition of Jesus reports: 'Christ said, "Till when do you describe the road to travellers by night while you yourselves remain behind with the perplexed? Only a little religious knowledge suffices, but many should be your deeds."' It does not seem to me at all surprising that a Muslim reference to Christ may introduce the thinking of a distinguished (and most unperplexed) Jewish scholar and participant in interfaith dialogue. The reader will find in this volume that both the extent of Professor Rabbi Magonet's religious knowledge and the distance he is prepared to accompany travellers are very great. By publishing this collection of essays, which I hope will inspire the widest possible audience, Professor Magonet adds to a list of many deeds of his that have bettered and will continue to better our understanding of each other and, through each other, our understanding of humanity and God.

Prince Hassan bin Tallal

Preface

My colleague, Rabbi Lionel Blue, who is a true pioneer in the area of interfaith dialogue, and who appears from time to time in these pages, finds my prose too tentative. Perhaps he is right. But the world of interfaith relations is a delicate one, with many traps for the unwary and an infinite number of potential misunderstandings. So some caution is warranted in how things are expressed. It has been suggested that for dialogue to succeed, those engaged in it should show the outside world the places where they are in agreement, while they can focus on where they disagree within the process. There are certainly short-term gains in such an approach. But for the longer term there are no secrets any more, and the difficulties and divisions are present for all to see. As dialogue moves from a marginal exercise for a few into something on which the spotlight is increasingly turned, and becomes something on which more and more hopes are lodged, the issues, the problems and the opportunities have to become ever-more transparent.

There are any number of people I want to thank for what they have given me throughout the stages of my own development in the world of interfaith dialogue. First and foremost Lionel Blue and Leslie Shepard, both of whom were extraordinarily influential at an important stage in my life. Many others have been religious 'teachers' in the broadest sense of the term at different stages in my own journey. If I name only a few here it is because they are the ones who have accompanied me and continue to do so even when they are no longer alive. Among Christians Anneliese Debray, Pastor Rudolf Stamm, Pastor Winfried Maechler, Pastor Hermann Denkers, Dr Charlotte Klein, Rektor Heinrich Spaemann, Gisela Hommel, Edith Möser, Ute Stamm, Fr Gordian Marshall, the Rev. Marcus Braybrook, Dr John Bowden, Dr Dorothee von Tippelskirch, Dr Sung He Lee Linke, the Rev. Ruth Scott, Karen Armstrong and Hans Küng; among Muslims, Professor Umar von Ehrenfels, the Sufi mystic Salah

Eid, Dr Smail Balic, Dr Khalid Duran, Professor Khurshid Ahmad, Dr Zaki Badawi, Dr Farid Esak, Sheikh Bashir Dultz, Chadigah Kissel, Amira Abdin, Halima Krausen, HRH Prince Hassan bin Tallal.

My thanks are due to Iradj Bagherzade and Turi Munthe of I.B. Tauris for helping me turn a collection of essays into a coherent book and Richard Stone of the Stone Ashdown Trust, himself a pioneer and activist in Jewish–Muslim relations, for underwriting the project.

A final tribute belongs to my wife Dorothea for sharing important parts of this journey with me, especially in the early years. But she has brought also her own wisdom, bound up with the Alexander Technique which she teaches and exemplifies. It has a physical reality that can only be experienced, but it carries also a partially articulated philosophy about pausing and waiting before acting. That too fits in well with the extraordinary process that turns the rough and tumble of meetings and encounters into something we call 'dialogue'.

Jonathan Magonet
April 2002

1
Interfaith Dialogue – A Personal Introduction

This book is over 30 years in the making. But they are years made up of fragments. Moments of encounter, breakthroughs in understanding, papers and lectures delivered and received, extraordinary friendships and embarrassing mistakes – above all, late-night conversations at conference centres, in hotel lobbies, railway station waiting rooms and cafes – wherever the journey led me. And behind such opportunities for meeting and learning, endless hours of hectic work – preparing conferences, resolving misunderstandings, frenzied translations of late-arriving lectures, sweating over recalcitrant photocopy machines, stuffing envelopes and hunting for that extra sum of money to ensure that a particular programme could actually take place. Much of the work of interfaith dialogue goes on behind the scenes and owes a lot to an invisible army of 'enablers'. To the above must be added occasional moments of reflection on the mysteries of human interaction and the question of what the Jewish religion has to offer to a world of many religions, or of none, in the opening years of the twenty-first century.

The immediate trigger for finally writing this book is the event that shattered our understanding throughout the world about how life needs to be conducted between peoples of different religious faiths in this new millennium. The attack on the World Trade Centre in New York on 11 September 2001 brought home the horror of terrorism as never before. But it also revealed the depth of our ignorance of one another, and hence the mistrust and often hostility between different faith communities.

President Bush's initial talk of a crusade unleashed memories of the horrors perpetrated in the name of Christianity in the Middle Ages. The language of 'Jihad', used almost cynically by the supporters of terror to summon Muslims to a holy war against the demon America, and used uncritically by our own media, fed Western fears and fantasies about the nature of Islam. There is a massive task of education and rethinking that needs to be done alongside the actions taken at least to curtail the power of those who practise terror. Part of that task is also to attempt to eliminate the injustices, poverty and despair that breed the desperation that leads to terror.

Against this background, this book sets out to address two questions. Firstly, what can Judaism contribute out of its tradition and teachings to interfaith dialogue – issues such as pluralism, multicultural society, conflict resolution and universal values? And secondly, what is the actual experience, and what issues arise for Jews and their partners, particularly Christians and Muslims, when Jews engage in dialogue?

Of course, the theory and practice are not totally separated. It is precisely in the course of the dialogue itself that one discovers the questions that need to be addressed to Judaism, and the answers too are influenced by what the partner brings to the encounter. Nevertheless, the book is conceived in two parts. The first deals with the particular values that Judaism brings to a range of dialogue-related issues, the second with my own experience, particularly in addressing Christians and Muslims.

To the latter part there is a second element – namely, how does one address 'the folks back home', one's co-religionists who may view the whole enterprise with suspicion or at best scepticism. Yet this element is crucial if dialogue is to change attitudes and develop new adherents.

In order to understand Jewish values and teachings it is helpful to have some background knowledge of Judaism: where we come from, what forces have shaped us. So much of Jewish history is actually the result of interaction with surrounding nations and religions, though 'dialogue' has rarely been the appropriate term to understand such interactions. Aspects of this history will be given where appropriate. At this point it is helpful to point to one particular factor. Judaism is composed of two elements. Judaism is the religious expression of a particular people, and the interaction between faith and peoplehood is a constantly changing factor, particularly in the past few centuries. This twofold combination makes it radically different from either Christianity or Islam, at least in theory, and leads to some confusion for those who think of religions purely in terms of a community of believers.

To round off the book, a number of appendices document important multifaith events that sadly relate to the Israel–Palestine conflict. Since the platform for a rabbi tends to be the pulpit, I have included two sermons that reflect on the event of 11 September and the Israel–Palestine conflict, the latter delivered to a mixed Jewish-Christian-Muslim audience. At the end is a contemporary Jewish prayer on the value and need for interfaith dialogue.

Since dialogue is about encountering the 'other' in their own terms, it feels appropriate to introduce myself and some stages in my own journey. I have always been struck by a line from Molière's *Bourgeouis Gentillhomme*, at least insofar as I remember it from schoolboy French. In his quest to become a 'gentleman', Molière's comic hero takes lessons in the arts of civilised behaviour, including dancing and fencing. One of his teachers introduces him to the concepts of poetry and prose. This leads to the moment of revelation when he discovers 'I've been speaking prose all my life and I never knew it!'

While putting together this book, I began to realise that in a variety of ways I have been 'speaking dialogue' for most of my life and have only gradually come to know it. So inevitably some of what is to be found in this book is personal. Dialogue is something that I 'do' – and have done throughout my career as a rabbi. But it is also about who I am, or at least seek to be. So I think it is helpful to sketch out something of my own journey that has led a middle-class, British Jewish boy out of a comfortable ghetto into encounters and friendships, as well as challenges and responsibilities, I could never have imagined.

The very nature of the Jewish experience of the last century places us at the heart of issues that affect the whole of society, and we have to respond as best we can. It is particularly the responsibility of Jews who are committed to the Reform or Liberal end of the spectrum of Jewish religious practice to be at the forefront of the dialogue with modernity in all its various guises, and obviously at the interface with the outer world and other faith traditions. The times determine what is essential, and the situation of Jews in an open society is not merely affected by outside forces but to a large extent defined by them. So areas like interfaith dialogue, that might have seemed marginal at various times in the past, are now much more central.

My own experience of interfaith work began before I qualified as a rabbi. Of course on one level, any Jew growing up in England, attending school and university, faces on a daily basis an outside world that is overtly Christian. Decisions about whether to attend Christian services at school, how to cope with Christmas, what to do about the occasional manifestation of antisemitism – these are all part of the unconscious forces that impinge upon one's Jewish identity.

But I owe my first conscious approach to Jewish-Christian dialogue to Rabbi Lionel Blue. One of the first graduates of Leo Baeck College, Lionel had once contemplated conversion to Christianity while still a student at Oxford University, and had explored many aspects of the religion.[1] When he entered the rabbinate it was with a great awareness of the values, particularly in the area of personal spirituality, that he had acquired from his explorations of Christianity. When he and I collaborated in organising the youth section of the World Union for Progressive Judaism during the early sixties, I learnt from him to respect religious teachers and teachings, from whatever source they came. We were very conscious at the time that our own Jewish world was lacking in spiritual leaders as a direct consequence of the war. A generation of rabbis and teachers was missing, and in our own rabbinic training we were aware that we lacked models and indeed 'father figures' against whom to measure our own spiritual growth.

The Judaism that I had experienced in my childhood in an orthodox synagogue in south London was very uninspiring, geared to a series of practical dos and don'ts without much intellectual or spiritual underpinning. The Reform world that I entered through the youth movement was itself not much more than a social club with good ethical intentions but limited Jewish content. The few rabbis available were good congregational workers but lacked the charisma and overt spiritual grandeur that I was looking for in my somewhat romantic way. What Lionel managed to do was find amongst his acquaintances people with a far clearer grasp of their own spiritual centre. Amongst them was Leslie Shepard, an English folklorist, Reichian analyst and Vedantist who taught me my first guitar chords, but, as we only half-jokingly put it, helped us keep our metaphysics straight. Certainly it was in dialogue with such people that we began to clarify what was uniquely Jewish and what was missing in the Judaism that we saw around us. I suspect that we were experiencing in our own small world something of the spirit of the sixties. That decade was a powerful time for me personally, enhanced by living through the Six-Day War in Jerusalem, where I found a circle of Jewish writers, artists and teachers who gave me back some confidence in Jewish spirituality as well.

Looking back, especially from my position as principal of Leo Baeck College, I can see that we were in the process of defining a kind of Judaism and spiritual searching that was appropriate for a postwar, emerging pluralistic society in Britain and elsewhere. Old barriers between religious communities were breaking down, and indeed the people who were committed to a religion often felt themselves to be in a minority in a growing secular environment. It was this need to create alliances in such a situation that led to one particular initiative from Lionel that I helped develop. Our work was triggered by the success in elections of the neo-Nazi party in Germany and concerns about a fascist revival. Lionel posed the question: in Germany the only ideology offered after the war was that of the *Wirtschaftswunder*: ever-growing material success. To put it crudely, the answer to every spiritual problem was to buy a new refrigerator! The only groups that seemed to be offering any ideological input into this vacuum were the right-wing movements – this predated the emergence of the new left.

So who was offering a more universal, international, spiritual ideology to counter them? Lionel thought of creating a kind of alliance of the 'good guys' – religious youth movements, organisations that arranged work camps in underprivileged areas, those that sought to do reconciliation work. Out of this emerged an organisation with the rather threatening title 'European Action'. It had a short-lived career promoting a few conferences and work camps. We planned one such programme in Wolfsburg, the home of Volkswagen, where there had been a large support for the neo-Nazi party and elections were soon to be held. With the help of a local pastor we arranged for a conference, some public lectures and a work camp activity in the area. (Voluntary work camps were by then beginning to disappear, partly because it was difficult to find appropriate work. We ended up painting a locomotive in a children's playground as our contribution to world peace!)

The organisation did not survive very long. One of the main reasons was what turned out to be a key lesson for us. It was one thing to invite on board organisations that saw themselves as working towards the same religious goals, but it was quite another to deal with the political manoeuvring and questions of official representation and voting rights that took place from the very beginning. I suspect we were just naive about the whole business and could have 'pulled it off' with more experience – but we learnt that whereas we could work with individuals whom we came to know and trust, working with existing institutions was extremely difficult, time-consuming and disillusioning.

Then something new crystallised what we were trying to do. In the period leading up to the Six-Day War, Lionel pointed out that beyond the limited political entities of Israel and the Arab states were the three great monotheistic faiths, with many shared beliefs. Could they not create channels for mutual understanding that would help resolve the political conflict? Together with Pastor Winfried Maechler of the Evangelische Akademie in Berlin and other Christian and Muslim colleagues, they arranged the first meetings in Berlin to try to build such new relationships. This time the organisation we set up was called the Standing Conference of Jews, Christians and Muslims in Europe, which meant that it only existed when a conference was held. Though the Berlin Akademie, the Leo Baeck College in London, the German Muslim League in Bonn and the Hedwig Dransfeld Haus in Bendorf are partners in creating the conferences, it remains without organisation and officers but has continued to be effective for over 30 years.

I have rather moved ahead of my own personal story and would like to return to that for a moment. The conferences for Jewish young people that Lionel and I organised in Holland in the early sixties brought us into contact with young Jews from Germany. They challenged us by pointing out that many Jewish organisations invited them to attend conferences abroad, but no-one came to Germany. We took up the challenge by arranging the first international Jewish youth conference in Berlin since the war. I myself hitched a ride to Berlin with these young people, as I did not want to impose something on others I was not prepared to experience for myself. It was on returning from my visit there that I knew that I had decided to become a rabbi, so the experience of encountering Germany has had a profound effect on my subsequent religious journey.

I have to admit that I found Germany attractive for a variety of reasons, not all of them particularly religious. At school I had had a year of German and my teacher had introduced me to the plays of Brecht. Lionel introduced me to Lotte Lenya singing the marvellous melodies of Kurt Weill, and I found myself particularly drawn to that pre-war world of German culture, with its strong Jewish component. Also, I met on my travels a number of young, left-wing German pastors who became friends and who opened up for me a very different Germany from the one of Jewish fears and fantasy. Or rather, in their struggle as a postwar generation to build a new Germany, I found a moving counterpoint to our own attempts to rebuild Jewish life in Europe after the catastrophe of the Shoah (Holocaust). What became tragically clear to me was that there existed in Germany young people, both Jewish and non-Jewish, who were unable to understand or come to terms with their past. They could not communicate with their parents – the Germans because of what they might have done in the war, and the Jews because their parents could not justify why they had remained or settled in Germany. And yet these same young people whom, it seemed to me, somehow held the key to each other's dilemma, never met. Perhaps in the feelings of frustration at this lack of communication my own interest in dialogue was unconsciously born.

The decisive factor in changing my approach to the whole issue was the meeting with Anneliese Debray, the director of what was then a Catholic conference centre, the Hedwig Dransfeld Haus, Bendorf/Rhein. Anneliese was a remarkable woman who set about transforming the Haus into a centre for reconciliation work after the war. She instituted German-Polish and German-French conferences, transformed the Haus into an ecumenical centre and then an interfaith one, initially by seeking out Jews with whom to dialogue and subsequently Muslims. I first visited the Haus one Whitsun with some fellow rabbinic students, and the impact of our presence was so powerful that we were invited to the summer Christian bible study week that same year. The result was to transform it into what has become the annual Jewish-Christian Bible Week, now in existence for well over 30 years.

A number of elements were important for me in these early encounters, firstly the seriousness with which the German participants approached religion, and their hunger to learn about Judaism. I am, and was at the time, aware of the many dimensions to this curiosity, including amongst some a kind of neurotic philosemitism, a desire to 'love' Jews out of a feeling of guilt about the past. And yet beyond that, there was a genuine interest, because of both the recent past and their curiosity about the origins of Christianity itself and the Jewish background of Jesus. My faltering German did not allow me to understand all that was going on in those early years, but I did come to value many of the participants and the genuineness of their searching. Indeed, the kind of questions they posed to me about Jews and Judaism went far deeper than anything I had experienced in my own community. Religion here was a live issue, and the questions that were asked and the answers that were given had consequences for the lives of those who asked them.

I have no doubt that there are factors on my part that are also less than purely holy. It was enormously flattering to be suddenly so important in the lives of these people. With my relatively limited knowledge of Judaism I was being asked very profound questions which sent me scurrying back to my books, but which also required me to mine my own spiritual intuition. Nor was this simply a one-way traffic. Many people became part of a circle of spiritual teachers and colleagues, each very different, but each part of a nourishing fellowship. In a way, the two annual Bendorf Conferences, the Jewish-Christian-Muslim (JCM) Student Conference in the spring and the Jewish-Christian Bible Week in the summer, remain for me touchstones on my religious journey, and they have generated enormous spiritual gifts for others. Moreover, they have become models for what is possible, particularly in the complex dialogue between Jews and Muslims, that are important far beyond their immediate impact. (I will explore something of the lessons obtained from the JCM conferences in the chapter on 'Risk-taking in Religious Dialogue'.)

This kind of religious encounter, which falls under the label 'dialogue', is about the meeting of minds and spirits in an attempt to understand and develop a shared commitment to the spiritual life of this society. In most cases it is the personal relationship that comes first; the accident of a particular religious background is secondary, or rather is merely the excuse that has brought us together. Again I have to stress this, because I believe that it is the mutual trust and love that this kind of meeting generates that allows each of us to operate effectively and constructively within our own home communities, and the institutional frameworks for interfaith dialogue that we support. People whose lives are dedicated to giving to others, whether it is in the ministry or other caring professions, need such opportunities to recharge their spiritual batteries and be reassured that their situation, in which they often feel isolated, is not unique, and that others share their commitments. These conferences are a kind of 'safe space' in which much may happen if people are prepared to allow it. The dialogue with the other is as much a dialogue with oneself.

Unfortunately, dialogue is often regarded as a kind of luxury for a few people on the edge of their own religious communities. A nice hobby but of no significance in terms of the real things we should be doing within our own religious home.

Nevertheless, sometimes it is precisely that which seems peripheral that may prove of value for our inner concerns. Moreover, there are urgent issues within our society as a whole that may overshadow our self-absorption and make our relationship with others especially important.

I am not naive about the difficulties of creating and supporting a multicultural society – they will form the basis of chapter 3. Reason and common sense alone do not touch the emotional issues that underlie intercommunity prejudices and fears. Something more is needed if we are to treat the underlying problems and emotions and resist those who exploit differences for their own personal or political ends. Dialogue is the only approach I know that builds trust, mutual respect, friendship and love. The first step is the same as it is in every other kind of relationship – we have to learn how to listen to each other, to those who are 'other', to take a chance on meeting and to create the frameworks for sustaining these contacts and deepening them.

There is a verse in the Psalms which says '*bikkesh shalom v'rod'fehu*', 'Seek peace and pursue it' (Psalm 34:15). The rabbis pointed out that for most other commandments, we are only instructed to do them when they come our way – but when it comes to peace, we are to be actively engaged in seeking it out, working for it and maintaining it. Interfaith dialogue is one of the tools available to us for seeking peace and pursuing it. It is not peripheral to our religious task today, but absolutely central.

2
The Challenge to Judaism of Interfaith Dialogue

There is undoubtedly considerable ambivalence about interfaith dialogue both within Jewish tradition and amongst Jews today. We are torn between welcoming the possibilities of building better relationships with all peoples and faiths and an anxiety about what the effect will be upon us, and indeed upon our very survival as a unique people with a unique perception of God. A variety of factors contribute to that anxiety. They include the historical memory of our minority status among other faiths in the Middle Ages and the experience of forced conversion to Christianity, and sometimes also to Islam. Undoubtedly, part of our fear today is coloured by the traumatic events of the twentieth century when one-third of the Jewish people were exterminated. Another factor is the seemingly insoluble range of issues surrounding the relationship of the state of Israel to its Arab neighbours and above all the Palestinian people, a problem compounded by the opportunity it provides for recurrent outbreaks of antisemitic activity against Diaspora Jewish communities. Beneath the surface is an awareness of our vulnerability as a people through sheer lack of numbers. There are between 15 and 16 million Jews in the world. Put us on a chart next to the hundreds of millions of Christians and Muslims, let alone other faiths, and we would hardly appear.

The roots of this uncertainty about the value and risks of interfaith dialogue can be found in the earliest periods of Jewish history. One reason for such ambivalence seems to be connected to the very idea of the oneness or unity of God. As the children of Israel in the biblical period struggled to understand the nature and demands of their God, they found themselves both attracted to and repelled by the religions of the nations that surrounded them. They rejected the rituals, values and mythologies of their neighbours because these often offended their sense of sexual propriety or human justice. But internally they were also engaged in a constant struggle to establish their own understanding of God, and of God's demands on them as a people, in a variety of changing circumstances. If one simply follows the biblical record, the descendants of the patriarch Abraham went from a semi-nomadic existence through a period of slavery in Egypt, affected by the culture and religious beliefs of that nation, through the experience of wandering in the wilderness, to a settled existence in the land of Canaan – all of which exposed them to very different concepts and experiences of the divine. They created a kingdom and even a small empire, but then experienced disintegration into two conflicting kingdoms with different religious approaches, and finally the horrors of national destruction and exile from their land in Babylon – the other major centre, alongside Egypt, of religious and cultural traditions. (As a small example of the influences of both of these 'world powers' of the time, the Bible employs two numbering systems, one using 'ten' as the base, taken from Egypt, the other using 'sixty' as a base, taken from Babylon.) The defeat of the nation must have meant to many the defeat of their God, and might have led to the end of their existence as a people and as a faith community. But through the power of the teachings of their prophets, they were able to transform their seeming defeat into a larger conception of God's plans for them, and of God's powers that could embrace the entire world.

Through all these experiences and challenges, they learnt to guard jealously and zealously their understanding and experience of the 'oneness', the 'otherness', the omnipotence and the universal nature of the God who addressed them and to whom they were tied with a legal covenant and bonds of love and devotion. This monotheism that came to be shared by the three 'Abrahamic' faiths, Judaism, Christianity and Islam, the idea of one God, a single unity behind the plurality of the world, suggests that all the rich diversity of life in its endless variety addresses itself to that one God. But do we learn from this that each individual and group are free to serve God in their own way, or do we hold the view instead that the one God can only be worshipped in 'one' way, our own particular way, in which case all other ways are wrong and untrue? It is only a small step from a monotheism that is universalistic and pluralistic to something we may call 'monolatry' that is possessive and monopolistic. This latter view is often accompanied by the need to correct by persuasion or by force the view of everyone else.

The Jewish people of the biblical and Roman periods knew that trap, the danger of identifying their own power and success with the will of God. It is a trap they fell into at times and one into which individuals and religious groups fall time and time again throughout history. While any group is passing through such a phase of triumphalism, interfaith dialogue as we understand it today is impossible. The very fact that the movement for such dialogue is growing is an indication that we are moving out of such a phase into the rediscovery of the possibilities of monotheistic pluralism.

But there is another situation that gave the Jewish people their ambivalence about dialogue. It was their other experience – not as a nation secure on their own territory but as a people in exile from their land. Their temple in Jerusalem, where direct communion with God was possible, had been razed to the ground. Jerusalem itself, their holy city, was likewise destroyed and occupied by others, initially the Babylonians and subsequently by the great Roman Empire. They were living as a minority – sometimes tolerated, more often exploited or persecuted – among the nations and religions of the world. As a minority, their survival was dependent upon the whims of those in power and the extent to which they could accommodate themselves to changing landscapes and circumstances. For 2000 years Jews lived under siege, trying to preserve their identity as a people and their perceived task as bearers of a particular religious tradition. Inevitably, throughout that period they were affected by and reacted against the religious influences around them, and yet also translated them into their own terms and assimilated them, in what was sometimes a fruitful two-way traffic.

Nevertheless, in such situations of social or political inequality, 'dialogue' in any formal sense becomes impossible, except perhaps in private encounters between individuals, because the two potential partners do not meet as equals. Too many issues of power and dependency, of implicit threat or coercion, stand in the way. Whether the host culture is sympathetic or aggressive, the possibility of exploitation is always present, and 'dialogue' becomes distorted.

One Jewish response to this reality of having a minority status was to put aside our pride of ownership of the idea of monotheism and to acknowledge the legitimacy of other paths to the one God. The rabbis, those who created what we know as Judaism in the post-biblical period, based on the opening stories of Genesis, identified seven basic moral laws that they taught were given by God to the sons of Noah, that is to say, to the whole of humanity. (We will explore them further in the chapter on 'The Ten Commandments and the Quest for Universal Values'.) These 'seven commandments of the descendants of Noah' gave Jews a moral checklist for assessing the behaviour of the surrounding nations and religious communities. In the Jewish view, any person who led a just life and obeyed these basic moral principles was assured a place in 'the world to come'. You did not have to go through Judaism to reach God. It is as if the experience of defeat and the bitter struggle to survive in exile among the nations had burned out of the Jewish people any claim to sole ownership of the truth about the ways and expectations of the one God, while they remained convinced that their way was the right one for themselves. The possibility of a genuine religious pluralism existed within the Jewish tradition, and is in some ways pre-visioned in the writings of the biblical prophets, most famously in the following passage that appears in the writings of Isaiah and of Micah.

> In the last days
> the mountain of the Eternal's house shall be set firm
> on the top of the mountains,
> and raised up above the hills.
> All nations shall flow towards it
> and many people shall go there, saying:
> 'Come, let us go up to the mountain of the Eternal,
> to the house of the God of Jacob,
> so that He may teach us about His ways
> and we may walk in His paths,
> for Torah (teaching) shall come out of Zion,

and the word of the Eternal from Jerusalem.'
Then He shall judge between many nations
and decide for great powers.
Then they shall hammer their swords into ploughshares
and their spears into pruning-hooks.
Nation shall not lift up sword against nation,
Never again shall they train for war.
But each man shall sit under his vine and under his fig-tree
and no one shall terrorise him,
for the mouth of the God of creation has spoken. (Micah 4:1–4)

Later, Jewish thought could make a distinction between the political reality of Jewish treatment at the hands of other nations, and this same belief that all people of religious conviction and righteous behaviour were acceptable to God. The most authoritative formulation about the Jewish view of Christianity and Islam belongs to the twelfth century Spanish philosopher and legal scholar Moses Maimonides (1135–1204). A Jew who was deeply imbued with the religious culture of Islam, he could see in the existence of Christianity and Islam, as daughter religions of Judaism, part of the divine plan for bringing God's rule to all humanity.

> But it is beyond the human mind to fathom the designs of the Creator, for our ways are not His ways, neither are our thoughts His thoughts. All these matters relating to Jesus of Nazareth and the Ishmaelite (Muhammad) who came after him, only served to clear the way for King Messiah, to prepare the whole world to worship God with one accord.[1]

Even earlier than Maimonides, in the Mekhilta, one of the earliest examples of rabbinic commentary on the Hebrew Bible, probably edited in the second century of the Common era, we find the following:

> The Torah, the revelation of God at Mt. Sinai, was given in public, for all to see, in the open. For if it had been given in the land of Israel, Israel would have said to the nations of the world: 'You have no share in it.' Therefore the Torah was given in the wilderness, in public, for all to see, in the open, and all who wish to receive it, let them come and receive it.[2]

But even the most tolerant and open-minded classical Jewish statements about other faiths do not quite share today's underlying assumptions about the nature and value of interfaith dialogue. Presumably individuals in the past had the same pluralistic views, but there is a radical difference today. It lies in the move from defining the nature and legitimacy of other faiths out of our own language and understanding of them, into accepting other faiths at their own self-valuation and self-definition. It is the move from what we may call religious 'colonialism' to religious 'pluralism'. And it is a difficult and disturbing change of perception.

There are many roots to this change. In the West we can point to the Enlightenment and the rise of humanistic thought as the intellectual sources. But there have also been transformations in our consciousness brought about by science and technology. The enormous advances in communications have given reality to the concept of the 'global village', and with it a knowledge of the fragility of our world under threat from nuclear and ecological disasters. We are aware as never before that we are a single humanity living in a finite and limited world, and that our survival depends on our mutual collaboration. This may seem a paradoxical idea in the face of so many regional conflicts and the emergence of so many new nations and people, each demanding their autonomy. But that may also be an expression of the need to preserve some sort of unique identity in a world becoming increasingly uniform. We are merely defining our individuality and our shared humanity in new terms in the face of the wider changes.

The political expression of this, which may also stand as a model for the new explorations of interfaith dialogue, is well summed up by Walter Lippmann: 'The complexity of modern civilization is a daily lesson in the necessity of not pressing any claim too far, of understanding opposing points of view, of seeking to reconcile them, of conducting matters so that there is some kind of harmony in a plural society.' I have used this secular, pragmatic view because we have to acknowledge that part of the interest in interfaith dialogue stems from changing social and political realities. For over a century religions in the West have found themselves under siege from secular culture and values. Many see this as threatening, but it can also be argued that the secular critique of organised religion has brought about a necessary self-purification and re-examination of things we had taken for granted. In the developed West we no longer have the religious power to enforce allegiance, and must compete in the marketplace with other ideologies. So we have had to learn to reach out in new ways to people and have come to realise that we share the same problems with other faith communities who may be our real allies in this difficult time.

I suspect that in the early days of interfaith dialogue, practical necessity began to bring us together and the ideology of dialogue came later – with the exception of a few notable individual pioneers. If you have power you do not need to meet the other. I do not think this makes the results any less valuable or sincere, and anyway, once begun, dialogue takes on a momentum of its own. But we should always try to be honest about what different factors bring us together.

All of the above factors, traditional religious values and contemporary realities, play a role in determining Jewish attitudes to dialogue today. While much of what I have described holds good for individuals, there is also an additional dimension that colours all of Jewish thinking with the creation of the state of Israel. Issues as complex as the guardianship of the holy places in Jerusalem and elsewhere, religious attitudes on all sides that fuel the struggles between Israel, the Palestinians and the Arab states, and the longtime reluctance of the Vatican to establish diplomatic relations with the state, all add political complexities to the pursuit of interfaith dialogue for its own sake. Certainly, for Jews and Muslims alike it is difficult if not impossible to separate 'politics' from the central task of building God's kingdom on earth, in all its pragmatic and detailed reality. So the attitudes and lessons of dialogue are open to real testing in the public and not just the private arena.

What Jewish sources are available to help Jews open up the area of interfaith dialogue? The rabbis taught that '*ma'aseh avot siman l'vanim*', the actions of the founding generations of the Jewish people are models for their descendants. Hence the Jewish custom of scouring the tradition for precedents in any new venture. Perhaps interfaith dialogue seems to be the least likely arena in which to find some such precedent, especially given the biblical attitude to most of the neighbouring societies and the ongoing battle with idolatry. Yet within two chapters of the call of Abraham in Genesis, we find the first recorded interfaith encounter in our tradition, when the patriarch meets Melchizedek, king of Salem, who asks his God, El Elyon, to bless 'Abram', as he is still known.

The ensuing dialogue is carefully crafted. Abram does not respond to Melchizedek directly, but speaks instead to the King of Sodom, swearing an oath in the name of 'YHWH El Elyon',[3] thus combining the name used by Melchizedek and Abraham's own name for the God who had called him (Genesis 14:18–22). Now it is possible that the divine name 'YHWH', Israel's term for God, has been added here for some later editorial apologetic purpose, but as the text stands before us, Abram has recognised in Melchizedek's El Elyon, 'Most High God', another name for the God that he has forsaken everything to follow. Whatever their other differences, these two figures, Abram and Melchizedek, meet and offer each other mutual support and blessing in the name of the same God. The possibility of true interfaith dialogue is signalled at the very outset of the biblical record and the birth of the Jewish people.

Abram and Melchizedek meet on a theological level. Moses and Jethro, his father-in-law, the priest of Midian, as well as being united by direct family ties, collaborate in a more practical way. It is to Jethro that Moses owes the political and legal infrastructure that enables him to lead the Israelites in the wilderness period (Exodus 18). Thus, the two key formative figures in the origins of the Jewish people and their religion, Abram and Moses, are crucial witnesses to the possibility and significance of interfaith activity of both a spiritual and a practical kind.

In neither of these episodes is the primary impetus for dialogue a theological one. The exchange with Melchizedek emerges from a collaboration forged in the course of a war; Jethro's relationship with Moses is the result of an alliance made by a political exile. Practicalities have determined the need for human contact, mutual recognition and the defining of their relationship. These subsequently extend into the religious arena. In neither case, however, does some kind of new religious symbiosis emerge. Israel continues to be Israel, the other two peoples go their own way, the only record of their passing being that preserved by the biblical tradition itself.

As we have suggested, it is once again out of practical necessity that new engagements and alliances need to be made. But there are barriers from the Jewish side that stand in the way. As we observe our numbers dwindling, an investment in interfaith activity is counter-intuitive. Add to this the physical and psychological wounds caused by the Shoah, and we have the current tendency for Jewish communities to look inwards rather than outwards, to focus on survival and continuity as ends in themselves, and to look with suspicion at any conscious attempt to relate to other faith communities. Though we often tend to think of ourselves as going our own unique Jewish way, in these particular trends we are also acting out tendencies in the world at large.

Whereas it is possible to point to Jewish values, born out of necessity, that would encourage an openness to dialogue, we must not be dishonest about the internal barriers within Jewish tradition itself. For every universal quote we can find out of 4000 years of Jewish tradition we can also discover contrasting ones that are as intolerant as any available elsewhere. If our minority status under Christianity and Islam for so many centuries has held in check our own sense of holding the absolute truth and wishing to impose it on others, with the re-emergence of the state of Israel, there are triumphalist tendencies within Judaism, backed by political power, that need to be carefully controlled. Interfaith dialogue is particularly the métier of liberal religious movements, so fundamentalist tendencies within Judaism, which question the validity of liberal values and religious movements, are equally antagonistic to dialogue unless it is carefully circumscribed. A celebrated opinion from an Orthodox leader allowed for dialogue to take place at the level of practical issues affecting our different communities, but ruled out any theological discussions. In explaining why, he pointed out that to discuss the intimate relationship between Israel and God was akin to discussing the private conversations between a man and wife in bed.

And yet unless we are able to enter also into such 'intimate' areas, once a basis of trust has been established, we will fail in the ultimate task of finding theological space within our tradition for the 'other'. The threefold challenge in this regard has been well defined by Hans Küng in his ongoing masterly exploration of the religious situation of our time.

> No peace among the nations
> without peace among the religions.
> No peace among the religions
> without dialogue between the religions.
> No dialogue between the religions
> without investigation of the foundations of the religions.

Küng's manifesto could as easily be a progressive Jewish formulation. In particular, the last element represents one of the points where Reform Judaism found its initial impetus – the scientific investigation of the origins of Judaism and the attempt to discover what of the tradition could be maintained in a post-Enlightenment world. Needless to say, for many who do not share this ideological position, this must prove the most problematic part of Küng's manifesto. But there is still plenty of work that can be done on the first two axioms alone within the broader sweep of Judaism.

What will be the price paid if Jews undertake dialogue on this level? First and foremost we can no longer use the method of cheap comparisons to indicate an alleged Jewish superiority to other faith traditions, a kind of reflexive reaction to our own religious insecurities. But this is something that will take a lot of educational work on our part – no less in the area of correcting our own standard textbooks. Our usual foil in such matters is Christianity – understandable, given the experience of Jews over two millennia. But in the light of major Christian attempts to re-examine the basis of their understanding of Judaism since the war, it is no longer sufficient for us to set up certain Christian beliefs, not always well understood, as Aunt Sallies for us to knock down. In fact, the issue goes much deeper than that. The last few decades have seen any number of Christian documents, particularly from the churches of Germany, Catholic and Protestant alike, in which they have tried to reformulate their perception of Judaism and the Jewish people, including the vexed issue of the Jewish claim to the land of Israel. In all these attempts, with their occasional setbacks, one can see a serious attempt at *teshuvah*, a regret for the past, with its horrific occurrences during the Nazi period, and a desire to prevent such things happening ever again in the future. But only now are some preliminary attempts being made to create a new expression of a Jewish understanding of Christianity on similar lines, the location of Christianity within a Jewish religious view, and the formulation of appropriate guidelines that flow from it. In some ways that is a reflection of the lack of central authorities within the Jewish world. Nevertheless there are enough Jews in Israel and the Diaspora with sufficient experience of interfaith dialogue to develop such positions, and the very attempts would be an important contribution to mutual understanding and respect. A first attempt from a number of Jewish scholars in America under the title '"Dabru Emet" ("Speak the truth")…', has recently appeared – see further discussion on page 132.

The absence of our own contemporary theological formulation of the significance of other religions is a cogent reminder that for all the wealth of rabbinical and theological expertise we have in our Jewish seminaries and academic institutions, our concerns remain surprisingly and perhaps dangerously parochial. Let me illustrate this from another perspective. I remember a conference in the very early days of the Jewish-Christian-Muslim dialogue in Europe, at which one of the speakers produced a kind of checklist of qualities that belonged to religious faiths. He listed, for example, 'social justice', 'purity of monotheistic belief', 'preservation of authentic traditions' and so on. He then checked off each of the three monotheistic faiths according to these criteria, and to no-one's surprise found that his own religion recorded positively on all his criteria, while the other two were found lacking in one or more areas. It was a naive exercise, but no different from the one we actually use in our daily converse about each other – it is simply that we win out because we make our own selection of criteria without taking the trouble to understand the inner workings of the other faith we are 'defeating'.

Living with religious pluralism and diversity means that we can no longer make such pronouncements without taking into account the sensitivity of the other we are discussing, whom we have effectively invited to overhear our conversations. Those who have experienced interfaith dialogue know that from now on there is an invisible partner forever present who acts as a new kind of superego watching over our more inflated claims and dubious comparisons.

At first this seems like some kind of self-imposed censorship that may prevent genuine disagreement, but that is not actually the case. It simply means that in our internal discussions about others we become more careful and modest in our claims – and we understand that such issues as divide us may only be properly addressed in the presence of the other. We come to realise that what we are conventionally doing is really talking about friends behind their back, and that it is no longer acceptable. We of all people, who bewail the distortions of Judaism that we perceive as being taught by others, need to accept that same premise in our dealings with other faiths. Dialogue begins at home.

What can Jews bring to interfaith dialogue? Here I can only speak out of my position within 'progressive' Judaism, which has always seen itself as standing at the interface with contemporary issues and the wider society.

Precisely because of this, we have a particular task in the pioneering and furtherance of interfaith dialogue. Our openness and flexibility give us the freedom to work with other communities on all levels, social, political and theological. Moreover, our liberal tradition should give us certain valuable qualities we can bring to the dialogue process, particularly the kind of humility that empowers us to listen before we feel the need to speak or pass some kind of judgment on what we have heard. Our commitment to the values of the Enlightenment should give us the necessary detachment and clarity to create understanding where so much misinformation and confusion abound. Our lack of false pride should allow us to accept the criticism and self-criticism that inevitably have to be faced when we have an honest encounter with the other. What we stand to gain is exactly that which arises from accepting the challenge provided by such dialogue, namely to find within ourselves the inner spiritual resources to build trust, friendship and love in situations where so much fear and suspicion abound. This is the challenge and the hope offered to Judaism and the Jewish people at this turbulent beginning of the twenty-first century.

Having asserted the necessity of engagement in interfaith dialogue, what are the resources that Jewish tradition can bring? In the next chapter we will look at relevant ideas about multicultural society.

3

Chances and Limits
of Multicultural Society

At the centre of this part of the book is the question: what does Jewish tradition have to offer to contemporary issues in a multifaith, multicultural society? To answer this question it is necessary to explore Jewish traditions as far as possible within their own terms. The value of such an exploration, apart from any ideas that may emerge, is that any serious attempt to enter the inner world of a particular tradition is itself an exercise in dialogue, in seeing the world through the eyes of the other. Since Judaism has existed for more than three millennia in a variety of different cultures and social situations, not all teachings may have a bearing on today's concerns. Nevertheless, some general ideas and even principles may emerge.

The biblical tradition knows one example of a multicultural society, but is distinctly pessimistic about it – the society that built the Tower of Babel. The story of Babel can be found in Genesis 11. It follows a long chapter containing a genealogy that seeks to account for the existence of the 70 different peoples that, in the biblical world view, inhabit the earth. It also imagines a remarkable world in which the entire earth used 'one language and words that were one' (Genesis 11:1). This statement is not altogether clear, but seems to suggest that objects and the words used to describe them were identical. A series of word plays shows how transforming materials from one form into another was exactly matched by the transformation of the words used to describe them. Thus by making a 'brick' (Hebrew: *l'venah*) it could be used in place of a 'stone' (Hebrew: *l'even*). The intimate relationship between objects and the names given to them is reflected in the Hebrew word *'davar'*, which means both 'word' and 'thing' — human speech and the material universe that human beings inhabited were united.

But this united humanity decided to build a tower reaching up into heaven, the domain of God. Whether this is simply the direct consequence of their ability to manipulate the material world or reflects a desire to storm God's heaven is not clear from the biblical text. It suggests that the attempt to build such an awesome tower reflected an intoxication with their own science and technology — if it can be done, let us do it, irrespective of the possible consequences. God is sufficiently concerned to intervene, and attacks at the central factor that unites them — their common language. God scrambles their language so that people cannot communicate and as a result they split up in disarray and go off in their different directions to populate the earth as God had intended.

The final ironic touch in the story is also appropriately dependent upon a word play. The name of the place where this happened is *bavel* in Hebrew, Babel, (Babylon), because God confused (Hebrew: *balal*) their language. Babel became babble.

But what is it that actually forces the people to separate from each other? The Hebrew text is different from the usual translations. Most of them read: 'God says "Come, let us go down and confuse their language there so that a man will not understand the language of his neighbour."' (Genesis 11:7) However, the word translated as 'understand' is the Hebrew word *'shema'*, which usually means 'hear' or 'listen', and is rarely translated as 'understand'.[1] In fact, I suspect that it is so translated in an attempt to explain this strange story, that the people no longer understood one another and so went their separate ways. But I would prefer to translate the word in its conventional sense of 'hear', and read the sentence in a different way: so that a man did not 'hear' or 'listen to' his neighbour. For even when we do not have a common language, it is possible for human beings to communicate with each other if the will is there.

The builders of the tower were simply too impatient or unwilling to listen to each other, to hear each other, now that this difficulty had been put in their way. Their separation was the result not of a lack of comprehension, but of a failure of imagination, patience and will. They could not meet each other across the boundary of language. In retrospect, their former unity can be seen as the accidental result of an unquestioned similarity of language and purpose. It could not be maintained when challenged, because, despite appearances, it was not underpinned by a deeper level of commitment to one another.

There is a second factor in the story that similarly touches on the nature of this human tragedy. Appropriately, it is also expressed through nuances in the language of the text itself. Describing the start of the project, the text utilises a commonplace Hebrew idiom: *'vayom'ru ish el re'ehu'*, 'they said, a man to his neighbour'. This is simply a biblical way of separating a collective action into the several individual parts – and at this stage in the story it carries no more meaning than the English 'they said to each other' or 'they said to one another'. The word 'neighbour' carries no particular weight in this idiomatic phrase. But when they can no longer 'hear' each other, the sentence reads, as we have seen, 'so that a man did not hear his neighbour'. Suddenly the 'neighbour' that we could take for granted in the idiom becomes a real person, a neighbour with whom it is no longer possible to communicate, whose speech we can no longer hear. The relationship is broken, and the one who was a neighbour is now an alien being, incomprehensible in his otherness.

There can be no more painful parable of the tragic divisions that erupt so often within societies or between nations when the simple reality of assumed, unexamined and undeveloped neighbourliness breaks down and incomprehension, mistrust, fear and violence take its place.

It is surely no accident that when the Hebrew Bible wishes to express the highest value it can understand in terms of human relationships it turns again to that same word 'neighbour' and says, as it does in Leviticus 19:18, 'You shall love your neighbour as yourself'. Without going too deeply into the complex Hebrew grammar of that statement, its real meaning may be more like 'you shall act in a loving manner towards your neighbour as you would act towards yourself', or even, 'towards your neighbour, who is like you'. However it must be noted that this statement, so often quoted out of context, is actually the climax of a carefully orchestrated set of laws about behaviour towards one's neighbour – laws which also play on four different terms for one's fellow Israelite: 'You shall not hate your brother [*ahikha*] in your heart; you shall surely reprove your fellow citizen [*amitekha*] …you shall not take revenge or bear a grudge against the children of your people [*amekha*]; but you shall love your neighbour [*rei'ekha*] as yourself. (Leviticus 19:17–18)[2]

The whole passage is bounded by the two opposite 'emotions' – 'you shall not hate…but you shall love'. These sandwich two sets of commandments that similarly define the outer limits of behaviour. If your fellow citizen or one of your own people wrongs you, you must confront them with their actions and work it through – but not simply keep it to yourself so that it becomes a grudge that you store up or that leads you to take revenge. 'Reprove' is a somewhat confrontational term, in keeping with the style of much biblical rhetoric, but the point is clear – the society cannot survive unless issues between people are clarified, discontents addressed and resolved. The transformation of hatred into the 'loving attitude' central to the Israelite covenant, the contractual agreement with God which is to be the constitution of their society, requires a commitment to fostering the relationship between people and an active engagement with issues that might damage it.

But who is the neighbour in question? Clearly in this immediate context in Leviticus it means a fellow Israelite, and were that the end of the matter this passage could say little to us about multicultural situations. But in the same chapter of Leviticus, in a section located as a parallel to this passage in the latter part of the chapter, comes a verse that applies the identical formula to the *ger*, the 'stranger' or 'resident alien':

> When a 'stranger' dwells with you in your land, you shall not oppress him. Like a home-born amongst you shall he be to you, the stranger who dwells amongst you, and you shall love him as yourself, for you were strangers in the land of Egypt, I am the Eternal your God. (Leviticus 19:33–34)

The Hebrew Bible knows situations of unquestioning neighbourliness, of the tragic breakdown of neighbourliness and of the quest for a conscious relationship of respect and support for the neighbour – all of which are reflected or challenged in the issue of a multicultural society.

The covenant legislation of the Hebrew Bible envisaged the creation of an Israelite society on its own land and therefore had to address the issue of the presence of non-Israelite elements. Two terms are used to distinguish different categories of people. The first, which we have already seen, is the word *ger*, which occurs 92 times in the Hebrew Bible and is often associated with the phrase 'remember that you were strangers in Egypt'.[3] The implication is that having experienced exile and oppressive slavery, the Israelites should have a special sympathy for those who are in a similar plight; their natural inclination should be towards generosity to others who are strangers in their midst; not oppressing them in the way they themselves had experienced. But it is all too often the newly freed slaves, the victors of the revolution, who may in turn impose on their former masters, and on others who wander into their orbit, the oppression and cruelty that was directed against them. The frequency of the repetition of this admonition in the Hebrew Bible suggests that it is not simply an affirmation of the natural state of Israelite generosity but an awareness that a different psychology must be created, even imposed, on the newly emergent nation.

The term *ger* may refer to the local Canaanite population, to Israelite refugees from the Northern kingdom,[4] or to proselytes who wished to adhere to the cult of Israel's God.[5] The *ger* occupies a middle position between a native-born Israelite and a *nokhri*, a foreigner, someone from another people who is only passing through, and has no permanent stake in Israelite society.[6]

Biblical society was built upon family and tribal structures. Therefore those who were displaced from their family connection for any reason or who came from outside, were vulnerable – hence the need for special legislation to cover their situation and the frequent linking together in the Hebrew Bible of the 'widow, orphan and *ger*'. Special divine concern was expressed for their welfare; God was their protector and the guarantor of their safety, which presumably means that society as a whole, the 'state' had a special responsibility for them. They were to be supported from welfare – all landowners were obligated to set aside specific parts of the harvest for them (Leviticus 19:9–10; Deuteronomy 24:19), and clothing was also to be provided (Deuteronomy 10:19). But the biblical legislation also recognised that the *ger* could prosper to the extent of acquiring Israelite bondmen who were indebted to him (Lev 25:47), though it fell to debtors' families to buy their freedom.

Since the Hebrew Bible does not distinguish between social and religious laws, the *ger* could share fully in the religious life of the community, and, indeed, they were obligated to keep the laws of Shabbat like anyone else. However, there seems to be some stage of transition between being simply a 'visitor' and becoming a fully fledged member of the Israelite community. Thus, a male *ger* could only attend the Passover ritual, the one that most celebrates the national and religious identity of the Israelites, after he had been circumcised. That is to say, he became that way a full member of the covenant with God, and his children would wholly assimilate into the Israelite people. It is this legislation about circumcision in Exodus 12:49 that concludes with the fundamental principle that affirms the full equality of the *ger* in certain areas: 'The same law shall apply for the home-born [native Israelite] and for the stranger [*ger*] who dwells amongst you'.[7]

How far this legal equality went is not clear, but it is evident from the historical texts that Israelite society had people of many nations within it, some fully assimilated and accepted, others perceived as problematic. Attitudes were also affected by current political and religious realities. Biblical Israel existed in a complex situation of semi-independence, its fate determined by the changing fortunes of the larger empires that surrounded it. Inner political pressures determined how far alliances could or could not be made, and this would doubtless affect the status of particular non-Israelite inhabitants, the whole being made more complicated by religious issues.

The model here is that of a society made up essentially of a single people, amongst whom lived minorities to whom certain civil and religious rights were granted. But Israel was also to experience the opposite situation during its own times of exile. Virtually the entire leadership of Judea, the southern kingdom, was deported by the Babylonians in 586 BCE, and Jerusalem and the temple, the spiritual centre of the people, were destroyed. The same factional struggles that had preceded this disaster continued to be played out after it. The nationalists saw this as a temporary setback, soon to be over, for surely God could not abandon His chosen people. Against this overinflated optimism, itself a desperate response to the reality of utter defeat and destruction, stood the figure of Jeremiah. Because he had envisioned the destruction and exile as a necessary purging and punishment by God, however painful, he looked upon the exile as a positive opportunity. In his celebrated letter to the exiles he spelled out what was to become the Jewish strategy for survival and development over the long centuries of exile.

> Thus says the Lord of hosts, the God of Israel, to all the exiles whom I have sent into exile from Jerusalem to Babylon: Build houses and live in them; plant gardens and eat their produce. Take wives and have sons and daughters; take wives for your sons, and give your daughters in marriage, that they may bear sons and daughters; multiply there, and do not decrease. But seek the welfare of the city where I have sent you into exile, and pray to the Eternal on its behalf, for in its welfare you will find your welfare. (Jeremiah 29:4–7)

David Biale has examined this policy in his book *Power and Powerlessness in Jewish History*.[8] Paradoxically, the yielding to the power of the host nation was the political strategy that contributed to the success of Jewish life. By relinquishing their desire for sovereignty, the Jews managed to obtain maximum internal autonomy in regulating their lives under their own Jewish law. Under the motto *'dina d'malkhuta dina'*, 'the law of the land is the law', the community was able time and again to base the right of Jewish self-government in the law of the particular host society. Its earliest formulation by the Babylonian Rabbi Samuel in the third century CE affirmed the authority of the gentile rule in financial matters such as taxation, but left all other internal matters within the jurisdiction of the rabbis and the community leaders, a pattern that was to persist throughout the Middle Ages. Moreover, by anticipating what the government would demand of the community in the way of taxation or other kind of requirement, the community could ensure that such things were accommodated through their own internal decision-making and administrative processes. As a rabbinic saying has it, 'A person must at all times be yielding like a reed and not unbending like a cedar' (Ta'anit 20a), for the latter is easily uprooted in a storm but a reed bends before the winds and survives. Being pliant before the pressures of the government meant survival at the worst of times and considerable success at the best.

The image of the reed is potent, and the theory proved remarkably successful as long as the regime played by the rules of the contract. But it was precisely this pattern of accommodation to the governing power that was to prove so disastrous in the Nazi period. The belief that the impositions of the Nazis were ultimately no different from those of previous difficult regimes led the Jewish community to accommodate to the demands in the same way, not realising that government policy was not a temporary aberration but a strategy for their annihilation. Part of the resistance to seeing this was presumably precisely the feeling that it was simply a rerun of a familiar scenario; only this time, anticipation and accommodation amounted to collaboration in their own destruction.

Two lessons in particular may be learnt from this latter experience, and indeed from the two biblical illustrations we have seen: the treatment of the *ger* within the biblical community and Jeremiah's programme for survival in exile. Firstly, that unless there is some sinister hidden agenda, it is theoretically possible to define a constructive relationship between a minority community and the majority society, provided the rules of the game are clearly defined, including the opportunities and limitations. But an essential element is the existence of a system of justice that stands above the particular interests of the two groups, one that ensures that no abuse of the minority or exploitation is allowed to take place, whether on religious, ethnic, economic or social grounds. This is self-evident, but tragically its absence, or perceived absence, is the primary cause of civil conflict, and it is often the first thing to go when relationships break down. That curious biblical figure Kohelet (Ecclesiastes) was quite clear about this two-and-a-half thousand years ago: 'Because judgment on an evil deed is not carried out speedily, men's hearts are encouraged to do evil' (Ecclesiastes 8:11). Kohelet could have meant by this that unless they are punished the perpetrators are encouraged to do further evil acts, but also that the victims themselves may have to respond in kind. The rabbis had this latter possibility in mind when they taught: 'Because of the delay of justice and because of the perversion of justice...the sword comes into the world'. (Pirqe Avot 5:11)

Work has been done in recent decades in documenting the abuse of the rights of minorities and in seeking to derive laws and forms of intervention that can be introduced for their protection.[9] Laws do not eliminate prejudice against others, but they serve to make prejudice less respectable, hinder some from taking unacceptable action and ensure that corrective measures against abuse can be instituted. Such laws, and the degree of their enforcement, set a yardstick against which the values of any society should be judged.

So what needs to be addressed practically if multiculturalism is to work? Here I would like to draw an analogy with what happens when a marriage breaks down. Suddenly a whole number of issues between the couple that had been tacitly ignored while the relationship was sound burst out into the open. That he snored or that she wore curlers in her hair at night were matters that must have been tolerated for years. Indeed the willingness to accept such irritations was part of the cement of their relationship. But when the marriage unravels, these and other minor irritants become major factors to compound the anger and bitterness that emerges. However, is it inevitable that they become matters of contention? Part of the process of marriage-guidance counselling in such situations is to enable the couple to talk through such sources of unhappiness, to adjust them where possible, to make compromises when choices have to be made and to agree to tolerate things that cannot be changed. In the light of the deeper awareness of the other that emerges from the counselling process, provided that the relationship has not broken down irretrievably, a new level of mutual understanding and commitment may become possible. That at least is the theory. I am fond of quoting something told to me by a friend who had gone through such a process with a counsellor. He introduced his programme by pointing out that at the end of the three-month period of working together, the two partners would come to understand each other and would be friends. They may not any longer be married to each other, but at least they would be friends!

On the basis that prevention is better than cure, it can be argued that counselling of the sort that enables couples to address the issues between them at an early stage, before a major crisis occurs, should be encouraged and supported, and it may indeed be effective. By analogy, it is tragic that the problems that arise in a multicultural society tend to be addressed only at times of crisis or when the situation has already broken down. The equivalent process of mediation, clarification and mutual acknowledgment takes place in the area of 'dialogue'. Unfortunately dialogue is rarely promoted as a pre-emptive measure, let alone as an essential constructive policy, wherever potential conflict exists. Where it does occur it tends to be confined to those at the margins of their respective communities. And yet, provided the legal safeguards mentioned above are in place, it seems self-evident that a proactive programme of dialogue is absolutely essential if two or more communities are to address all the fears, prejudices, misunderstandings and sources of conflict that are either overtly or latently present amongst them. And this should be done at all levels, both as private and as institutionalised activities. Whether in schooling, between religious communities, at the workplace or during leisure-time activities, a more conscious attempt at creating frameworks for interaction and consciousness-raising would seem to be vital – if only for coming to understand the nature of the conflicts that may arise.

Such activity would have to address questions of the different perceptions of the other that arise depending on whether the partners have a minority or majority status within their particular society. These and other socioeconomic factors distort the power balance between the 'partners' and must also be taken into account in the kind of dialogue programme that is inaugurated. Moreover, where obvious sources of injustice exist, they have to be addressed if any kind of honest meeting can happen. But unless we become proactive in this manner we are doomed to be shocked time and again by situations of interracial, intercultural, interethnic or interreligious violence that suddenly overwhelm us. Tragically these are conflicts which, in retrospect, could often have been prevented if only real communication was present. We know enough about the mechanisms of conflict – we need to do more to create the ongoing programmes that help prevent it and at the same time promote the richness in personal growth and empowerment that are created by the best kinds of dialogue experience.

However, when thinking of the ways in which communities have tried to explain themselves to each other, I am haunted by a particular book, the *Philo Lexikon*. It was published in Berlin in 1935 as a survey and summary of the great Jewish contributions to the world. It lists three pages of names of doctors of medicine and their special scientific achievements, five pages of leading Jewish writers in the German language, two pages of famous Jewish sportsmen, and statistics about the number of Jews who died fighting for Germany in the First World War. It was an attempt to offer a reasoned response to anti-Jewish legislation, actions and propaganda. But reason alone could not resist a threat that went beyond rationality and reason. In 1938 the same Jewish publishing house published the *Philo Atlas*, a handbook for Jewish emigration.

I cite this example because I am not naive about the difficulties of creating and supporting a multicultural society. Reason alone does not touch the emotional issues that underlie intercommunity prejudices and fears. Something more is needed if we are to treat the underlying problems and emotions and resist those who exploit differences for their own personal or political ends. Dialogue is the only approach I know that builds trust, mutual respect, friendship and love. If the Babel story is a warning but also a possible guide, then the first step to sustaining a multicultural society is the same as it is in every other kind of dialogue – we have to learn how to listen to each other, to those who are 'other'. For the act of real listening turns the one who seems to be 'other' into 'your neighbour who is like you', into your neighbour whom you can come to love as you love yourself.

Nevertheless, precisely because dialogue is not the norm and conflicts do arise, is there anything that Jewish tradition can offer to address this eventuality? Before addressing this issue, it may be helpful to take a brief detour and do an exercise in 'listening' to the self-understanding of a particular minority community, namely Jewish society in Britain. As an immigrant community, well established over a couple of centuries, it exemplifies something of the changes that have taken place within it, and within British society itself. Such an study may also offer indications about how other such immigrant communities experience themselves and might develop over time.

4

Reflections on the Jewish Immigrant Experience[1]

No two groups of people have the same history, culture or traditions, so it is always a mistake to project from the experience of one onto another and say: this is how it was with us and so you should follow our example. Nevertheless, it may be helpful before returning to more theoretical Jewish teachings to give a brief overview of the history of Jewish immigration into Britain and indicate some of the stages in our integration here.

I would like to take as my starting point some of the changing aspects of Jewish life in this country. The Jewish community of Britain refers to itself as Anglo-Jewry, which already shows a particular focus of identity, since there have been significant Jewish communities in Scotland, Ireland and Wales. But whatever we call ourselves, the Jewish community is a good example of a conscious minority living and flourishing within a majority culture. We will have to examine both the gains in this situation and the price we have paid.

The US recognises itself as a pluralistic, melting pot culture made up of many ethnic immigrant groups. As Michael Billig has pointed out with regard to nationalism in general:

> The assumptions of nationalism are fundamental within modern common-sense. These are assumptions that the world is naturally divided into separate nations, each with its own particular history, destiny and culture; and that every individual properly belongs to one of the nations of the world. Such assumptions are 'natural' to the modern individual…Nevertheless, nations are not 'natural' units…The modern nation is an 'imagined community'.[2]

Britain still tends to see itself as a monolithic, cohesive, national society made up of what we might call mythic English people, as well as real Scots, Irish and Welsh. British society is actually made up of people of many origins, including descendants somewhere along the line of various invading armies. This reality has never bothered the nationalists and racists who proclaim the unity and essential uniformity of the British people.

There were probably a number of Jews in Britain who came here at the time of the Roman occupation, but the first major settlements followed the Norman invasion, with communities in London, Lincoln, Norwich, York, Oxford and other towns – though the total population probably never exceeded 5000. In 1189, 2000 Jews were massacred by a mob during the coronation of King Richard the Lionheart. The following year in York, under siege from a mob in the royal castle, members of the Jewish community, led by their rabbi, committed mass suicide. In 1255, Jews were accused of the ritual murder of a child, Hugh of Lincoln, and some 90 prominent Jews were executed. The Jews were expelled from the country in 1290 under King Edward the First, something that happened frequently to Jewish communities in Europe throughout the Middle Ages. Though a few could be found here over the next few centuries, they were only formally readmitted under Oliver Cromwell in 1656.

The first to arrive were Sephardi Jews (of Spanish and Portuguese origin) who had settled in Holland after being expelled from Spain in 1492. Later they were joined by Ashkenazi Jews (of German and East European origin) who were part of the communities that had gained a degree of freedom and emancipation in Western Europe. By the end of the eighteenth century the Jewish population was about 20,000 and by the mid-nineteenth century they were a well established community, no longer immigrants, and gaining a degree of rank within society. In 1847 Lionel de Rothschild won a seat in parliament, but was not permitted as a Jew to take it – as a Jew he was not prepared to take the oath. It required an act of parliament changing the nature of the oath before he was able to take his seat in 1858 – the House of Commons repeatedly voted in favour but the House of Lords blocked it. There was thus a gradual gaining of civil rights through-out the nineteenth century – the religious disabilities that Jews faced were also shared by Catholics and the non-comformist churches.

The community remained relatively small, but in the years between 1881 and 1914, vast numbers of Jews fled from the Russian Empire seeking a new home away from forced conscription into the army, repressive measures, persecution and outbreaks of violence against them. A million people were on the move, the vast majority of them settling in the US – but the British community grew to some 350,000 within this short period. Inevitably there were strong reactions against this vast influx of 'foreigners' into the country – with local organisations like the British Brothers' League warning against these new immigrants. You only have to look at the newspapers of the time to see just how threatening these new arrivals seemed to be. The fears were about their bringing in disease, creating ghettos, increasing overcrowding in houses and driving up the rents, and accepting lower wages and so taking away jobs from local people. Obviously they make for very familiar reading. They could be paralleled by reactions to each new wave of immigration into this country.

What is uncomfortable to record is the reaction of the established Jewish community to this sudden influx. There was a great feeling of anxiety that the status that Jews had established here would be threatened by the new arrivals who came out of the poverty of East European villages, spoke Yiddish and not English, and in general did not conform to the middle-class Victorian values of the settled population. Adverts were placed in the European ports of embarkation for the newcomers discouraging them from trying to settle in Britain and some tens of thousands who arrived here were persuaded to return to Eastern Europe. Others were encouraged to go on to America or to the colonies.

At the same time a number of institutions tried to encourage the newcomers to assimilate to English norms as soon as possible – they created Jewish schools, welfare organisations, Jewish equivalents of the Boy Scouts and church brigades for them, as well as institutions for adult education. In some ways these were sincere attempts to look after the needs and welfare of the new arrivals and help them find their way here, but there was also a recognition that the sooner they conformed with British behaviour the better for everybody.

The last major influx of people came in the thirties with the rise of the Nazi party in Germany and the beginning of Jewish disabilities and persecution. By the time of the outbreak of the Second World War, some 60,000 refugees had arrived here, from Germany, Austria and Czechoslovakia. Ironically, despite being the victims of the Nazis from whom they fled, many of them became officially classified as 'enemy aliens' and were interned throughout the war. They were even accused in the press of being fifth columnists. (Someone who managed to find a place here told me that he was reclassified as a 'friendly enemy alien'!)

Since the war there has been a growing assimilation of these different waves of immigration into a lower-middle-class or middle-class Jewish community. There have been very few proper demographic studies of the Jewish community, so it is very hard to know exact numbers. After the war we spoke of a Jewish population of about 450,000. In the seventies a survey gave figures of about 330,000. The latest statistics put the number below 300,000. However, these figures too are only approximations. Nevertheless, the impression is clearly of a community shrinking in size. Whereas in the past, and more commonly on the continent of Europe, this would have been through conversion to Christianity, today Jews merely lose touch with the Jewish community, marry non-Jews in civil ceremonies and cut their ties. Whereas the East European immigrants had large extended families, Jews today conform with the norm of the small nuclear family, so do not reproduce themselves in large numbers. We are affected by the same high divorce rate as is the general society – despite the myths that still persist about the cohesiveness of the Jewish family (perhaps such myths are simply part of the stereotyping of immigrant communities). A few Jews emigrate annually to Israel, and more will follow the classical brain drain-path to the US or other countries where there are new opportunities. Certainly those seeking a vibrant Jewish community find it hard to locate it here.

I would like to return to the immigrants at the turn of the century – who included my own grandparents. Partly because of the hostility they encountered, but also out of a respect for British society as it then was, the Jewish community until relatively recently has largely seen itself as a minority whose position was to be safeguarded by maintaining a degree of invisibility. Individuals assimilated to the British way of life at virtually all levels in society, but did so by playing down their Jewish origins.

For example, there have been relatively large numbers of Jewish MPs at various times, in earlier years on the Labour side, more recently on the Conservative side, even reaching cabinet rank. But most of them, although Jewish by birth, had and have almost nothing to do with the Jewish community and would never claim to be motivated by Jewish values. From outside, and particularly from the perspective of other minorities here, such a relatively large Jewish presence might indicate a goal to aim for as well. Though there is also a downside in that some see it very negatively as proof that Jews secretly control everything. But most of these MPs bend over backwards to avoid having anything to do with Jewish matters in an attempt to prove their utter neutrality. I suspect that unless things have drastically changed, the same tension may also affect people from other ethnic groups if they advance either in local or national politics. The price for acceptance in the wider society, at least in the past, has been to cut oneself off from one's roots, or at least become much more careful about being overidentified with one particular group or cause. In a truly multicultural Britain this too may change.

Jews have tended to create organisations, especially during the last century, that paralleled British national institutions. The most obvious is the office of the Chief Rabbi that was set up as a kind of Jewish version of the Archbishop of Canterbury. In fact he is only the Chief Rabbi of a part of the community and his actual power is relatively limited, though he is seen as a spokesman by the outside world. Another example is the Board of Deputies, which was set up as a kind of Jewish representative body, modelled on parliament. In line with the older situation, the Board too has kept a deliberately low profile. It used to be run by people who represented the older Jewish families, the so-called Anglo-Jewish aristocracy. After the war the leadership was transferred to people who had made a success in their business enterprises and who were wealthy and willing to make a contribution to the community. The current leadership tends to be drawn from the professions, though those with wealth do have a major influence on the community through other organisations. The Board of Deputies in the past has prided itself on its quiet diplomacy, its discreet approach to government on matters concerning the community. This kind of paternalistic approach has increasingly come into conflict with Jewish groups that prefer to take a more public stance on particular issues. And though the Board has undergone periodic self-examinations, it is still seen by many as not being really representative of the community at large and not very effective. That some such representative organisation is important is clear, but how best to constitute it and make sure that it is relevant to the changing needs of the community is a major challenge.

Just to pick up one other aspect of the ways Jews have tried to blend in very quietly and discreetly, we have only to look at the new synagogues that were built during the postwar period when Jews began to move into the suburbs. Often converted churches or schools, on the whole they are very nondescript buildings, functional but in no way reflections of Jewish pride in our faith. One has only to compare them with the bold and artistically challenging synagogues in the US to realise just how self-effacing are those over here. I remember the impact here of the Lubavitch movement some years ago. These are very traditional Chasidic Jews who feel they have a mission to bring other Jews back to Judaism. Coming out of a totally different, American, experience, they are not shy like we are and are quite happy to make a big public display of their Judaism. A few years ago they began to put up huge eight-branched candelabra in public places to celebrate the Festival of Chanukah, which comes about the same time as Christmas and is almost a national holiday in some parts of America. It came as a real shock and embarrassment to many Jews here to see Judaism on public display in this way, and reflected a real clash of culture. The fact that these things are now more or less taken for granted is another signal that Jewish attitudes have been changing here.

(I must add that not everything that comes from America has been so readily accepted. There is another kind of missionary movement, Jews who have become Christians but claim to be still authentically Jewish – 'Jews for Jesus' is one such group. Their missionising attempts to win over Jews have been seen by some as a considerable threat to a community already shrinking. The anger they arouse is disproportionate to their size or success rate, but does reflect a genuine level of insecurity about the future of the community here. It is well reflected in the title of a book by Chief Rabbi Jonathan Sacks – 'Will We Have Jewish Grandchildren?')

Behind the desire to assimilate into British life and virtually disappear as a Jew are a number of issues. Some have to do with the inner life of Jews after centuries as a minority, often persecuted, often forced to change countries. In the new open society it seemed possible to simply leave all that painful past behind. But to do so leaves behind a residue of guilt about having abandoned Jewish tradition and our extraordinary history. Sometimes this has been experienced as Jewish self-hatred. Unfortunately this concept of the self-hating Jew, which has a certain reality, has also become a kind of term of abuse levelled against any Jew who is not one hundred percent supportive of whatever is currently considered important for the Jewish people.

Perhaps this is the right place to make a particular point about the long-term impact of the Jewish experience in Europe. I have to start with an analogy. One of the problems left behind for the native population when the colonial powers leave is exactly this kind of psychological distress. Colonised peoples have been subjected to the denigration and contempt of the ruling power, and suffer also from insidious policies of divide and rule. When the colonial power leaves, much of this negative experience has been internalised and may affect the way people deal with each other as they try to build their new society. It may take generations before a new kind of equilibrium is reached.

Jews were effectively a colonised people for centuries – except that it all took place within Europe and not somewhere in Africa. Entire Jewish communities were bought and sold, often for the sake of their ability to trade, and when they ceased to be useful, or conflicts arose between the church and the local rulers, the Jews were simply expelled. Worse still, under Christianity they had to put up with attacks and abuse that derive from the negative Christian attitude to Judaism. I need hardly point out that within this century Jews experienced the attempted genocide at the hands of the Nazis and their collaborators throughout occupied Europe. One-third of the Jewish people were murdered, and the impact of that horror will also take generations to work through.

If these events and pressures have resulted in internal conflicts and anxieties, Jews have also had to address legitimate concerns about anti-semitism in Britain. It was certainly a major issue at the turn of the twentieth century and again in the thirties with the appearance of the fascist movement and Mosley's Blackshirts. Nevertheless, British antisemitism has proved to be relatively mild and restricted to fringe groups. But things are never static. What Jews find worrying today is the threat of violence from groups who identify with the Middle East conflict – and the reality of terrorist attacks on individual Jews as well as bombs at Jewish centres. Such incidents are fuelled by a heady mixture of classical antisemitic stereotyping: Jews are rich, Jews control the media, there is a Jewish world conspiracy; and today's political anti-zionism linked with the extremism of some religious groups. Jewish students at university in particular have found themselves under attack. Where a legitimate engagement with political problems slides into prejudice, racism and violence are complex issues, but ones that we all have to address in our home communities.

As a Jew growing up in Britain in the forties and fifties, and attending public school, I must have absorbed the prevailing closet mentality and the feeling I should not display my Jewishness too overtly, unless it was directly invoked or challenged. I was once called a 'kike' by one of my schoolmates and I hit him. He was most upset, as if I had completely overreacted to what he probably saw as a mild bit of teasing. I was scared for the next week that he and his friends would retaliate, but nothing happened. Clearly a certain level of anti-Jewish sentiment exists, just as there is here a kind of latent hostility to any other 'outsider'. But it does remind me of what they used to say about pre-war Hungary: an antisemite was someone who hated Jews more than was necessary.

It is important to remember that Judaism begins with a complex interaction between a religious belief and set of values and a very particular group of people – we are both a faith and a people at the same time, and it is almost impossible to separate these two aspects. Not all Jews are religiously motivated or faithful to their tradition or even sure what its relevance is to them – nevertheless they may feel themselves very strongly to be Jewish, and identify with the people or some aspect of Jewish life. That means that it is very hard to speak about Jewish 'behaviour' and assume that we are dealing with a religious phenomenon and not a cultural one.

Though I have referred to outer events, I think there is also an inner pattern that happens over a few generations. The immigrant Jewish population had to struggle to establish itself here. This meant abandoning a lot of the religious practices they had brought with them from Eastern Europe. Perhaps the most serious was the necessity to work on Saturday, the Jewish Sabbath, simply to earn enough to live on. But since the Sabbath is at the core of Judaism, it was felt to be a particularly problematic betrayal.

Part of the aim of these immigrants was to build a better life for their children, to ensure that the next generation had all the advantages in this new society that they had never known, including a university education or entry into one of the professions. So their children grew up with a British schooling and acquired British values. This often set them at odds with their parents, who still tried to hang on to old values and practices when they could. So you had parents insisting on sending their children for religious studies at the synagogue on Sunday mornings, at least until the age of 13 when boys come of age religiously. But all the things that the children learnt in the synagogue about Judaism they never saw at home, because their parents had been forced to abandon them or at least amend them. What the parents saw as a regrettable but necessary compromise, the children saw as a kind of hypocrisy.

The situation was not helped by the problem in many cases that the parents were not able to speak English, or else did so badly and with such a strong accent that their children may even have been embarrassed by them. So this first generation born here grew up with a lot of ambivalence about their Judaism, which often led them to reject it altogether. They might keep up one or two activities: usually the Passover Seder (home ceremony and meal) which has always been a major family gathering; and the annual visit to synagogue, on Yom Kippur, the Day of Atonement, that still kept its grip on them, even if they did not know much about what it meant and could not follow the service.

If they married a Jewish person, they may well have joined a synagogue once they had children, because they wanted them to have some kind of Jewish knowledge, even if there was very little of it to be found in their homes. If their potential wife or husband was not Jewish they may have been ostracised by their family. If the new spouse was willing to convert to Judaism, they would probably have to join a Reform or Liberal synagogue which would welcome them, but by doing so they often cut themselves off from their families and friends who still retained an emotional loyalty to the Orthodox synagogue of their youth.

With the third generation something different might happen. If they were lucky as children and had a good Synagogue youth group, they might begin to find Judaism of interest. But knowing very little, and with almost no support at home, they would have to set out to build a kind of Jewish identity for themselves – with the help of their peers and perhaps a rabbi or teacher who was able to understand their difficulties. But this generation brought to their Judaism a whole range of questions and assumptions that they had acquired from their own British cultural and spiritual background. So that the Judaism they began to build for themselves had a different emphasis from that of their grandparents. In a way they reinvented Judaism after their own likeness, but this is how the religious tradition changes and evolves in each of the new places where it is transplanted.

That is not to say that some Jews did not remain within or find their way back to more traditional Jewish practices. And many remained associated with the synagogue of their parents or grandparents out of a sense of loyalty or simply inertia. But the fate of many Jews today, and the degree to which they will wish to remain consciously within the Jewish world, will depend on the kind of community they can find, the welcome they receive – especially those who have married out of the faith – and the openness of the spiritual leaders of the community to respond to the different kind of questioning that they bring.

The desire to keep a low profile as a Jew, so typical of the first two generations, has undergone major changes during the last decades of the twentieth century. In the absence of any formal study of the reasons for these changes, I would suggest at least three factors for today's greater Jewish self-confidence and public openness about our identity in Britain.

Firstly, there is the impact of the Six-Day War on the consciousness of Jewry as a whole. However problematic we might now see some of the consequences, it is clear that that event brought home to Jews the reality of the state of Israel more even than the actual granting of independence in 1948. It also unleashed a new kind of Jewish pride, lost since the Shoah, which allowed Jews, particularly in Europe, East and West, to express their attachment more publicly and openly.

The second factor, I would assume, is the changing nature of British society as it becomes more pluralistic, with the arrival of large numbers of immigrants from former commonwealth nations and the appearance of their second- and third-generation children. This has also had troubling consequences, including the rise of racism and nationalism, but it does mean that Jews no longer feel so exposed as the only recognisable minority. The negative side of this is the crass kind of view, sometimes expressed by those outside the Jewish community, to the effect that Jews should not worry any more as others would be the victims of racism before them. The positive side is that it is possible to identify as a Jew in many more ways, including through a newly emerging public Jewish cultural life, with Jewish book weeks, music weeks, film festivals, some public political actions and the like.

The third factor is the general tendency in Western society, presumably influenced by the black civil rights and women's liberation movements, for various groups to step out of their particular 'closet' and make their unique, individual presence felt. In this respect, 'Jewish pride' can take its place alongside 'gay pride' and 'black pride' and a more forceful Islamic self-expression, as a reflection of a new openness in society and corresponding self-confidence of minority groups.

However, it must be noted that in Britain we are still in a transitional stage between the old-style 'don't make waves' assimilation and the newer desire to assert Jewish individuality and to take on higher profile Jewish activism in the wider society.[3] A remarkable example of the paradoxes inherent in this situation was the ferocious debate about the establishing in north London of an *eruv* (a notional 'wall' around a district that extends the ability of Orthodox Jews to carry things on Shabbat, thus enabling, for example, pushing a pram). Certain Orthodox rabbis wished to set it up, supported by a newly emergent younger Orthodox Jewish community in the area. It was vehemently opposed by other Orthodox rabbis and also by the residents of Hampstead Garden Suburb, including local Jews whose arguments ranged from it disfiguring the urban landscape through unsightly poles and wires to an attack on these primitive, ghettoising religious practices. As has often been observed, dialogue within religious or other communities is often much harder than that between communities.

What the next stage in the development of the community will be is hard to say. It is clear that many of the best initiatives are arising at grassroots level. One of the most exciting events in the Jewish year now is a study conference called Limmud that takes place over the Christmas period. Up to 2000 Jewish people, of all ages, alone or with their families, take part in a major study experience, with literally hundreds of courses on offer, from reading classic texts with a rabbi to experimenting with family education to exploring art or music. This resurgence may be part of the wish of the third or fourth generation to rediscover their Jewish roots, but also to find a place for themselves within the tradition and the comm-unity. Time alone will tell how deep it goes, how many of the community are affected by it, and what its long-term effect will be. My own question is whether I have accurately identified this cycle of immigration, assim-ilation, rediscovery and commitment as part of Jewish experience, and how far it can be seen in other communities.

To summarise, the Jewish settlement in this country during the last century has three or four stages. First came the struggle to survive in a new land and to secure a proper future for our children. Then came the assimilation to British life of the second generation, with a degree of rejection of past culture and tradition and faith – partly because of the need to conform with the new society, partly because of an inherent cultural clash between traditional Jewish life and western secular values. The third and fourth stages have been a decline in numbers and religious affiliation – though some have looked for a strengthening of their national or ethnic identity, for example by creating a number of new Jewish schools. There is also evidence of a spiritual renewal. This can be seen in the postwar rise of fundamentalist groups and at the same time the growth of the Reform and Liberal Jewish religious movements – which reflects a greater religious polarisation within the community. There have also been new groups appearing that are seeking Jewish spiritual values in a variety of ways. How far these changes are special to Judaism, and how far they are part of a broader cultural phenomenon, is hard to tell.

We are a community in flux. Deeply torn by a variety of inner conflicts – between Orthodox and 'progressive' religious views of our tradition and the role of Judaism and the Jewish people in the world; between religious and secular; between those who defend the state of Israel in all circumstances and those who are deeply distressed at the plight of the Palestinians, support the peace process and accept the logic, justice and inevitability of a Palestinian state; between those who want the Jewish world to be self-contained and inward-looking, and those who want it to speak out on the wider issues of society; between those who want to preserve tradition and the status quo and those who champion new issues, notably the role of women in Jewish life or a more positive Jewish attitude to sexual minorities.

In short we have a smaller but still vibrant community, one which is beginning to revive again after a long, dormant period. It is a community that plays a distinctive role in the wider British society through individual contributions and as a whole, but is still overly conscious of its minority status and not sure just how far it can press its own claims or make its own demands. It is a community in great spiritual and religious turmoil – which again reflects the problems of the host society. It is a community that has enjoyed a freedom from persecution and a rich variety of opportunities that can only be made available within a democratic society – with all the temptations to assimilate and disappear that come with this. In short, we have experienced Britain as problematic in some ways, but ultimately as a source of blessing.

For 2000 years Jews have experienced themselves as a community in exile, totally dependent on the goodwill of their host society. We have learnt, in one rabbinic image, to be flexible like bullrushes so as to survive the winds and waves buffeting us, and that can include both passive and active measures. But we have also respected and valued our host society and our responsibilities towards it.

It is my personal hope that all other minorities in this country will experience the same opportunities, and work successfully through their own problems and never regret the freedom they have found here.

It is our Jewish tradition to recite a prayer for the welfare of the land or nation or state in which we live. When we came to write our own British Reform prayerbook, we composed such a prayer, partly based on traditional models, but also containing the following words:

> May God give us all the strength to do our duty, and the love to do it well, so that justice and kindness may dwell in our land. May God's peace be in our hearts, so that

every community of our nation may meet in understanding and respect, united by love of goodness, and keeping far from violence and strife. Together may we work for peace and justice among all nations, and may we and our children live in peace. So may this kingdom find its honour and greatness in the work of redemption and the building of God's kingdom here on earth. May this be God's will.

Whether this is God's will or not, the reality of conflict between communities is a part of daily life throughout the world. In the next chapter we will return to examining Jewish teachings on the nature of controversy and conflict.

5

Controversy for the Sake of Heaven

ACKNOWLEDGING CONTROVERSY

In the previous chapter we examined some biblical and rabbinic views on what might be needed to underpin a multicultural society. Central to the passage from Leviticus 19, culminating in the command to 'love your neighbour as yourself' is the requirement that one 'reprove' one's neighbour when misunderstandings or wrong behaviour create problems or tensions. Yet to do so in a way that is acceptable and does not simply compound the source of conflict is one of the hardest of human tasks. The rabbis were strongly in favour of reproof: 'It is written: "Reprove a wise man, and he will love you"' (Proverbs 9:8). 'Rabbi Jose ben Hanina said: "A love without reproof is no love". Resh Lakish said: "Reproof leads to peace; a peace where there has been no reproof is no peace"' (Genesis Rabba, Vayera 54:3). But they were equally sanguine about the difficulties of giving reproof in a way that did not shame the recipient and of receiving it in the right spirit.

> Rabbi Hanina said: 'Jerusalem was destroyed only because nobody reproved his fellow.' Rabbi Tarfon, who saw the destruction, said: 'I should be surprised if there is anybody in this generation who knows how to give reproof rightly, or how to receive it. If one says to another: "Take away the splinter from your eye", the other replies: "Take away the beam from your own eye!"' (Babylonian Talmud Arakin 16b)

At the heart of these sayings is the assumption that controversy is an inevitable part of any social interaction, and yet that if handled in the right way it can become a positive force for reconciling differences and maintaining civilised discourse. Hence the starting point for this chapter is a rabbinic saying from the 'Pirqe Avot', the 'Chapters of the Fathers', an independent unit of the Talmud which assembles a number of the favourite sayings of the rabbis of the first two centuries of the Common era. This particular passage has no attribution and comes within a collection of sayings based on numerical sequences: 'With ten sayings the world was created…', 'there are seven marks of a cultured person and seven of an uncultured one' etc. The latter part of the chapter examines a number of character traits: there are four qualities among those who sit before the wise etc. The passage immediately before the one we will be considering sets a new kind of pattern. It reads: 'Whenever love depends on some material cause, when the cause departs, love departs; but when love is not dependent upon a material cause, it will never depart'. The text then cites two biblical examples to back up this statement – the love of Amnon for Tamar did not survive when his lust for her had been satisfied (2 Samuel 13); but the love between King David and Jonathan, the son of King Saul, did survive.

Our passage reads as follows:

> Every controversy which is for the sake of heaven, in the end it will endure; but one that is not for the sake of heaven, in the end it will not endure. Which controversy was for the sake of heaven? That was the controversy between Hillel and Shammai. And which one was not for the sake of heaven - that was the controversy of Korach and his company [Numbers 16]. (Pirqe Avot 5:20)

What is intriguing is this distinction between controversies that 'endure' or, as another translation would have it, 'lead to a permanent result', and those which do not. By implication, and as borne out by the examples given, there is a positive side to controversy. In fact, a little thought reminds us that most of our life is taken up by controversy in one form or another, usually taken so much for granted that we hardly even notice it. For we define our place in the world, our relationship with people and institutions, from our first experiences within the family onward, by a process of negotiation with others. We set our own perceived best interests, insofar as we are capable of recognising them, against the constraints imposed upon us by the outside world. From the withdrawal of the breast when we want it, to sibling rivalry for the love or attention of parents, to the complex display and competition for a mate, to negotiations in the workplace, to the choice of a location for a summer holiday, even to the decision whether to die at home or in a hospital, we spend our entire lifetime making choices, arguing, reaching some kind of compromise or agreement with other forces or people, or else attempting to avoid the whole difficult and often painful exercise. It is not that controversy is absent from our lives – rather the problem is how best to acknowledge and work with it, and how to cope with the point at which controversy gets out of control and spills over into conflict, when it ceases to be something that 'leads to a permanent result'.

The two illustrations that the rabbis bring need further elaboration. Interestingly, they do not choose a biblical illustration of a controversy for the sake of heaven, though there are examples that could be used. Moses and his father-in-law Jethro debated the best way to organise Israel's legal system and agreed on the structure suggested by Jethro (Exodus 18). David and Jonathan could have fought each other for the throne but the latter yielded to the former. Moses found his leadership betrayed by his brother when Aaron constructed the golden calf, but accepted that he had acted out of a pragmatic assessment of the situation. Instead, the rabbis select two crucial figures from the beginning of the rabbinic period, Hillel and Shammai, both masters of Jewish law, both founders of academies that continued to debate with each other long after their founding teachers had died. Hillel was the more lenient in his judgments, Shammai the more strict, and their fundamental disagreements threatened to tear the Jewish people apart. Things got so bad that people spoke of two Torahs, two revelations of God seemingly in conflict with each other. The resolution came with a heavenly voice that declared: '*eilu v'eilu divrei elohim hayyim*', 'both these and these are the words of the living God' (B. Talmud Erubin 13b; Gittin 6b), both are legitimate interpretations of the tradition to be equally respected. The debate itself, with its contradictory conclusions, is sanctioned by God. But since these matters were not of merely academic interest but affected the life of the entire community, some guidelines were needed to resolve their differences. The solution was that when it comes to making practical legal decisions, one should follow the more lenient opinion of Hillel. Thus affirming the needs of the community and acknowledging the dangers of imposing on it a law that might not be kept.

Presumably these broader ramifications lay behind the decision to use the Hillel/Shammai illustration rather than a biblical one. The whole rabbinic methodology of interpretation and argument, the democratising of revelation, with all the attendant risks of divisiveness, is at stake here. Arguing one's way into heaven is a radically new religious approach.

Whereas in the Hillel/Shammai example both parties to the controversy are named, in the second case the controversy that was not 'for the sake of heaven', only one set of the protagonists is named, Korach and his company. The rabbis are referring to the rebellion against Moses in the wilderness by Korach and a group of disaffected leaders, each of whom had somehow lost out in the new structure set up by Moses (Numbers 16). Korach as a Levite could have had the role of high priest that went instead to Aaron and his family; his followers, Dathan and Abiram, the Reubenites, had lost their former political leadership to Moses. The 250 leaders who joined the rebellion, and whose identity is alluded to but not made explicit, may have been firstborn males who had lost to the Levites their former right of offering sacrifices. The implication is that Korach's rebellion was not motivated by the needs of the community or the 'democratic principles' Korach seemed to be asserting – if everyone is holy, what makes Aaron so special!? Instead, they would seem to be driven by motives of ego, pride, jealousy and the desire for power. It is therefore, in the rabbinic view, Korach and company's controversy alone, and Moses is not to be mentioned in the same breath as him.

The rabbinic commentaries on this passage tried to establish what was the difference between the two controversies. In the former case, that of Hillel and Shammai, the intention of the controversy was to find the truth: to hear each other's arguments, to refine each other through the process of debate, so that the truth that emerged had greater validity and was something that would come to endure in time. But in the latter case it is not truth that is at issue but a conflict with authority for the sake of gaining power. Again, the former case illustrates an important principle governing the recording of debates in the Talmud. Whatever the conclusion that is reached by majority vote, the minority opinion is recorded – both out of respect for those who argued and so that it is available for the argument to be reopened at a future time should this prove necessary.

Thus both the 'truth' that is discovered and the nature of the controversy 'endure'.

This kind of approach shown throughout the Talmud has even deeper ramifications, as indicated by Daniel Boyarin (1993:29):

> …the point is not that there was more or less dissent and controversy within the rabbinic culture than in the cultures of other forms of Judaism or Christianity but that in this culture, as in some of the others, it is precisely dissent that was canonised. The cultural model is one in which 'these and these are the words of the Living God', in which even God is not allowed to decide whose interpretation is correct (Boyarin 1990, 34-37). This particular structure must be taken very seriously in any attempt to describe rabbinic culture or any sub-system of it. We must be able to recognize not only that there were different views at any given time but also that the very fact of the existence of contradictory views all being asserted at the authoritative level would have fundamental effects on the nature of social practice and ideology…

What provides the common ground for legitimising the controversy of Hillel and Shammai, but not that of Korach, is that they should be '*l'shem shamayim*', literally, 'for the name of heaven', 'for the sake of heaven', even 'for the reputation, the "good name", of heaven'. Somehow in the debate between Hillel and Shammai and their respective schools, however divisive the arguments and the potential damage they might have caused to the community, in the end something held them in check, a higher aspiration motivated them and enabled them to reach the kind of agreement or compromise that was life-affirming and constructive. Being 'for the sake of heaven', they remained this side of conflict and breakdown. Korach and company crossed that boundary, and indeed the Reubenite faction turned up armed, ready for insurrection if they did not get their way. They were prepared for violence and it was through violence that they were stopped – the earth opened and swallowed them up living into the underworld.[1]

Whether we like it or not, our opponents rarely get swallowed up conveniently by the earth, and more often than not when things get to a certain state we are more likely to resort to our own acts of violence than wait for divine intervention. Yet certain questions emerge from this rabbinic passage and the illustrations it employs. What is that element, 'for the sake of heaven' that can keep a controversy within bounds, however tough and heated it may become? In particular, does the legitimising of controversy and debate within the religious tradition have an impact on this issue?

All human life is experienced in some way as controversy and potential conflict. This cannot be wished away, either by ideology, sentimentality or sloganeering. Nevertheless, once this reality is acknowledged, then we have a basis for regulating it and seeking to hold it within bounds and even transmute it into some greater kind of human harmony.

HOLY COMPROMISE

It is important in this context to stress that Judaism is based on a legal covenant or contract. Therefore it is legal thinking, alongside all the other human dimensions, that determines some of the forms of Jewish religious expression. The arguments between the rabbis in talmudic literature are hard-fought, on occasion with the trading of insults and even political action taken against each other in extreme cases – but all these examples are organised in a dialectical structure within the Talmud, so that the reader shares in the nature of the argument as much as the particular conclusions. This is reflected indirectly in the rabbinic preference for a neg-otiated settlement in a legal dispute between people – *pesharah*, (arbitration) or *bitzu'a* (adjustment, compromise), rather than the handing down of a legal judgment. A judgment is absolute, favours one side or the other, creates winners and losers, leaves emotions unresolved and unaddressed. A negotiated settlement may leave both sides equally frustrated having to give something up, but that is an equalising factor, and the human relationship between them may be restored in the process of seeking an agreement. It is this concern with, and indeed tension between, justice on the one hand and the healthy continuity of human society on the other that seems to be at the heart of rabbinic thought. Rabbi Joseph B. Soloveitchik, one of the leading Orthodox thinkers of the last century, describes the role of *pesharah* as follows:

> In *pesharah*...social harmony is the primary concern of the *dayyan* (rabbinic judge). The fine points of the law and the determination of precise facts are of secondary importance. The goal is not to be juridically astute but to be socially healing. The psychology of the contenders, their socio-economic status and values, as well as the general temper of society, are the primary ingredients employed in the *pesharah* process. These considerations are evaluated within the broad halakhic (legal) parameters

...and the final resolution of the conflict is a delicate and sensitive blending of both objective legal norms and subjective humanistic goals...(Soloveitchik 1979:54)

He continues by indicating the biblical verses cited to justify the use of arbitration.

The first verse reads: 'Execute the judgment of truth and peace in your gates' (Zechariah 8:16). The Talmud explains: 'Surely, where there is strict justice (*mishpat*) there is no peace. And where there is peace, there is no strict justice! But when do justice and peace coincide? Only in *pesharah*...(Babylonian Talmud Sanhedrin 6b – *bitzua*).

Where there is strict adherence to *din* (legal judgment), there is justice but no *shalom* (peace), because one of the parties is humiliated and antagonized. The immediate issue is resolved but the conflict persists, with ensuing social discord. The secular judge is seemingly indifferent to this failure since justice, not harmony, was his objective. *Shalom* is for social workers and psychologists to attain; it is beyond his jurisdiction. The Torah, however, wants the *dayyan* (the religious judge) to be not only a magistrate but a teacher and a healer. He should seek to persuade both parties to retreat from their presumed points of advantage, and he should preach to them about the corrosive personal and social effects of sustained rancour. His responsibility is primarily to enlighten, rather than to render decisions on points of law...

The second verse states: 'And David executed justice and righteousness toward his people (2 Samuel 8:15). The Talmud explains: 'Surely, where there is strict justice (*mishpat*) there is no righteousness (*tzedek*), and where there is righteousness there is no justice. But when do justice and righteousness coincide? Only in *pesharah*!' (Babylonian Talmud Sanhedrin 6b)

The *halakhah*...believes that absolute right and wrong can be realized only in heaven. In dealing with imperfect man, we posit that no man is totally wrong or right and that in the case of the litigants, both are partially right and wrong. The application of *din* can only take account of obvious surface conditions; it fails to perceive subtleties underneath, which dilute our certainty about the right and wrong of the litigants. Each has some responsibility for the situation and is partially guilty of the misunderstanding for misleading innuendoes, and for contributing indirectly to a climate in society which places others at a disadvantage. Strict justice deals with plain facts and salient reality; real responsibility, however, goes much deeper and is obscured from the scrutiny of the court. Metaphysically, no one is entirely absolved in situations of conflict. (Soloveitchik 1979:55–57)

In this view, in any controversy between apparent equals, both are responsible in some measure for what is happening. Only where there is an obvious imbalance of power between them, is it legitimate to hold one party more responsible than the other. However, equality is also to some extent a subjective matter, compounded of historical, cultural, economic and religious factors. Nevertheless, the success of arbitration lies in helping both sides to recognise their own contribution to the conflict, and how both stand to win and to lose in the resulting solution. That is to say part of the art of arbitration is to open up the normal experience of dialogue, that each protagonist comes to see the world, and particularly themselves, through the eyes of the other.

SACRED NEGOTIATION

The distinction between the logic of judgment and the logic of arbitration is well illustrated by comparing certain kinds of commercial practice in the West and the East. I heard this in a lecture by Dr Jonathan Webber, and as I recall it, the argument runs as follows.

Consider the difference between buying a house in the West and what happens in an Arab marketplace. In the West the seller's estate agent sets a price for the house, the prospective buyer looks around, sends in a surveyor and then the following discussion takes place. The buyer points out to the seller that the roof leaks, that there is dry rot in the basement, that the plumbing and all the electric wiring need repairing. Because of all these faults he can only make an offer considerably below the asking price. The seller protests that he had a new roof put in only five years ago and that the whole central heating system is new. After some haggling the two agree – but the seller is disappointed and feels cheated, having received less than anticipated. On the other hand, the buyer has now seen all the problems in the house and is aware of the extra money needed to find to repair it. In short, both leave the transaction bruised, disappointed and unfriendly.

Contrast the *shouk*. You stop to admire something and the owner invites you in for a coffee. You ask the price of the article and he gives you a figure. You say: 'It is truly a magnificent article and I would love to own it. Unfortunately my financial situation is such that I can only afford to pay you so much for it.' The seller responds: 'I am truly sorry that this is the case because you are such a nice person and I would dearly love to sell it to you. In the circumstances, I am willing to reduce the price to such and such.' More coffee is drunk, you discuss your respective families and exchange photographs. You say: 'You are really most generous and the article is of surpassing worth, but with the best will in the world, I fear that the very highest price I can offer is so much.' The seller will reply with further praise for your taste and generosity of spirit, and offer the next price down. In the end a deal is struck, but in the process a relationship has been created, a kind of friendship created and human contact, including the pleasure of the game itself, has been achieved.

The difference in approach is significant. It is also evident how the lack of awareness between a Westerner and an Easterner in how the game is to be played, how the two systems operate, must inevitably lead to misunderstanding, hurt pride and potential conflict.

Now I do not want to sentimentalise the *shouk*. Elias Canetti (1978:17–22) writing about Marrakesh, suggests that there is actually a real price for the article that someone at the back of the store knows – and he is the one who will determine when the reduction has gone on long enough. He also points out that the price is always greater for someone who is poorer, presumably because the richer person will more likely return for a second purchase. But cynicism apart, the point is that negotiations of this and other sorts, as suggested by the rabbinic debates recorded in the Talmud, involve a process that is itself life-serving, irrespective of the particular outcome.

Perhaps it is worth noting at this point how many illustrations of the art of negotiation are included in biblical narratives. Abraham bargains for a plot of ground in which to bury his wife Sarah (Genesis 23); Moses negotiates with Pharaoh for the release of the Israelites (Exodus 5–11); Ruth, through her display of humility and gratitude, actually inserts hints that elicit a considerable elevation of her status from Boaz (Ruth 2:8–17); indeed God, with occasional signs of irritation, has to negotiate with Moses to persuade him to return to Egypt, and reassure him after each of his objections, before finally losing the divine temper. Conversely, Moses becomes the arch-negotiator with God on behalf of the children of Israel after the episodes of the golden calf and of the spies in order to win a reprieve for the people. He has to make the most of the few bargaining points in his hand, God's promise to the patriarchs, God's self-declared mercy and compassion, even God's reputation in the eyes of the nations.

Most significantly, the revelation at Sinai itself is actually also part of an elaborate process of negotiation as God offers the children of Israel the opportunity to enter into a covenant, but only after they have had the chance to examine its detailed provisions.

BACK FROM THE BRINK

In all the above biblical cases, with the exception of the negotiations with Pharaoh where violence intrudes, those engaged in the process stand to win by the reaching of some kind of agreement. But what of the situation where violence seems to be inevitable? One biblical example of this is Jacob's return home and his dread at the encounter with his twin brother Esau, whom he had cheated out of his blessing some 20 years before. The narrative is complex and subtly woven together (Genesis 32–33). Jacob sends gifts ahead of him to appease his brother; he prays to God for help; he sends his family ahead of him over the river. And then comes the struggle with the mysterious man/angel in the middle of the night. He wrests from him a blessing and a new name, but leaves the struggle limping. When finally he comes to meet Esau and makes obeisance to him, his brother, instead of attacking him as expected, embraces him and all seems to have been resolved, though it is noteworthy that Jacob is careful to maintain a discreet distance between the two camps in the future. Coexistence is a delicate exercise that only begins at the moment of reconciliation and can never be taken for granted.

The text itself is very suggestive. Jacob carries with him the burden of 20 years of exile, memory and guilt at what he had done – stealing the firstborn's blessing. Does he have a real sense of the Esau whom he is going to meet, or does he see instead some fantasy figure bent on revenge? What indeed is the intention of the Esau who comes towards him? Is he approaching as an enemy with a troop of armed men ready to fight, or as someone coming with an honour guard to welcome a long-lost brother? Who is the figure with whom Jacob wrestles? The text is mysterious and open enough to allow for many interpretations: whether angel or man, Esau's guardian angel or Esau himself, the figure may also be at the same time something within Jacob with which he must fight, the fear he carries within him. Indeed, the matter seems to be resolved after the fight, even before he meets Esau. Considerable play is made on the word *panim*, 'face'. Before the struggle, Jacob is forever sending gifts and people 'before his face' (Genesis 32:4) as intermediaries between himself and Esau. But after the struggle, he stands 'before their face' (Genesis 33:3), suggesting that he can now 'face up to' his brother, having overcome the inner demon. Hence also the plays on the name of the place, *peniel*, meaning 'the face of God' (Genesis 32–33).

In the rabbinic view, Jacob's ploys were valuable signs to his descendants on how to deal with a threatening enemy. Firstly send a gift to appease, seek to buy off the danger. Only then, having done all that one can on the diplomatic front, pray to God for help. But in the last resort, arm yourself and be ready to fight. Battle might be necessary, controversy may have to spill over into conflict, but only after all other civilised methods of resolving matters have been given a fair try.

The case of Jacob and Esau is particularly significant because of the recognition that it gives of the backlog of fears, betrayals, hatreds and projections that are inevitably present when old controversies between individuals and peoples are resurrected. Moreover, the closer people or groups are to each other, the more their antagonisms are likely to reflect the dynamics of sibling rivalry. The irrational feeling of competition for the imagined love of a long-departed parent, the sense of being cheated out of something that was really destined for oneself and, conversely, the awareness of unacknowledged guilt on either side about past behaviours towards the other – all these colour and confuse the apparent cause of the current dispute. The story of Jacob's struggle with the 'angel' suggests that it is only when one, but preferably both, of the protagonists are willing to examine their own past responsibilities and guilt, wrestle with the fantasy image they have of the other and be willing to set it aside, and approach the other prepared to offer some appropriate gesture of appeasement, that reconciliation is possible.

Tragically, that degree of self-confidence is rare in a people and its leadership. There is a verse of the Psalms that is cited at various times in the Jewish liturgy. It can be translated in various modalities, but one version would be: 'May God give strength to His people, may God bless His people with peace' (Psalms 29:11). The objection is raised in one of the rabbinic commentaries: surely if God grants strength to Israel it will make them warlike and aggressive. To this comes the reply, it takes a great deal of inner strength and security to take the risk of seeking peace.

BETWEEN CONTROVERSY AND CONFLICT

So what happens when conflict seems inevitable, when the basis of the controversy is not 'for the sake of heaven'? It is instructive to take a further look at the story of Korach's rebellion and the way in which Moses actually handled it.

Biblical scholars have tried to disentangle the different sources that make up the story as a kind of composite. Nevertheless, the narrative does work quite clearly in the form that we have inherited. Moses, after a series of disasters in the wilderness that have almost brought the entire experiment to an end, must now face a rebellion, as if all the discontents that had been smouldering under the surface, and all the factions that had a particular grudge against the leadership, had now coalesced into a single expression. Moses and Aaron are summoned before an assembly of the people. Moses reminds the Levites, who have accused them of taking over the spiritual leadership, specifically of making Aaron and his sons into the Priests, that they too have been chosen to take on a special role in the cult, bringing the offerings of the people to God. He challenges them to stand before God the next day with their censers, the symbols of the priestly office. In the course of his argument he actually separates Korach out so that he is forced to stand beside Aaron, exposed and not hiding behind the rest of the Levitical group.

Similarly, Moses summons Dathan and Abiram, the Reubenites, whose argument is political: why did you take us out of Egypt, a land flowing with milk and honey, so that we die in this wilderness? Do you want political power over the people? (The Hebrew suggests something like: Will you 'lord it' over us?) Moses responds with an oath before God indicating that there is no evidence of his abusing the power granted to him as a leader.

The next day when they assemble, Moses pleads with God not to destroy the rebels, asking him, 'if one man sins will You rage against the whole community?' Then Moses goes with a delegation of elders, the other remaining ruling group from the Egyptian period, and warns all the different factions to separate themselves from Korach, Dathan and Abiram, who have emerged with their family in full military array. When the people move away from them, the earth opens up and swallows the political rebels living into the underworld. Also, fire comes down from heaven and devours the 250 would-be priests holding their censers.

It is an extraordinary story – but certain things emerge about Moses's strategy. First he seeks to differentiate the motives of the different groups – to separate the factions into their various parts with their different grievances. But beyond a simple policy of 'divide and conquer', Moses does seem to address the grievances of the Levites so as to persuade them to recognise what opportunity they have been given to express their desire to serve God. To the Reubenites, who have settled for war, he responds with war, at least a supernatural onslaught that buries them. The 250 who had wished to dedicate themselves to the service of God are indeed enveloped in a flame that comes down from heaven – symbolically, they are burned up in their own zeal.

Both this story and the previous one about Jacob share certain characteristic ploys when confronting potential or real conflict. Create a situation in which talking is possible before resorting to violence. Take seriously and address the concerns and discontents of those who are in opposition – Jacob addresses his brother's anger at the stealing of the blessing for fertility and success by offering financial compensation and, when he meets his brother, by adopting a position of subservience; Moses rehearses both the unspoken desires and the achievements of the Levites, raising their awareness that all their arguments are not with Aaron and the role he plays, but eventually about the service of God…Dathan and Abiram refuse to come to a discussion so, swallowing his pride, Moses goes to meet them. But in vain. Without a willingness to meet and negotiate there is no way forward – and violence becomes the only remaining option.

CONCLUSION

I am conscious that there is little in these teachings that is new or even particularly hopeful. When matters can be negotiated between potential antagonists, everything must be done to seek an agreed settlement – and certainly Jewish tradition contains a deal of teaching that would encourage this process. But there are also situations, like the Korach rebellion, in which conflict seems inevitable – though here too at least an attempt can be made to separate the factions, address real issues and limit the damage as much as possible.

By the time matters come to a head, however, it is usually too late. It is only in addressing the injustices, real and perceived, that are present before they reach the point of conflict that hope lies for our world. The rabbis already warned in another saying from the 'Chapters of the Fathers': 'The sword comes into the world because of the delay of justice and the perversion of justice' (Pirqe Avot 5:11). But the acknowledgment of inequalities usually requires the setting aside of our own perceived self-interest, not to mention our power and advantage in a given situation.

Why is the issue that sparks a conflict always so self-evident after conflict has arisen and never before? Or rather, why do we never wish to see it before the situation breaks down? Perhaps the fear of controversy itself, precisely because it implies change or may demand a re-examination of things we take for granted, is enough to make us ignore problems till it is too late. Perhaps we prefer to imagine that our own particular society or faith community is really united, despite the evidence at every moment that this is not the case. Perhaps we prefer to stay safely behind our own perceptions rather than risk seeing things through the eyes of the other. But any denial of reality must inevitably break down – and the greater the walls of defence we have built up against reality, the greater the destruction that will occur when they fall. In the next chapter we will look at what happens when controversy slides over into conflict.

Personally, I prefer the security of religious insecurity, of a dialogue with others that continually challenges, that opens up new dimensions of my own self. With Jewish tradition I celebrate the quest for negotiated truth and for holy compromise. God is always greater that the systems we devise. And, as the heavenly voice continues to remind us: both these and these are the words of the living God.

6

Between Controversy
and Conflict

The work of dialogue presupposes the existence of a willingness on the part of the particular groups or individuals to meet. Once that process starts and continuity is maintained, and provided that the dialogue is nurtured and not betrayed or hijacked by any of the partners, then with patience and trust, in the course of time, others might be persuaded to give at least their tacit assent to its continuity or find in it something of value for themselves or their community.[1]

What are the preconditions for such an activity to be effective, particularly when real issues of past or current conflict are involved? There needs to be the willingness of at least one side to acknowledge their own failings and sins of the past vis-à-vis the other as a crucial preliminary step. The internal will to acknowledge past faults, and the acceptance of a present responsibility to take an initiative towards the other, are the essential preconditions for dialogue and, ultimately, reconciliation. This view finds one classical Jewish expression in the talmudic tractate 'Pirqe Avot', the 'Chapters of the Fathers', in the statement: 'who is a *gibbor*, a "mighty person" or "warrior"? - one who controls his passions' (4:1). To this, a later rabbinic commentary added: 'and who is the mightiest of the mighty? - one who controls his passions and makes his enemy into his friend' (Avot d'Rabbi Natan 23).

Whether at the personal level or in the cases of groups or even nations in conflict, much may depend on the help of outside parties to act as mediators or facilitators, or simply to hold the ring. A rabbinic statement, again in the 'Pirqe Avot', points to the very special role played by the High Priest Aaron, brother of Moses:

> Be of the disciples of Aaron, loving peace and pursuing peace, [loving creation and bringing them close to Torah]. (Pirqe Avot 1:12)...If a man quarrelled with his wife and sent her out of the house, Aaron would go to him and ask him, 'Why do you quarrel with your wife?' The man might answer, 'because she acted shamefully to me.' At which point Aaron would say, 'I shall be your guarantee that she does not do so again.' Then he would go to the wife and ask her, 'Why did you quarrel with your husband?' She would reply, 'Because he beat me.' Aaron would say, 'I shall be your guarantee that he does not do so again.' Aaron would do this day after day until the husband took her back. When subsequently the woman had a child, she would say that without Aaron's help she would never have been reconciled, and so would name the child 'Aaron'. Some say there were more than three thousand children called Aaron. (Avot d'Rabbi Nathan 25:25b)

Aaron's role as the classic mediator is well described. He listens to both parties, acknowledging the issue as each sees it. He offers himself as a guarantee that the conditions of their resuming a relationship will be properly kept. He is prepared to continue negotiating patiently till the parties agree.

In another version of Aaron's actions he goes a step further in his reconciling work:

> When two men quarrelled, Aaron would go and sit with one of them and say, 'Look how your friend beats his breast and tears his hair out, saying: "How can I face my friend! I would be too embarrassed because I am the one who acted offensively towards him!"' He would sit with him till he had removed all anger from his heart. He would then go and do the same thing with the other man. Later when they met one another they would hug and kiss. (Yalkut Shimoni, Hukkat 764)

This is clearly a riskier strategy, but again requires a serious investment of time and commitment by Aaron in the process. This works effectively as a parable, one in which the mediator acts like a catalyst, ensuring that the process of reconciliation takes place but without imposing his own agenda, beyond the belief in the necessity for reconciliation, into the process. Of course, to pursue the chemical model, the catalyst is actually affected during the transaction but is restored to its original state at the end. But for both parties to be able to trust the neutrality of the mediator is clearly an essential ingredient. Yet no mediator is without his or her own particular concerns or commitments, so it is important to have some idea of what they also might bring to the table. This thought is triggered by a debate I became engaged in in response to a contemporary Christian source that was advocating non-violent activity as a value to be pursued by someone who would attempt to work for the peaceful resolution of conflicts. It comes from the *Newsletter of the World Conference on Religion and Peace* (December 1988–January 1989, Geneva): 'True religion does offer an alternative to violence. It is the power of love. But it must be love linked to total commitment to accept the full consequences of love and to be obedient to death. Only then can love become an effective power greater than violence.'[2] From a Jewish perspective there seems to be here an inner contradiction between an ideology that on the one hand gives 'absolute respect to human life', hence the practice of non-violence in a conflict situation, and yet, in the name of love appears to expect the self-sacrifice of human life as an ultimate ideal. I can recognise that such a view might be comprehensible within the broad framework of Christian belief, given that the self-sacrifice of Jesus is a significant model for Christian behaviour.

But Judaism is a tradition which takes as one of its central texts the Akeda, the binding of Isaac (Genesis 22). In this, one of the most problematic texts of the Hebrew Bible, the patriarch Abraham is asked by God to sacrifice his son Isaac, only to have the request cancelled at the last minute. That the Hebrew text expresses God's words as a request and not a command is often lost in translation – God too has something at stake in Abraham's free will to accept or refuse. Moreover, the text explicitly points out at the beginning that this is a test, even though the nature of the test is not made entirely clear. Neither of these factors soften the horror of the story or remove the central moral problem of a potential child sacrifice for the sake of a religious belief. Nevertheless, a major lesson of the story is that the child Isaac is not sacrificed, hence the title of the section the 'binding' of Isaac, and not the 'sacrifice' of Isaac, as it is known in other traditions.

The reality of Jewish existence over the millennia has included many occasions when entire communities gave their lives in defence of their faith. But to propose self-sacrifice as an ideological goal for any cause, let alone in the name of the quest for peace, is not perceived in Judaism as a virtue. On the contrary, when it comes to a physical threat to one's life, Jewish tradition contains as a normative rabbinic statement 'If someone comes to kill you, rise up early and kill him first' (Babylonian Talmud Berakhot 58a; Yoma 85b; Sanhedrin 72a). That is not the last word on the matter, nor is it the only Jewish position, and for 2000 years Jews were rarely in a situation where self-defence of this sort was an option.

A truer reflection of the Jewish view on the priorities when life is endangered is the rabbinic reading we saw in the last chapter of Jacob's behaviour when about to meet with Esau, whom he thought was still intending to kill him. Jacob did three things: he sent a present to Esau in order to try to appease him, he prayed to God to intercede and, in case both of these failed, he prepared himself for war (Midrash Tanhuma on Genesis 32:9). Both these passages dramatise the passionate Jewish concern with survival and life – without which, incidentally, we might well have disappeared off the face of the earth centuries ago. It may be that, coming from a religious community that has always experienced itself as a threatened minority, one that could not count on vast millions of adherents, the sanctity of the individual life has been taken very seriously by the Jewish people. For us, the giving up of life is not something that should be set up as an ideal in any way – a necessity perhaps, but only as a last and ultimate desperate resort.[3]

To illustrate this let me note one particular talmudic discussion. It comes from a time when studying Torah was seen as a form of resistance to the Roman authorities, but to do so was to sign one's own death warrant and thousands of Jews were killed or took their own lives in defence of their faith. The rabbis asked the question, what are the circumstances in which one should be prepared to give one's life, and when should one not? Their conclusion was to limit martyrdom and permit it only when forced, under threat of death, to perform one of three cardinal sins: murder, idolatry or adultery (Babylonian Talmud Yoma 85b; Sanhedrin 74a). In the case of idolatry, when faced with the choice of forced conversion or death it was permitted to pretend to accept another religion, but not if that was a public act which would lead other Jews to following suit. In these three situations and these alone should one accept death rather than obey. They based their view on a reading of Leviticus 18:5 – that God's laws were given so that people should live by doing them, and not die because of them. What is important here is not the particular limitations, but that the rabbis were deeply concerned by the temptation of self-sacrifice. They saw life itself as the primary gift and living as the primary command of God.

We are a people of survivors, from biblical times onwards, and our assertion that human beings are created in the image of God means that we have no right to deface or destroy that part of God that resides within us as human beings, except under the most extreme circumstances. That is not to say that Jews have not gone involuntarily (and sometimes voluntarily) to their deaths by the thousands – and indeed today we can speak of the millions – because of their faith, but it should be as a last resort and in no way as a response to an ideological desire. Perhaps one may speak of a norm of expected behaviour, one that should only be set aside in exceptional circumstances. Or else it may be the private decision of an exceptionally pious person – it cannot be a rule for normal religious conduct.[4] The norm is well illustrated by a particular Jewish joke – and I apologise if it appears to include some Christian stereotypes.

Because of a series of freak accidents of nature, it is discovered that the entire world will be covered by a flood in three days' time. In their respective places of worship, different groups prepare themselves for the end. In the Catholic church, the priest talks to his congregants: 'as you know, in three days the earth will be flooded – this means that we have three days in which to confess our sins before God and prepare ourselves for the end'. In the Protestant church, the pastor addresses his flock: 'as you know, in three days the earth will be covered in water – this means that we have three days in which to reconcile ourselves with each other and ask one another for forgiveness before the world ends'. In the synagogue, the rabbi is addressing his congregation: 'as you know, in three days the earth will be completely flooded – that means that we have three days in which to learn how to live under water'.

I would like to add one other Jewish idea to the theoretical basis of our discussions before addressing the practical problems before us. The talmudic tractate, 'Pirqe Avot', contains the following statement: 'Rabban Simon ben Gamliel says, The world is preserved by three things: by truth, by justice and by peace' (1:18). Again, as we saw in the last chapter, the mere assertion of these three values is not the end of the matter, because, though any two of them may coexist, in our real human situation the three of them cannot operate together at the same time. If you want absolute justice or absolute truth, you will not have peace but endless conflict. Peace is possible when both sides are prepared to step back from their absolute demands, when injustices are addressed as far as is reasonably possible but both parties are prepared to yield something to the other. The same is also the case with regards truth claims. Negotiation, compromise and realistic goals are the heart of human community and shared survival.

I would like to bring together three points from these more theoretical aspects and examine them in relationship to certain Jewish attitudes towards the Israeli–Palestinian conflict. The first is the primacy of 'survival'. As well as being built into a traditional Jewish value system, the need to survive has had to be cultivated through two millennia of exile living 'under-water', under the power of others who have been at times benign and at times demonic in their behaviour to the Jewish people. Add to this the unimaginable impact of the Shoah, in which one-third of the Jewish people were destroyed within living memory. There is no way that anything can be achieved from the Jewish or Israeli point of view without addressing this distrust of the outside world – a distrust that at times threatens to verge on paranoia, were it not for the fact that Jewish fears have all too often been confirmed by tragic and bitter experience. The current Jewish preoccupation with 'survival' and, in Israeli terms, 'security', is deeply coloured by the Shoah and has resulted in a feeling of the need to 'go it alone'. We live with the suspicion, confirmed for Israelis by their experience of the period prior to the Six-Day War and certainly during the Yom Kippur War, that in the eyes of the world we are still expendable. Perhaps the Gulf War has restored a little confidence that others are prepared to support Israel, but it is also recognised that a neutral Israel served the purposes of others. Unless these fears are addressed on political, psychological and spiritual levels as well, it will be very hard to move Israel to any change of status that seems to threaten a current perceived relative security.

If I understand the Palestinian situation, similar mechanisms exist amongst them based on their own experiences of dispossession as refugees, and under occupation. The recognition by both sides of this conflict on the baggage carried by the 'other' is another dimension that needs to be taken seriously if anything remotely like trust is to be established. What is needed is reassurance rather than a constant reinforcement of such deep-seated anxieties.

Secondly, since the beginning of the second Intifada and the events of 11 September 2001, we have seen the devastating effect of a doctrine of self-sacrifice in the name of a particular cause, especially if underpinned by a selective reading of religious scriptures. There is already too much emotional confusion and turmoil, enough real sacrifices and martyrs, both within the current conflict and deep within the folk memories of both peoples. Until now, the contribution made by religion in the region has been more to exacerbate things, to make absolute demands and claims, to raise emotions and heighten tensions, rather than to move anyone in the direction of peace – with the possible unique exception of that fateful encounter between Anwar Sadat, Menachem Begin and Jimmy Carter, all of whom seem to have had some level of religious motivation. There is a common view that ascribes the past failures of religion to the mistakes of individuals or groups, while asserting the ultimate innocence of religions in what goes wrong. Yet surely it is a fatal mistake to confess the sins of the past without exploring and acknowledging the inbuilt potential for destructiveness that is endemic in our religions themselves. This may appear shocking, but it should not be. Religion attempts to explore and sanctify all aspects of human existence, but it cannot bring out the best in human beings unless it is prepared to tackle the worst in them as well – and thus risk becoming itself affected in the struggle and even acquiring its own harmful characteristics. Religion can be a resource for good or for evil in this conflict, as anywhere else, and we who claim to act on its behalf must be honest about the traps built into our own traditions and continually seek ways for our own self-purification. There are no guarantees, and the higher our aspirations, the greater the possibilities of our failure. So those who wish to intervene need to be very cautious in their rhetoric, and the values and emotions they evoke, both consciously and unconsciously. What is needed in those who would play a role is a proper modesty, a passionate detachment and a very patient love.

Thirdly, I would raise the question of the use of the word 'peace' itself. I am very influenced by an old Yiddish proverb – 'better an insincere peace than a sincere war'. So many claims have been made for the desire for 'peace' by all sides in the current conflict that it has become part of a political game to claim the moral high ground – often with little to justify their protestations. Peace is a high ideal, and many are the sentences from rabbinic literature that could be quoted to show how Jews value it and are encouraged to seek it. But as I have indicated above, peace has a realistic price and we need to go beyond rhetoric to spell out the options that are really available. Those who would intervene out of their own religious conviction to help secure peace must try to set aside their own ideological claims on the word, to cease absolutising it, and to inject pragmatism, enlightened self-interest and modest proposals into the arena.

I would like to raise three further issues that I think must be addressed directly in terms of the specifics of this conflict.

The first has to do with the problem of the imbalance of power at all levels within the conflict. I was told prior to the Gulf War that a number of long-standing Israeli–Palestinian dialogue groups had already begun to fall apart for a particular reason. Whereas the Israeli participants entered into such discussions out of a genuine desire for peace and friendship, as had indeed the Palestinians, at some point they came up against the Palestinian need for what they saw as a matter of justice for their people. As a Palestinian colleague once put it: 'The Israelis have everything – so all they need is peace. But we have nothing!' The inability of the Israeli partners to deliver justice, and their growing realisation that dialogue did not seem to alter the macro-dimensions of the conflict, led to a painful frustration and parting of the ways. The outbreak of the second Intifada has had an even more catastrophic impact on the Israeli 'peace camp', which suggests that at a deep level there has been a tragic lack of communication. In any attempt to address the problem we must consider the difficulties of the imbalance of power between the various protagonists.[5]

If that is dramatised in the case of the Palestinians vis-à-vis the Israelis, it is important to remember that we have here a set of perceptions with several layers. The Palestinians feel themselves overwhelmed by the Israelis, but in some sense gain emotional strength from being part of a larger Arab world, even if frustrated by its seeming failure to support them adequately. Similarly the Israelis feel threatened in attempting to deal with the Palestinians because of their own perceived relative weakness compared to the vast masses of the different Arab populations around them. Beyond even them lie the forces of the superpowers with their old regional rivalries. Somehow, unless these particular perceptions and realities of complex imbalances of power can all be addressed at once, no-one will be able to break out of this interlocking structure.

The tragedy for the Palestinians is to find themselves at the bottom of this heap, which leads into my second point to be addressed. Both Jews and Palestinians, and indeed the entire region, suffers on some level from the experience of previous 'colonialism'. Whereas this is recognisable for the other people in the region, it applies equally to the Jews — though in our case the colonial exploitation did not take place in some far-flung part of an empire, but instead within the heart of Europe. Jewish communities were bought and sold and shifted around from one exile to another, from one comfortable home to another bolthole, at the whim of a myriad regimes, Christian and Muslim alike. They were subjected, just as were the classic victims of colonisation, to the same techniques of divide and conquer. They too were conditioned to experience feelings of inferiority and shame and self-hatred, of fear and paranoia. All the parties to the conflict have a wealth of similar experiences, half-acknowledged and half-denied, that colour their responses today. There is even a tragic irony in the particular problem faced by the Palestinians, as one of them remarked on a television programme. He pointed out in despair that of all the people in the world by whom to be persecuted, it was their bad luck that it was the Jews who were their oppressors, because in the recent tragic history of the Jewish people, their pain and suffering were so enormous that Palestinian suffering appeared to outsiders as insignificant in comparison. That is not to say that Palestinian suffering is not just as bitter and painful and tragic for those involved, but in his view, in the perception of the world the Palestinian problem could only appear tiny in comparison. In addressing the conflict the experience and psychological consequences of this past historical conditioning have also to be taken very seriously into account in seeking a solution. We are dealing with the victims of real trauma with all the psychological syndromes that arise from this.

The third point has to do with the problem of the Western demonisation of Islam. If virtually every image we see on our television screens is the same stereotype of masses of people or violent behaviour, we who choose, create and show ourselves these images constantly reinforce our own fear about the Islamic world. In the same way we have our own set of terminology, speaking of militant Islamic fundamentalism, as a catch-all phrase for every manifestation of Islam. My own experience of working with Muslims has been completely different from this, but there are times when I also wonder if I am only dealing with a select minority and am somehow misguided. Certainly within Israel these religious stereotypes exist and reinforce their fears of the Arab world as well. It seems to me that there is a major task here that must also be tackled. In place of the demonisation of Islam we need to work for the 'domestication' of Islam – the transforming of these images alongside a genuine attempt at dialogue and clarification and trust-building, particularly amongst the three monotheistic traditions. Much of this must begin away from the Middle East, because the political struggles too readily confuse the religious issues. Support should be given to all dialogue (or trialogue) programmes. There should be far more resources put into academic work in the West on the history of the golden age of Spain, when Islamic and Jewish civilisation worked hand in hand, and on ways found to portray and dramatise and disseminate this knowledge. And there should be a concerted effort to ensure that Islamic studies, taught by Muslims, feature within Jewish institutions of higher learning, and that Jewish studies, taught by Jews, feature in Muslim institutions of higher learning. The possibility of normal relationships that exist among friends, acquaintances and neighbours, that are not disturbed by religious or political differences, should be encouraged, so that both sides can move beyond their stance of mistrust of each other, even where the immediate conflict does not exist. It can only be a small beginning, but it is the sort of lateral activity that will eventually change the consciousness of those at centre stage.

I have attempted to indicate some of the factors from a Jewish perspective that might hinder the building of trust in a specific situation of conflict – both because of the presuppositions of those who would wish to take on the role of mediators and peacemakers, and because of some of the baggage carried by at least the Jewish side of the conflict. In the next chapter I want to move back to Jewish teachings that may contribute to the quest for universal values.

However to end this chapter it is worth considering a Chasidic teaching, mediated by Martin Buber, that suggests the great inner responsibility we must take on if we seek to create peace for others.

> Rabbi Bunam taught: our sages say: 'Seek peace in your own place.' You cannot find peace anywhere save in your own self. In the psalm we read: 'There is no peace in my bones because of my sin.' When we have made peace within ourselves, we will be able to make peace in the whole world.

7

The Ten Commandments
and the Quest for
Universal Values

At the centre of the impulse towards interfaith dialogue, as in any dialogue process, is a paradox. On the one hand the practice assumes, even asserts, the need to recognise and accept the otherness of one's dialogue partner in his or her uniqueness. Indeed, it is precisely because of some perceived difference, in gender, culture, faith, class, race, nationality or other feature that makes it necessary in a particular situation to meet, understand our differences and the effects they have upon our relationship, our mutual alienation and potential or actual conflict. Yet the very process of dialogue is based upon the premise that it is indeed possible for us to meet, share and, to at least a limited extent, learn to see the world, and ourselves, through the eyes of the other, to 'stand in their shoes'. What makes this possible is the awareness that ultimately all human beings are part of the same species, have the same physical, intellectual and emotional equipment, despite all the overt differences between us, and, in terms of the religious teachings of the three Abrahamic faiths, are all created equal in the image of God.

Hence, alongside the quest for understanding and indeed celebrating our differences, there are ongoing attempts to find shared values and common objectives that reinforce the ultimate unity of all human beings. One of the key attempts today to seek out this 'unity within diversity' is the work of Hans Küng in terms of what he describes as a 'global ethic'. It is in response to this quest that it becomes important to explore the sources within Judaism for elements that could contribute to such a universal system of values, perhaps inevitably focusing on the most widely recognised statement of principles, the Ten Commandments (or Decalogue).

From a study of the sources of Judaism, particularly the Talmud, it is quite possible to assert that a particular point of view on a given subject is 'authentically' Jewish. But it is also possible to prove that the opposite opinion is equally authentic. This is not altogether surprising because such a plurality of interpretations is an inescapable consequence of the nature of 'revealed' religions. Once the word of God has been given, canonised, and thus fixed 'for all eternity', interpretation becomes essential so as to make it relevant to changing circumstances and realities. Moreover, if God is 'infinite', 'transcendent' or 'greater', whatever terminology one wishes to use, then the 'word of God' revealed to human beings must itself reflect this infinity.

Human ingenuity is almost limitless when it comes to creating seemingly closed systems of belief, and then finding ways to open them up. The very fact of having a fixed sacred text presents the challenge to every generation to understand it afresh. As the rabbis expressed it, there are 70 faces to Torah by which they meant an infinite number of possible interpretations for a given passage, sentence, word, letter, the decorative crowns on top of the Hebrew letters – even for the seemingly empty spaces between the letters because 'the Torah was written as black fire on white fire' (Jerusalem Talmud Shekalim 6:1 49d).

The particular circumstances of a given generation contribute to the direction those interpretations will take, and the vagaries of each new direction will in turn offer precedents for future reinterpretation. Perhaps that is what actually defines a 'scripture' – that it can never be simply ignored or taken for granted but demands of those who have received it that it be listened to, questioned, challenged, reinterpreted and then reapplied in the changed contemporary circumstances.

Our own time, as reflected in the quest for a 'global ethic', is one in which our particular world view demands that religions dig into their myriad treasures to find those teachings that encourage mutual understanding, solidarity with and generosity of spirit towards each other. This seemingly 'self-evident' quest for mutual respect, understanding and tolerance of today was not always the case. Indeed, this same religious moment that calls for interfaith dialogue has also seen the renewal of the politicisation of religion on an unprecedented scale, interreligious conflict and the sanctioning of brutality, witch hunts and genocide. The exhilarating sense that we belong to 'one world', and hence the need to find ways of mutual support and sharing, seems to be accompanied by the terrifying sense that we do indeed belong to 'one world' and therefore that which gives us our individual identity and uniqueness, our way of life, be it through our tribe, nation, people or religion, is under threat. Every expression of universal hope seems to call forth the contrary need to assert a particularistic identity, to be strengthened by a return to our 'roots', to that 'old-time religion', as remembered, imagined or reinvented for today. Thus the quest for a meeting across the religious traditions, one anchored in the sources and resources of our religious traditions, is actually one feature of a global religious revival that is in some ways as problematic as it is full of opportunity and hope.

It is therefore very important that in seeking those formulations that express the universalism of our faith we do not sentimentalise what we find or deny that it has at the same time its own implicit dark side. For that must inevitably be the case. Religion seeks to address all aspects of human life and activity so as to 'redeem' them in some way, to offer them back to God who is their source. Yet the exploration of our complex human nature has built-in traps. In another context, my colleague Lionel Blue expressed it by saying that religion seeks to make the world religious, yet all too often ends up by itself becoming worldly. The very beliefs and ideal forms of religious expression contain their own risks. We tend to assert that there is somewhere a pure religious ideal in our tradition that is perfect and can never do wrong – and that the crimes and disasters done in the name of our tradition are merely the incidental fault of human error, weakness or mischief. There may indeed be a level at which this pure religion exists, but it is higher than the religious systems that we actually operate. Within the 'Abrahamic' faiths, our monotheism can easily become an exclusive monolatry, our obedience to God mere subservience to human authority, and our enthusiasm fanaticism. So it is not only the formulations of the 'values' and 'truths' that we must investigate in the religions to which we belong, but their methods of achieving them, and their commitment to self-criticism, self-purification and repentance, *teshuvah*. Religious formulations are conventionally life-enhancing, tolerant and generous-spirited – how do we ensure that they are real?

All this is by way of introduction to examining a Jewish contribution to the quest for global ethical values. As suggested above, it is possible to find within Judaism both a tendency to seek out such general principles and an equally strong wish to view them with caution. In early rabbinic debates about the importance of the Ten Commandments, great care was taken to limit their prominence because of the fear that they would be seen as some kind of 'essence' of Judaism, whereas the rabbis asserted that the Torah in its entirety was the word of God. Whether the 'laws' within the Hebrew Bible were immediately relevant or seemingly inexplicable, they carried equal weight and called for the same obedience. Who were we to judge what significance God placed upon them? (Though, at the same time, reason and pragmatism were immediately introduced when it came to establishing how any given law was to be carried out in practice.) Nevertheless, the Ten Commandments remain a central expression of a universal Jewish ethic. Moreover, the tendency to seek guiding principles remained a concern of rabbinic Judaism. It can be seen in the following talmudic passage:

Rabbi Simlai taught: Six hundred and thirteen commandments were given to Moses.
Then King David reduced them to eleven in Psalm 15, beginning: 'God, who may live in Your tent, and dwell on Your holy mountain? One who follows integrity, who does what is right and speaks the truth in his heart.'
The prophet Micah reduced them to three (Micah 6:8):
'Act justly, love mercy and walk humbly with your God.'
Then came the prophet Isaiah and reduced them to two (Isaiah 56:1):
'Keep justice and act with integrity'.
The prophet Amos reduced them to one (Amos 5:4):
'Seek Me and live!'
Habakuk also contained them in one statement (Habakuk 2:4):
'But the righteous shall live by his faith.'
Rabbi Akiba taught: 'The great principle of the Torah is expressed in the commandment: 'Love your neighbour as you love yourself; I am the Eternal' (Leviticus 19:18).
But Ben Azai taught a greater principle:
'This is the book of the generations of humanity. When God created the first human being, God made him in the image of God' (Genesis 5:1) (Makkot 23b–24a; Genesis Rabbah, Bereshit 24:7; Sifra 89b).

This last debate between Akiba and Ben Azai is recorded more than once, and reflects a central religious issue. What is the difference between the two verses? The Leviticus verse finds our obligation to our fellow human beings in their 'likeness' to ourselves, though the phrase is difficult to understand. However it must be noted that our 'neighbour', in its context in Leviticus, is somewhat narrowly defined as a fellow Israelite. (Nevertheless, a broader obligation is also present in Leviticus 19:34, where a complementary verse demands that we love 'the stranger', the 'resident alien', the *ger*, 'as ourselves'.) In contrast, the Genesis quote puts every human being into the category of a person made in the image of God, and therefore not only 'like us', but equally bearing the imprint of the creator. As expressed in our passage, the two verses together define the essential oneness of humanity and our obligation to mutual support, fellow-feeling and responsibility.

To Akiba is ascribed another attempt to sum up the 'whole of the Torah' in a single teaching (Avot d'Rabbi Natan XXVI 27a – Schechter ed.) It is the same formulation of the 'golden rule' earlier attributed to Hillel. Interestingly, the context of Hillel's answer is the request of a pagan to discover the 'essence' of Judaism. The story is worth repeating:

> A pagan came to Shammai (whose academy rivalled that of Hillel) and said to him: 'Accept me as a proselyte on the condition that you teach me the whole of the Torah while I stand on one foot!' Shammai drove him away with the measuring rod he held in his hand!
>
> Then he went to Hillel (renowned for his patience!) who received him as a proselyte and taught him: 'What is hateful to you do not do to your fellow; that is the whole of the Torah, all the rest is commentary. Go and learn.' (Shabbat 31a)

All the above reflects a broad universalism within Jewish teaching that can ultimately be traced back to the opening chapters of Genesis. Beyond this recognition of the oneness of humanity, the rabbis asserted that certain key responsibilities are incumbent on all people. This they expressed in the concept of the Seven Noachide Laws, universally binding moral obligations given to Noah after the flood, and hence through his sons to all of humanity. They include prohibitions on idolatry, blasphemy, bloodshed, sexual sins, theft and eating a limb from a living animal, as well as the positive command to establish a legal system for one's society (Tosefta Avodah Zarah 8:4; Sanhedrin 56a).

In any attempt to find a core set of universal values to which all different faith communities might be expected to subscribe, these seven laws are a possible starting point and offer a Jewish contribution to the debate. Clearly, problems will emerge over definitions of idolatry, particularly given the strictness of the monotheistic faiths on this issue. The demand for establishing courts of law, so as to ensure justice for all, is an essential factor, even though societies disagree with each other as to what exactly constitutes 'human rights' within a particular legal system. However, one element seemingly missing in this list is anything that addresses the question of how societies are to meet across their particular boundaries – whether the 'society' in question be a national, ethnic, religious or other kind. Where is the ethical demand to create a positive relationship with others?

In fact it exists elsewhere in a rabbinic concept: '*mipnei darkei shalom*', 'in the interests of peace'. This phrase appears in the Mishnah (Gittin 5:8), in a series of regulations designed to prevent unnecessary conflict within Israel. The last in the series discusses the parts of the produce of the harvest that are to be left for the poor – the individual stalks of grain (gleanings), the 'corner of the field', *peah* (Leviticus 19:9) and an entire sheaf if it has been overlooked in the gathering (Deuteronomy 24:19). They do not try to prevent the poor among the gentiles from gathering 'gleanings', the 'forgotten sheaf' and 'the corner' – in the interests of peace.

The Talmud then elaborates: 'One provides for the poor of the gentiles as well as the poor of Israel, and visits the sick of the gentiles as well as the sick of Israel and buries the dead of the gentiles as well as the dead of Israel - in the interests of peace' (Babylonian Talmud Gittin 61a). A variation reads: 'In a city where there are both Jews and gentiles, the collectors of alms collect both from Jews and from gentiles: they feed the poor of both, visit the sick of both, bury both, comfort the mourners whether Jews or Gentiles, and they restore the lost goods of both - in the interests of peace' (Jerusalem Talmud Demai 4:6).

Presumably this idea can be traced back to Jeremiah's letter to the exiles in Babylon, encouraging them to 'seek the peace of the city to which I have exiled you, for in their peace will be your peace' (Jeremiah 29:7). At its face value, Jeremiah's call can be seen purely in terms of 'enlightened self-interest'. But pragmatic motivations are of enormous importance in establishing the base-line, common sense presuppositions for any human interaction. The process of operating on such a basis has its own rewards in the mutual respect and ultimate affection that it creates. Thus, the ethos of establishing norms for relationships with the 'other' on the principle of 'in the interests of peace' has enormous long-term value and importance. Indeed its apparent 'pragmatism' conceals a fundamental religious value, for its implementation must inevitably have an impact on the conventional attitudes, practices and formulations within the rest of the religious tradition.

It is surely no accident that the principle emerged in Israel in a situation of relative powerlessness in which accommodation of a majority power, the Roman occupation, made it an essential factor for survival. Where a faith community experiences itself as having some measure of power or, paradoxically, where that sense of power is under threat, the need for such considerations may well seem less relevant or urgent. But the challenge of Hans Küng's global ethic lies precisely in recognising the vulnerability of all human societies today and the need to reassess on all levels issues of seeming power and authority.

This latter consideration brings us back to the paradox I mentioned before – that the quest for a global ethic comes precisely at the time when enormous energies are pushing people in the opposite direction, towards a ghettoisation of their particular faith community, often accompanied by expressions of hostility towards others. Those who have been engaged in dialogue of any sort know that it is a two-way process. In addressing the other, we risk losing touch with our own community. In fact, it is usually easier to deal with those from the other faith who have a similar interest in dialogue than with our co-religionists. The hardest part of dialogue is often returning home and trying to convey to those who have not had our experience what it means and why it is important, and reassuring them that we have not simply betrayed them. The success of this new initiative will depend on both the degree to which we are able to enter the dialogue 'back home' and the way in which we help each other to achieve this. It is precisely at this point that formulations have to be translated into a new self-awareness, and that a transformation has to take place on intellectual, emotional and spiritual levels. Yet for this to work, we who are engaged in the task of dialogue with each other must work on such transformations within ourselves. In this case the mediator is the message. It is the committed individual who has to hold and somehow resolve the paradoxes of the different ideas within our traditions, the tensions between the particular and the universal. But more than that, to face and somehow work through the deep fears of powerlessness, alienation and dissolution that are the shadow side of our 'global village'

Such a transformation is nicely suggested by a story. A man sent his son to the *yeshiva*, the talmudic academy, to study Talmud for five years. When he returned the father met him, took him aside into his study and asked him what he had learnt. The son replied: 'I learnt that the greatest teaching is "you shall love your neighbour as yourself".' 'But you knew that before you went away!' said the father. 'You didn't need five years of study to find that out!' 'The difference,' said the son, 'is that now I know that it means: "I must love my neighbour as myself"!'

THE TEN COMMANDMENTS

Since the Ten Commandments play such a central role within the religious tradition of the Hebrew Bible and Judaism, and have their direct influence on Christianity and, perhaps more indirectly, on Islam, it is helpful to examine them in more detail. Though Jewish tradition has seen them as part of a specific divine revelation given to the Jewish people, the rabbis are insistent upon their universal relevance and indeed the possibility of other people accepting the Torah, the revelation in its entirety, for themselves.

> The Torah was given in public, openly in a place owned by no one. For if the Torah had been given in the land of Israel, the Israelites could have said to the nations of the world, 'You have no share in it.' But now that it was given in the wilderness in public, openly in a place owned by no one, everyone wishing to accept it could come and accept it. (Mekhilta, Ba-hodesh 1, on Exodus 19:1–2)

Another rabbinic homily has God offering the Ten Commandments to the other nations only to have them refusing to accept them when they see the provisions that would impact on their normal behaviour (Mekhilta, Ba-hodesh 5, on Exodus 20:2).

The Ten Commandments first appear in chapter 20 of the Book of Exodus as the preamble to the covenant between God and Israel, and Moses repeats them (Deuteronomy 5), with slight variations, in his closing address that takes up most of the Book of Deuteronomy. They include certain key affirmations that have become the basis of much of human civilisation. Indeed, they have stepped out of that biblical context and taken on a life of their own. Their very conciseness and formality of construction make them a touchstone for the quest for universal values and a model for other attempts at drawing up codes of values in many different kinds of context. Even the story that surrounds their appearance in the Bible, the two tablets of stone engraved by God, their subsequent shattering by Moses and his re-engraving of every word on a second set of tablets, gives them a powerful mythic quality, irrespective of their actual content. The image of Moses holding them up has become an iconic symbol of the rule of law in human societies. The fact that there are ten of them, itself a number of exceptional power with its relationship to the fingers of two hands, adds to the readiness with which they can be committed to memory.

But it is also this very power that proves problematic for the rabbinic Judaism that builds itself upon the Hebrew Bible. The rabbis struggled both to honour the Ten Commandments and at the same time prevent them being seen as some kind of essence of the biblical message. They feared precisely that tendency that led them to stand alone. For the rabbis the entire Torah, the five books of Moses, and all subsequent and derived laws and teachings, were all equally significant as the word of God. There was no 'essence', no simple formulation that could replace the rest of the body of the Bible. All laws within the Torah were of equal worth and significance – even if some of them seemed obscure whereas others appeared to be based on natural human expectations, even common sense. Their quest was the application of the Torah, in its smallest detail, to the conduct of individual lives and of society as a whole, so their method was to debate and work through specific cases and instances. They resisted the creation of principles, creeds or dogmas, preferring an openness to the extraordinary variety of human experiences and needs.

So it became important to them to prevent the Ten Commandments acquiring too prominent a place, overshadowing, and hence diminishing, the fuller revelation of God. Thus though they were originally recited daily in the temple liturgy and were contained in the *t'fillin* (phylacteries, small boxes placed on the head and hand while praying), they were subsequently removed from the latter and from too prominent a place in the post-temple liturgy. The reason given was precisely the concern that sectarians would assert that they were indeed the essence of the Torah (Jerusalem Talmud, Berakhot 1, 3c). When the commandments are read in the synagogue as part of the regular weekly cycle of readings of the Torah (in Exodus 20 and Deuteronomy 5) as well as at the Festival of Shavuot (Pentecost), the congregation customarily stands, but this action too was disputed in the Middle Ages as it again gave them undue prominence.

Before looking at the wider significance of the Ten Commandments we need to examine them in their biblical setting. The first point to be noted is that the term 'Ten Commandments' is not biblical at all. When they are repeated by Moses he refers to them as the 'ten words' ('*asereth ha-devarim*': Deuteronomy 4:13), the same expression that is used for the text inscribed on the second set of tablets engraved by Moses (Exodus 34:28): 'the words of the covenant, the ten words'. Later in the Hebrew of the rabbinic period the word '*devarim*' was replaced by '*dibberoth*', the term that was chosen by the rabbis to represent divine speech (Greenberg 1985:83–84). This distinction between 'commandments' and 'divine utterances' is reflected in Martin Buber's examination of the Decalogue within the setting of the creation of the covenant between God and Israel: 'What this means is that the intention to be recognized in it refers neither to articles of faith nor to rules of behaviour, but to the constituting of a community by means of common regulation' (Buber 1958:130–31). He goes on to explain that if one studies the individual laws separately, as has commonly been done in biblical scholarship, there is a tendency to distinguish between 'religious' laws and 'ethical' laws, all of which are addressed to individuals. But Israelite society did not make such a distinction between 'religious' and 'ethical', for all the laws come under the same divine command. Moreover the 'individual' saw him- or herself as part of a collective whole, part of a common life, unified by the conception of a divine sovereign.

In analysing the structure of the Decalogue, Buber recognises three divisions. By his reckoning there are actually five separate 'religious' commands within the first part, i.e. those determining the relationship between Israelites and God. Similarly, there are five closing 'ethical' ones – which deal with interpersonal relations. But between them stand two that Buber sees as the only ones dealing specifically with time – the laws about keeping the Shabbat and the honouring of father and mother.

> Remember the Sabbath day and keep it holy. You have six days to labour and do all your work, but the seventh shall be a Sabbath for the Eternal your God. That day you shall do no work, neither you, nor your son, nor your daughter, nor your servant, man or woman, nor your cattle, nor the stranger who lives in your home. For in six days the Eternal made heaven and earth, the seas and all that is in them, and God rested on the seventh day. Therefore God blessed the Sabbath day and made it holy.
>
> Respect your father and your mother so that the days of your life be fulfilled on the land which the Eternal your God gives you.

Buber writes:

> The two of them, and only these two among all of the Ten Commandments, deal with time, articulated time; the first with the closed succession of weeks in the year, the second with the open succession of generations in national duration…Both of them together ensure the continuity of national time; the never-to-be-interrupted consecution of consecration, the never-to-be-broken consecution of tradition. (Buber 1958:132)

Of the closing 'words' he explains:

> If the first part deals with the God of the Community and the second with the time, the one-after-the-other of the Community, the third is devoted to the space, the with-one-another of the Community in so far as it establishes a norm for the mutual relations between its members. There are four things, above all, which have to be protected, in order that the Community may stand firm in itself. They are life, marriage, property and social honour. And so the damaging of these four basic goods and basic rights of personal existence is forbidden in the most simple and pregnant of formulas. (Buber 1958:133)

Buber concludes his analysis by addressing the last commandment, against coveting those things that belong to your neighbour:

> There is one attitude, however, which destroys the inner connection of the Community even when it does not transform itself into actual action; and which indeed, precisely on account of its passive or semi-passive persistence, may become a consuming disease of a special kind in the body politic. This is the attitude of envy. The prohibition of 'covetousness'…is to be understood as a prohibition of envy. The point here is not merely a feeling of the heart but an attitude of one man to another which leads to a decomposition of the very tissues of Society. (Buber 1958:133)

A few more general remarks about the contents of the Ten Commandments are in order. Buber also draws attention to the fact that they begin with God's reminder about the exodus from Egypt, rather than focusing on God as creator of the world. Here the particular relationship to Israel is stressed. A rabbinic comment emphasises this point through a parable:

> It is like a king who entered a province. He said to them, 'May I rule over you?' They said to him, 'Have you done anything for our benefit that you should rule over us?' What did he do? He built the city wall for them, put in a water supply and fought their wars. He said to them, 'May I rule over you?' They replied, 'Yes, yes!' In the same way God brought Israel out of Egypt, split the Sea for them, brought down the Manna for them, raised for them the well in the desert, brought the quails for them and fought for them the battle against Amalek. [Then] God said to them, 'Shall I rule over you?' They replied, 'Yes, yes!' (Mekhilta Ba-hodesh 5 to Exodus 20:2)

Though this passage has an underlying humour, it emphasises the relatedness of God and Israel through a shared experience of loyalty and trust. That is the basis on which a lasting covenant can be built. But the opening reminder of the exodus from Egypt stamps another idea on the Ten Commandments in their totality and the society that Israel is to create through them. For it intends a liberation from slavery, a society in which the forced labour of Egypt is to be banished forever – and indeed the very first law in the following chapter in Exodus is the one about liberating slaves in the seventh year. Israelites are no longer to own each other. And though this emphasis is strictly internal to the covenant, and does not apply to the ownership of foreign slaves, the whole thrust of the Exodus narrative itself has similar universal implications. Indeed this fact is spelled out in the Book of Exodus, in which it is repeatedly pointed out that the liberation of Israel is also to be a lesson to the Egyptians (Exodus 7:5; 9:14; 11:7; 14:4, 18), the great world power of the time. Freedom is to become a universal value, and indeed the image of the exodus from Egypt continues to be a universal symbol of the struggle for liberation in every society and in every situation of slavery where the biblical story is known.

The second major emphasis in the Ten Commandments is on the rejection of idolatry. Based on the demand for absolute loyalty to God, the prohibition on making images of anything 'in the heavens above, or on the earth beneath, or in the waters beneath the earth' presents a challenge to every attempt to tie God down to some human limitation. That there are implicit problems in such an image of a God who is 'jealous' of idols leads to a rabbinic conversation with a 'philosopher'.

A certain philosopher asked Rabban Gamliel, 'It is written in your Torah: "I the Eternal your God am a jealous God." But is there any power in an idol that should arouse jealousy? A warrior can be jealous of another warrior, a wise person of another wise person or a rich person of another rich person. But is there any power in idolatry to evoke jealousy?' Rabban Gamliel replied, 'Suppose a man called his dog by the name of his father, so that when making a vow he would vow, "By the life of this dog". Against whom would the father be incensed [literally, impassioned, jealous]? Against the son or the dog?'

The philosopher said, 'Some idols are worthwhile.' Gamliel replied, 'What is your evidence for this?' He said, 'There was a fire in a certain province and the temple of the idol was saved. Was it not because the idol protected itself?' Rabban Gamliel replied, 'I will give you a parable. What is it like? Like a king of flesh and blood who went out to battle. With whom did he fight? With the living or with the dead?' He replied, 'With the living!'

Then the philosopher tried again. 'Since there is nothing useful in any of them why does God not just annihilate them?' Rabban Gamliel responded, 'But is there only one thing you worship? You worship the sun, the moon, the stars and planets, the mountains and hills, the springs and valleys, even human beings! Should God destroy the entire world because of fools?' (Mekhilta, Ba-hodesh 6 on Exodus 20:3–6)

Erich Fromm indicates the wider implication of this commandment:

God, as the supreme value and goal, is not man, the state, an institution, nature, power, possession, sexual powers, or any artifact made by man. The affirmations 'I love God,' 'I follow God,' 'I want to become like God' - mean first of all 'I do not love, follow or imitate idols.'

An idol represents the object of man's central passion: the desire to return to the soil-mother, the craving for possession, power, fame, and so forth. The passion represented by the idol is, at the same time, the supreme value within man's system of values. Only a history of idolatry could enumerate the hundreds of idols and analyse which human passions and desires they represent. May it suffice to say that the history of mankind up to the present time is primarily the history of idol worship, from the primitive idols of clay and wood to the modern idols of the state, the leader, production and consumption - sanctified by the blessing of an idolised God...The idol is the alienated form of man's experience of himself. In worshipping the idol, man worships himself. But this self is a partial, limited aspect of man: his intelligence, his physical strength, power, fame, and so on. By identifying himself with a partial aspect of himself, man limits himself to this aspect; he loses his totality as a human being and ceases to grow. He is dependent on the idol, since only in submission to the idol does he find the shadow, although not the substance, of himself. (Fromm 1966:36–37)

A similar insight into the problem of idolatry is expressed by the playwright Arthur Miller:

An idol tells people exactly what to believe, God presents them with choices they have to make for themselves. The difference is far from insignificant; before the idol men remain dependent children, before God they are burdened and at the same time liberated to participate in the decisions of endless creation. (Miller 1987:259)

Just as the closing 'ethical' laws have universal application, and could well belong to the legal systems of the surrounding nations, even the particular demand for exclusive loyalty to their own God must have its echo in the conventional religious expectations of the ancient Near East. Indeed, only two laws appear to step outside such conventions – precisely the two indicated by Buber as relating to time – the keeping of the Shabbat and the honouring of father and mother.

The Shabbat is unique in the ancient Near East. By stamping the regular rhythm of six days for work and a day for rest upon society, it effectively limits the power of the sun and moon in regulating human times and hence the danger of deifying them as well. Israel measures its time by the pattern imposed by God. But by asserting the right to rest one day a week, the Sabbath is an expression of human dignity. Indeed, in the Deuteronomy version, it explicitly requires that all within the household, including slaves, partake of that rest, thus underlining an essential unity between 'owners' and 'workers'. Once again, the contrast with the meaningless, destructive drudgery of the slavery in Egypt is emphasised.

The law about honouring parents may have had its counterpart elsewhere in the ancient Near East, but it is possible that it too is unique, or at least sufficiently radical to require some sort of reinforcement – the promise of a reward of length of days. The rabbis saw it as a transitional commandment between those relating to God alone and those relating to fellow human beings, because parents are 'partners with God' in the creation of their offspring. But it is also noteworthy that only these two laws are reinforced in the Deuteronomy repetition of the Ten Commandments by the phrase, 'as the Eternal your God commanded you', perhaps suggesting the unique nature of both of them.

While both represent important values, they remain 'particularistic' in their application within the biblical context. It is therefore not surprising to find them missing in the parallel set of 'commandments' that rabbinic tradition furnished – the Seven Noachide Laws. If the Ten Commandments represent the covenant with Israel alone, the rabbis believed that God had made a similar covenant with all of humanity. As noted above, these universal laws were perceived as seven in all, though with some variation as to their content. They represent basic requirements for the right conduct of any human society, or at least an opening programme for debate.

But just as the rabbis had reservations about the Ten Commandments in their own time, as we look at them today we must also raise questions about certain underlying assumptions they contain. Thus they are totally bound up with the nature of the society out of which they emerge. It is well expressed by the Israeli biblical scholar and feminist Athalya Brenner:

> The Ten Commandments - so most readers will probably agree - is a manifesto that expresses some basic religious, moral and social norms required for the survival of human communities. It presents a vision of divinely regulated social order, hence is widely acclaimed as universally valid. But to judge by its language and content, that vision is far from egalitarian: it accepts slavery, perpetuates otherness (of social inferiors, including the *ger*, the resident alien), and promotes gender discrimination. A reflection of its time and space, no doubt. Nonetheless, this latter observation hardly masks the obvious. This manifesto of religious and social obligation relates to females only as language objects and social inferiors. Women are affected by it but their participation is non-existent (as receptors in the story); and yet, it seems that they are supposed to be silently obedient (as implicitly sub-categorized addressees). (From a commentary on the Ten Commandments in *Forms of Prayer Vol. 2, Pilgrim Festivals, Reform Synagogues of Great Britain*, 1995:483).

The addressee, as in the case of all the other laws promulgated in the following passages of the Book of Exodus, is the autonomous adult Israelite male, the 'owner' of a house, a wife, servants (male and female), oxen and asses – the formal partner with God in the covenant. There is no way of circumventing this fact – rather, it presents us today with a challenge on at least two levels. For not only does the Decalogue accept a secondary status for women, it appears to assume a property-based society of owners and dependents, a power structure seemingly blessed by divine design. Of course it is not as simple as that, since that self-same autonomous adult male is also part of a complex family, tribal and national structure of inter-woven responsibilities and roles. Moreover, as the jubilee-year regulations in Leviticus 25 indicate, the land itself, the source of wealth, prosperity and power, is to be considered as only leased from God, to be returned at regular intervals to this rightful owner, who redistributes it to its original Israelite family and tribal inhabitants. These regulations place considerable limitations on the individual power of the Israelite – though in practice the system may never have worked very effectively.

These two question marks on the validity of the Ten Commandments in certain respects are a forcible reminder that none of the regulations can be taken for granted – either as self-evident for a particular society or as easy to apply.

Perhaps each generation in its own way recognises reservations in the unqualified acceptance of the Ten Commandments. In our own post-Marxist and post-feminist world we have to address these two particular forms of idolatry that seem to be implicit in the Decalogue itself, property and patriarchy, however difficult it is to acknowledge such issues, let alone tackle them.

However, there is a further challenge that contemporary Western society in particular must inevitably bring to the Ten Commandments: precisely the point that Buber emphasised – that the central role of God in constituting and holding together the society defined by the Ten Commandments, makes us uncomfortable. The long struggle for the separation of church and state, the redefining of religion as belonging to the private sphere, though free to enter the political arena through the democratic process like any other pressure group, militate against the simple acceptance of any such complex web of religiously ordained laws. Here the Ten Commandments may actually cause division rather than unity within religious traditions, between those religious individuals and movements whose faith is deeply imbued with the values of the Enlightenment, and those who have not yet encountered its full impact or who have defined themselves in reaction against it. Are the prohibitions of the Decalogue the binding, unquestioned and unqualified words of God, or merely evidence of a particular stage in the human quest to understand the divine? Are they to be literally understood and obeyed or measured in relative terms alongside so many other human 'truths'? Here, paradoxically, there is a meeting-ground at least for debate and shared exploration between the liberals and conservatives, reformers and so-called fundamentalists, who exist within and across the barriers of the three monotheistic faiths. Though much human interaction, confidence and trust-building needs to be undertaken before such a matter can be tackled.

So what remains of the Ten Commandments that can serve the task of building a shared religious ethos? Perhaps it is that single element that permeates the so-called 'religious' and 'ethical' laws that are to be found here. What is common to them all is a prohibition against the invasion of the space and integrity of the other, be the other God, whose honour we belittle through idolatry, or our neighbour, whose existence in its totality, physical, material and spiritual, we harm by our assault. Rather than define an ideal positive relationship that can never be realised, the Ten Commandments take the route of defining the damage we should seek to avoid doing to each other, the respect for the integrity of ourselves and of each other that we should seek to maintain. Here too is a minimal universal ethos that we would do well to accept and maintain.

As we saw above, this was the approach with which Hillel won over a would-be proselyte through his version of the golden rule: 'What is hateful to you do not do to your fellow'. But he added, with typical rabbinic insight and the same reluctance to reduce the whole of life to a single creed, 'The rest [of the Torah] is commentary - go and learn!' (Babylonian Talmud Shabbat 31a).

8
Risk-taking in Religious Dialogue[1]

In the previous chapters we have looked at some ideas from within Jewish traditions that may contribute to the process of interfaith dialogue – in terms of the value of dialogue itself and the quest for universal values that might support it. But in my own experience the activity of dialogue came first, with the theory being filled in over the years. The very situation of becoming a rabbi in postwar Europe led to encounters with Christians, especially in Germany, with a hunger to learn more about the 'Jewish roots' of Christianity. Often behind this interest were feelings of guilt and responsibility about the fate of the Jewish people during the Nazi period. Requests for 'information' about Jewish teachings or practices would open up much deeper questions about the past and the possibility of finding a way of living together in the present.

The dialogue with Muslims was initially a by-product of the Middle East conflict and the recognition that beyond the political struggles between Israel, the Palestinians and their neighbouring Arab states, there was the world of Islam. The recognition of the growing number of 'diaspora' Muslim communities in Western Europe, which shared many of the problems of Jews as a religious minority, opened further opportunities for mutual curiosity and possible support at least at a pragmatic level.

This chapter arises out of the practical experience of co-organising an annual JCM Student Conference for some 30 years, where we learnt by trial and error about each other's sensitivities and needs, as well as what each of the parties had to offer to the others.

The 'risks' in this title are of two kinds: the first is that of entering into dialogue with 'the other', together with the problems that need to be addressed in doing so; and the second, the risk of losing touch in some way with the community to which one belongs as a result of entering such a dialogue. Both of these aspects are sources of concern for those who have attempted dialogue and require serious consideration.

THE RISKS ON ENTERING DIALOGUE

Once there is a willingness to enter dialogue and an appropriate partner has been found, we begin the first phase of introduction and, to some extent, self-justification. Here it will depend upon whether the dialogue is taking place between equals or, as is so often the case, in an unbalanced situation where some degree of power belongs to one participant and the other is in a more dependent position. It need not be the case that real force is involved – in fact, such situations tend to make dialogue impossible. But I would rather point to circumstances where there is a host society, with a majority culture or religion or ethnic grouping, and a minority or minorities that live within it. Here there are a number of almost hidden issues that will play a major role in affecting the behaviour of the participants.

The participant from the minority situation will often be aware of a degree of threat to his or her status before the dialogue even begins. This may have to do with being a relatively new arrival in the host society, such 'newness' often stretching over a number of generations; or it may be because of the fear of loss of identity through assimilation or acculturation to the majority society, a deeply disturbing experience even when no overt threat is being posed. The minority partner in dialogue does not start off on the same footing, and is often acutely aware of the fragility of his or her position vis-à-vis the other. This becomes magnified because of the responsibility he or she bears as a representative figure to those back home.

In contrast to this, the representatives of the host culture may be totally unaware of any insecurity on the part of the minority partner, because it would never occur to the host that such insecurity could exist. By definition, the host is the one who feels at home in that particular environment.

He or she will be the first to assume that both parties are meeting as equals, each representing an ancient tradition. Thus, for example, I have often found that Christians entering into dialogue with Jews or Muslims within Europe are sometimes quite insensitive to the issue of power until it is pointed out to them, whereas their Jewish and Muslim counterparts are acutely conscious of it. It may emerge in quite simple ways. Consider, for example, the attitude of the host to 'established authority', be it the police or civil service or any other agency of the state. The Christian clergyman or theologian or committed layperson in Europe may have the odd brush with such agencies. Such encounters may be quite confrontational or merely irritate or cause inconvenience, but nevertheless they are experienced as encounters with representatives of our society – in a sense our servants, who can be regarded with a degree of equanimity. In sharp contrast, someone from an immigrant community, even into the second generation, may feel quite different about such agencies – depending on their previous experience elsewhere or the degree to which they feel at home in that culture. The police and civil servants may be experienced not as 'ours' but as 'theirs', their agencies that need to be regarded with a degree of caution. Issues such as the extent to which the minority may maintain separate schooling or have access to public buildings for their religious needs are seen as measures of the degree of respect, responsibility and authority given to the minority by the host society. And are such rights or opportunities given without question, grudgingly, or only after a struggle, or are they totally denied? Are they merely yielded or are they simply made available as of right? Such issues can feed the worst fears of the minority unless real sensitivity is shown.

When people with these two different sets of perceptions meet in dialogue, those from the minority situation may experience their new partners from the host culture as singularly insensitive to the matters that concern them. This insensitivity can be experienced in apparently quite simple matters: to what extent has the host taken steps to ensure that the food, prayer facilities or other factors that are important to the minority group, have been made available – and not just available, but explicitly offered? In such circumstances the host may take it as self-evident that if you need a room to pray in you will ask for it; the minority group may feel too insecure to make such a request, and a suppressed anger bubbles under the surface. Those of the minority group who have gained experience of dialogue may feel sufficiently confident to make the appropriate requests or suggestions and those of the majority culture may likewise, in time, learn to enquire as to what is needed. If we have guests for dinner we gradually learn to check out beforehand about particular food requirements if we are not to cause embarrassment or be embarrassed ourselves during the meal by someone's inability to eat a particular dish. Yet it is surprising how insensitive some groups are to such obvious matters when they enter the world of dialogue for the first time.

My favourite example concerns one of the first Jewish-Christian-Muslim meetings we held in Berlin at the end of the sixties. The senate invited us to a reception at the town hall and presumably the caterer was instructed to lay on reception number 5a, drinks and hot snacks. So we arrived to a sumptuous range of pork sausages and rolled ham pieces, forbidden, of course, to both Jews and Muslims; and some delicious German wine – which the Jews, not being Orthodox, enjoyed, but the Muslims could not touch.

I mentioned the difference between Orthodox and other Jews in this respect because that also raises problems. Not all Jews are Orthodox, but in such circumstances a sensitive host will assume they are and take appropriate action. The group of Jews, on the other hand, may find themselves asking for food to be prepared in such a way that Orthodox Jews would be free to participate, and themselves stick to the rules of kosher food, even if they might not usually do so in private. They will do so because of their feeling of solidarity with other Jews and to take seriously their own representative position. Such feelings may be compounded by the belief that it is necessary to show a unified Jewish position and not expose the internal divisions that actually exist. Sometimes the minority group may even insist on conditions that they would not dream of requiring in their private capacity, precisely because they feel the need to make the point to their hosts. It is a kind of inverted expression of power and control in a situation experienced as one of relative powerlessness either at the present time or during the past relationships between the two groups. The net result is often a curious situation in which, out of the best motives and with the best will in the world, everyone is acting out an artificial role. It may take a long time before sufficient trust is established for these hidden agendas to be acknowledged and examined.

These differences in perception between host and minority are very real, and relate directly to the degree of security that one feels within a given society. The Christian within Europe may have to report back to some organisation about what they experienced, but otherwise may feel no particular need to justify to anyone their presence at such a gathering. If anything it may be looked upon as rather worthy, if somewhat quixotic, for the Christian to take part in dialogue work. However, the person from the minority group may be far more conscious of a community, indeed a whole world, back home to whom he or she is in some sense answerable. There may be serious fears within the minority group about possible betrayals of loyalty by their representatives. The participants in dialogue may have to address these concerns on returning, and offer appropriate reassurances. If they are acting quite independently, they may still have internalised the values and fears of their own group, so will act in the same way. The nature of power is that if you have it you do not notice it unless its reality and implications are drawn to your attention; if you do not have power, then most of what you do is geared towards measuring, antici-pating and otherwise adjusting to those who do have it. So from the very beginning of the dialogue such an imbalance can affect and even seriously distort the perception of each side as to what is possible or desirable in the forthcoming meeting. As I have stressed, all too often this occurs on levels that are not overtly expressed or recognised, and much misunderstanding can occur. The net result may indeed be to reinforce the prejudices that the meeting was designed to overcome.

Such imbalances have particular consequences for the first phase of the dialogue – and this will also be the case if there is not such an obvious power difference, but there is some history of conflict between the two groups that are meeting each other. In the first encounters, at least one of the partners, and perhaps both, is not really speaking to the person who stands before them, but to their own people back home. Whatever the overt message to the dialogue partner, they are effectively saying to the invisible audience behind them, 'I have not let the side down, I have betrayed nothing either by coming here or by my opening remarks. Indeed, rather than waste a potential platform, I have used the opportunity to express a whole range of our grievances and concerns and they have been forced to listen.' If there is a real background of conflict, one side may well need to express a lot of anger at past hurts. In a way this is actually a tribute to the dialogue situation that someone feels sufficiently secure to express what may be very hurtful remarks against the new 'partner'. However, if something of the dynamics is not recognised, this can lead to an equally angry, self-justifying response with a resultant total breakdown of communication. Nevertheless, if this anger is accepted and held by one partner or the other, or by some accepted mediator, it can open the way to a new stage of encounter now that the level of hurt has been expressed and the degree of 'security' has been tested out. If this truly proves to be a 'safe space', where anything can be said without fear, then there is a real possibility of movement.

To return to the earlier point about the imbalance of power, the situation can become even more complicated where the minority group actually has power elsewhere, or has a cultural tradition for dealing with conflict that is not shared by the host. Though being in a minority situation, they may then act with the usual stratagems or behaviour they would use elsewhere where they did have a measure of power, only to cause a degree of incomprehension or even a feeling of threat on the part of the host. The host, if unaware of these dynamics, begins to feel rather hurt and insulted that these ungrateful people have become so belligerent or demanding. This, in turn, evokes a kind of defensive reaction. 'After all, we have invited these people into our homes and offered them our friendship, what more do they expect? They have to understand that living here they must conform to our standards of behaviour.' At least the latent power inequality is beginning to become more open, although, unless it is recognised, once again we are entering a possible breakdown and indeed confirmation of the worst fears about the other and the whole dialogue enterprise.

A further cause of confusion is when the two sides see quite different goals to be achieved through the dialogue. One group may have specific aims to achieve for their own status or situation vis-à-vis the other. They actually want a negotiation, whereas their prospective partner may be acting out of more general religious or humanitarian motives, wishing to broaden their own perception of people, to be friendly or simply to form a kind of alliance of like-minded people. It may take some time before the different agendas become clear, at which point there may be a great sense of disappointment or betrayal. An illustration of the problem concerns some of the many dialogue groups between Israeli Jews and Arabs, and between Israelis and Palestinians, that have been operating over the past few decades. Despite years of successful meetings, many of these groups begin to fall apart even when the outer political situation became favourable. The problem as I heard it from a number of those involved was that whereas the Israeli participants wanted to express friendship, support or solidarity with their Palestinian counterparts, the Palestinians, having grown increasingly more frustrated by the lack of change in their circumstances, were now calling for what they considered as 'justice' for their cause. Because their dialogue partners could not deliver this, communication between them broke down and some of the Israelis even turned anti-Palestinian, perhaps because they felt that their sincere commitment had not been properly reciprocated. Here we see the problem of unrealistic expectations of both sides coming up against a hard, seemingly unchangeable reality.

I am sure that parallel examples can be found in many other situations around the world. Essentially, both sides have made assumptions without taking the power relationship into account – and both have behaved quite logically, given their own circumstances. However, it is not always so easy to identify where power really lies in a given encounter. As well as the direct issue of power, it is useful also to think in terms of the freedom of action or the freedom of thought that may be available to either side. Perhaps it is best to illustrate this with a concrete example.

Early on in the establishing of the JCM Student Conference at the Hedwig Dransfeld Haus in Bendorf, Germany, we had to consider the issue of food. Out of that experience I prepared a little explanation that I tend to give at the start of each conference. It is delivered with a degree of humour as a way of lightening some of the tensions that are inevitably present at the opening evening. However, by addressing the issue directly, it is reassuring to those who are concerned about such things that their needs have been recognised and met. I point out that traditional Jews can only eat kosher meat that has been slaughtered and cooked in a particular way. Muslims similarly eat hallal meat, but are also allowed to eat kosher meat, though traditional Jews will not eat hallal meat. And Christians can eat almost anything!

Since the majority of people at these conferences from the beginning were Christians, with a gradually growing number of Jewish and Muslim participants over the years, in the first few years we laid on a special vegetarian table for the Jews and Muslims. It should be pointed out that not all the Jewish participants felt so concerned about the Jewish dietary laws, but, as I suggested before, it is often the case in such circumstances that they feel the need to show solidarity with traditional Jewish practices. This is a good example of how the loyalty issue can actually distort the real beliefs and actions of people from the minority group. However, the vegetarian table raised other problems. Some people felt that it defeated the purpose of a dialogue if some of the participants ate separately from the others, so out of solidarity with them they joined the vegetarian table. A few others did so as they just happened to like vegetarian food and thought this was a good opportunity to eat it. Soon the vegetarian table got so crowded that there was no room for the Jews and Muslims to sit there, at which point some of the Jews who were not so committed anyway to the Jewish dietary laws felt quite happy about joining a different table, which was good from the point of view of honesty, and mixing, but rather bewildering for the kitchen. The whole thing was further compounded by the difficulties that the kitchen had in understanding precisely what these strange dietary restrictions meant. They recognised that meat was to be banned so they removed the usual sausage meat from the dinner table and substituted it with cheese. What they often did not notice was the adventurous kinds of processed cheese on offer in Germany, including those with little specks of ham included. I spent many a breakfast and dinner in those early years running round tables confiscating suspect cheese before it got into an innocent mouth.

To return to the saga of the vegetarian table, we hit on an ingenious solution. The following year we would make the entire conference vegetarian and in that way all of us would be equal and no-one need be segregated or offended. And that is how we ran it, except that I forgot to explain this on the opening night. So two days into the conference I had delegations of Jews and Muslims, very few Christians for some reason, coming to complain that there was no meat on offer! So now each year I explain – because another of the lessons of dialogue is that on each occasion you have to start from scratch and can assume nothing. You may personally have moved on, but the new partners are only at the very beginning.

But there was a second food issue that is more directly on the point that I wish to make. I learnt early on that there appear to be two attitudes among Muslims to the presence of alcohol. Some not only object to it being available for Muslims, but also for anyone else in the vicinity to drink it as well. Others, though strict about it for themselves, have no objection to it being available for non-Muslims. On this basis we eventually decided to remove the customary wine bottles from the bar at the conference centre and provide only soft drinks or late-night teas. But there remained a problem. On Friday night, as an integral part of the religious ritual, Jews say a blessing over wine and drink it. The Muslims who are part of our organising team were perfectly agreeable to our drinking it, but insisted that the bottles in which it came should be very clearly marked so that no mistake could be made. We were happy to do this, and we had wine bottles and bottles of grape juice available for the Friday evening meal.

This was fine for the first year, however the next year the kitchen decided to intervene. They had learnt that Friday night was special and had indeed laid on a marvellous buffet meal for the occasion. This year they decided to go one better and provide some beautiful glassware on the tables for the drinks. So they produced two different kinds of glass carafes: into one sort they poured wine and into the other grape juice. But though the two were slightly different in appearance it was difficult to distinguish them, and you can imagine the problem for the Muslims when confronted with these virtually indistinguishable flasks. Some of the less-experienced ones were really upset, and it seemed to confirm all their worst suspicions about the dangers of dialogue conferences and attempts to seduce them away from their tradition. Fortunately the matter was cleared up pretty rapidly, and it became quite useful to discuss the incident.

However, I felt that it was necessary to do something to prevent another occurrence, and pointed out that since the Jews could equally well say the

Friday-night blessing over grape juice there was no need to have any wine at all. At that point I began to get objections from the Jewish participants – not questioning the legitimacy of this substitution, but asking why it was that it was always the 'liberals' who had to concede everything to the 'fundamentalists'! 'Why should we have to give up our wine?'

There are a number of answers to that question. The first is that in entering a dialogue everyone has to be prepared to make some sort of sacrifice in seeking the middle ground where meeting can take place. If this action made one of the partners more comfortable, then it seemed to me that it was a legitimate, and not very demanding, sacrifice to make. However, the discussion here was being overshadowed by the kind of argument that often occurs between 'liberals' and 'fundamentalists' within the same tradition – namely that such concessions by the 'liberals' may lead to further concessions and ultimately the delegitimisation of the liberal position.

Having thought it through, I pointed out to my Jewish colleagues that for them the journey to Bendorf for this meeting with Muslims was not a particularly long one, either geographically or spiritually. It is, after all, an essential part of our liberal tradition that we be open to the world and to others. In any event, we feel free of many of the constraints of our tradition, particularly in the matter of food, that make social intercourse difficult. But for those from a more conservative framework amongst the Muslims, the journey to Bendorf had required that a far greater emotional distance be covered. If we added to that the Muslim sense of solidarity with the Palestinians that made any meeting with Jews additionally suspect, and could even cause serious repercussions for some of them back home, we had to acknowledge that there was here as well a kind of imbalance of power. For the two sides to meet a symmetry had to be established, but it could only be achieved by acknowledging the difference between the intellectual, emotional, spiritual and political loads that each was carrying. With unequal weights on the see-saw, the fulcrum has to be moved closer to one end if the true point of balance is to be found. Both parties had made sacrifices and concessions within their own specific terms of reference for the sake of the dialogue – and it was a mistake to judge the journey taken by the other in one's own terms. Indeed, part of the purpose of dialogue is to come to understand the journey the partner has had to undertake for the meeting to be possible at all.

Just as power differentials can distort the apparent issues that take place in the early stages of dialogue, so also differences in freedom of action or thought, as between people from liberal or conservative cultures, can lead to misunderstandings. Part of the art of dialogue is recognising the point at which these unexpressed or unacknowledged subtexts are dictating what is going on, and bringing them out into the open in as delicate a way as possible.

I think there is another kind of issue with regard to the problem of meeting between so-called liberal groups and so-called conservative, traditionalist or fundamentalist ones. A natural polarisation of this sort seems to take place within every religious grouping. This means that people entering into dialogue with the other may have a preconceived idea about this polarisation from their own experience and project it onto their new potential partners. It hardly needs to be said that these terms are to some extent misleading. There are people who belong within a liberal organisation who are temperamentally conservative and even very narrow in their personal thinking, becoming dogmatic about the preservation of the particular liberal mores or forms of their group. Conversely, there can be 'fundamentalists' who are by temperament open and tolerant.

I recall a problem that faced us in the early days of the Jewish-Christian-Muslim work. As Liberal or Reform Jews we wanted to find our spiritual counterparts in Islam. But where was the equivalent of our middle class Reform Judaism? Instead in those early days we found a strong polarisation amongst Muslim participants. One was either a so-called 'traditionalist' or 'fundamentalist' or else a 'secularist', with very little middle ground between them. If one opened up a dialogue with one grouping, the door was to some extent closed to working with the other. We were fortunate in meeting a Muslim leader of impeccable traditional credentials who recognised the importance of interfaith dialogue as part of the integration of Muslims into the western European scene. And as the first tentative encounter began, we found a power, simplicity and directness in Muslim spirituality that was as enriching and refreshing as it was challenging. As 'liberals' we suddenly found ourselves stretched to meet these 'others', and learnt that the only point of meeting open to us was our shared experience of faith in

God. But it was a faith expressed with a directness and sincerity that was somewhat remote from our own more hesitant, qualified language. So we had to stretch our own faith to be able to find a common ground, and gained immeasurably from the experience.

One of the curious by-products was that entering the world of traditional Muslims and learning something of their concerns made me more sensitive to the concerns of traditional Jews. The dialogue with the 'other' had made me more open to dialogue with my own co-religionists. I do not know whether the converse applied to our more traditional Muslim partners, but looking at the journey some of them have made since those early days, I would guess that their sense of religious security has grown, and with it has come a greater openness to other views and positions.

THE RISK OF LOSING TOUCH

This seems a valid point at which to move on to a particular risk that arises at a later stage of dialogue, one that seems to confirm the worst suspicions of those who are opposed to, or at least ambivalent about, the whole exercise. Once the other has been met on a true personal level, and suspicion or anxiety has changed to respect, and then to friendship and to love, a whole range of consequences follow. For a new set of loyalties has been established alongside those one brought into the dialogue in the first place. It is almost a cliché that many people with a regular experience of interfaith dialogue find that they have more in common with their dialogue partner than with the mass of their own co-religionists. This should hardly be surprising since the people who are prepared to participate in dialogue may well share common assumptions and may already be to some extent marginal within their own world. The desire to meet the other, or the recognition that it is important, is already a step beyond the conventional wisdom and expectations of many groups. Some degree of affinity between dialogue partners might well be expected, however 'different' from each other they may seem to be at first glance.

In the event there is often a kind of 'double growing'. The religious impact of the meeting sends us back to our own tradition refreshed, open and curious about the spiritual dimensions that it contains that we have not previously explored. This may be due in part to a need to re-establish a degree of security in our own identity after the openness we have just experienced. But on a deeper level, a genuine religious encounter sensitises us to broader or newer personal questions, and the answers need to be found within our home tradition. Sharing our faith with another and finding it reciprocated leads to a mutual encouragement in the religious quest. Moreover we often discover particular qualities in the new partner that we would like to have in ourselves. The fact of recognising them suggests that they are already latent within us, but now the inner work begins of discovering and developing them. Since all the great religious traditions must, almost by definition, have addressed every human and spiritual dimension at some stage, there may be much in our own tradition to be rediscovered that might have been neglected in the immediate past or present. Dialogue often opens up channels for the renewal of a religious tradition on a personal and collective level.

But alongside this growth into our tradition there may be a realisation of the distance we have travelled from the regular set of assumptions, biases and even prejudices that are present within our own community. Meeting the reality of the other has called into question the conventional or stereotypical view of them which we inherited and, indeed, brought with us to the dialogue in the first place. It is thus a very painful experience to return home knowing the effect of our own prejudices on our new partner, and with our new sensitivity to meet the inaccuracy and unpleasantness of these biases that still dominate within our home environment. But even more difficult or frustrating can be the incomprehension and even hostility we may encounter when trying to explain how our perception has changed. Our loyalty may be called into question and hence the demand that we decide whose side we are 'on'.

There are no simple responses to such challenges. One way of regarding the situation is to recognise that there are two kinds of loyalties. There is a narrow, exclusive kind that demands that the self-interest of the group be placed above all other considerations; but there is also a broader more generous kind of loyalty that does not require that loving one's own group excludes loving the other as well. Those who have made the journey from the narrow loyalty to the broad may find themselves isolated and misunderstood and accused of betrayal – which is doubly painful, since they have actually experienced the dialogue as a way of helping their own group to a better expression of its own values, as well as gaining a new and positive relationship with the other.

What is effectively happening is that a new kind of division is being created in the world through the growth of dialogue. It is between those who have experienced it and been changed by it, and those who have not. The former now share with each other alongside their own personal 'historical' group identity, an identification with their new partners and indeed with all others who have made the same journey. They must walk a narrow tightrope as they try to bring back to their own group the lessons they have learnt without alienating those they would convince of the validity of what they have experienced. There is always a risk in any kind of leadership that we will move so far ahead of our constituency that it is impossible to get back in touch with them. In a way, all the skills of patient listening, sensitive argument, shared prayer and silence that have made the dialogue possible must now be applied with even greater skill in the attempt to re-enter our own world. Like the prophet Isaiah, whose mouth has been touched by the purifying coal from the altar (Isaiah 6), those who have experienced dialogue have become mediators between two domains, answerable to both but always potentially misunderstood by both. The risks inherent in participating in dialogue should not be underestimated by those who undertake it for the first time. The hardest part is returning home.

Perhaps it is important to note that the problems may not only lie with the 'folks back home'. The process of dialogue is no magical one with guaranteed results. In a way, precisely because we are laying ourselves open to the other, making ourselves vulnerable, it is possible to fall into traps. As I have suggested, we all come to such a meeting with different agendas. The very fact of the existence of dialogue, while being a tribute to the values of tolerance and mutual respect, is also the product of a new religious reality. In a sense, all of us, even the majority faith of a society, are religious minorities in a materialistic and secular society. In some ways, the desire to meet the other is a quest to find mutual support in a relatively hostile world. However much we may rationalise the new desire to meet, we are also huddling together out of a common need.

I do not think that this is a bad thing, because it has brought many gains. Moreover, perhaps because of the peculiarities of Jewish religious pragmatism, I do not find secularism so threatening, and in some ways it has challenged us to examine afresh our religious traditions and values. Nevertheless, having discovered a new group of allies through dialogue there is always the risk that someone will try to hijack the process for their own power ends. Precisely because of the various levels of insecurity that we bring to the dialogue process, it is easy to fall into the trap of seeking to build up a new alliance of the faithful against the unholy world out there. It may happen that people with a very urgent and particular agenda may seek to use the new partners as allies in their own special struggle, even challenging the validity of what has gone on between them if such support is not forthcoming. That is not to say that there are not occasions when such a request or even demand is legitimate. This is merely to sound the warning that precisely those elements of power and powerlessness that make dialogue difficult in the first place may still be operating. Caring for each other does not mean we should switch off our common sense.

In a way the real work of dialogue begins at these later stages – or rather, we begin at that point to carry the full responsibility for the joy we have come to experience because of the dialogue process.

THE LAST RISK

There is one final risk concerning dialogue that I would like to mention: the risk of not undertaking it today. It is a commonplace that we are seeing today the rise of nationalistic forces throughout Europe and alongside them racism, antisemitism, islamophobia and other abuses of human dignity and worth. But even where there is no overt violence, the presence of such extremism has a significant polarising effect on the whole of society. Thus the more extreme the violence of the far right, the more it pushes the entire society towards the right. Those with responsibility for government have a more radical model against which to measure themselves and justify themselves – look how humane our policies are compared to what they are doing. For example, the attacks on immigrants in Germany by right-wing extremists, beginning in the early 1990s, did not lead to immediate statements by the government of solidarity and support for the victims and a call to stamp out this form of violent racism – rather, they led to calls for a change to laws of asylum and immigration, the very policy the perpetrators of violence were seeking to achieve.

In such a situation, dialogue is one of the few activities and ideologies that can push attitudes back the other way. What we need for the health of our pluralistic Western societies are effective models of tolerance, co-operation, mutual respect and support, which at the same time preserve distinctions and respect individual and group identities. Those who have been engaged in dialogue of all sorts have much to contribute, and far more resources should be made available to help develop and utilise their experience. More precisely, those who carry responsibility within their own religious traditions should draw attention to the examples of tolerance and mutual respect for others that are contained within their tradition and use them to develop a greater consciousness of their significance. Like the issue of loyalty, we have within our traditions both narrow and broad perspectives, those concerned primarily with self-preservation and those that recognise a shared humanity and mutual responsibility. Unfortunately, calls today for religious renewal all too often mean a retreat into conservatism rather than a re-awakening of the openness and generosity of spirit that are the hallmark of religious faith. As in every generation, it is our religious task to choose where we place our own emphasis and commitment.

Where should the process begin? One place is clearly in the seminaries and other religious institutions that provide the leadership for our respective faith communities. The next chapter will explore some of the issues and opportunities involved when we admit the other into the intimate space of our own religious formation.

In a world that appears to be growing smaller but is actually becoming increasingly more divided and tribal, dialogue is no longer simply a religious luxury for a few well-meaning but marginal individuals. With all its inherent difficulties and risks, its experience and lessons can play a transforming role for the whole of our society. Martin Buber says that all authentic living is meeting, dialogue. I would only add that today all authentic religious living is risking.

9
Teaching the Teachers

If interfaith dialogue is to become a recognised part of the life of religious communities, the process has to begin with those who have leadership responsibilities. Were that indeed so self-evident, it would only be necessary to discuss 'how' to set about this. Nevertheless, my own experience suggests that we are not yet at the stage where it can be taken for granted that training in dialogue is acceptable or even welcomed in the institutions that train the spiritual leaders of different religious communities. There are still preliminary issues that have to be addressed and reassurances that have to be given. Having written about risk-taking in religious dialogue in the previous chapter, perhaps it is worth taking a small risk in presenting arguments in favour of a greater institutional commitment to dialogue. This will indicate the dimensions of the problem to be confronted, and also establish another level to the process. To set the scene I must turn, perhaps inevitably, to a Jewish joke.

The background to the following story is the mediaeval disputations that from time to time were the frightening background to Jewish life in Christian societies. Jews were called upon to defend their beliefs against the allegedly superior values of the church. The following story is a Jewish reaction to this situation, though I have no idea how old it is or where it first appeared. However, I should point out that there are a number of variations to the story itself, which belongs to the folk wisdom tradition, and that it exists in various forms in the popular literature of others as well. I hope that Christian readers will not be offended by it!

In this version, the Pope issues a decree that unless the Jews of a particular town can answer three questions they will have to be expelled. Having heard such stories before, the Jews start packing. All except a lad called Yankel, a tailor's apprentice, who decides to try his hand at answering. So he goes to the Vatican and knocks on the door. To cut a long story short, after all the appropriate protocol has been observed he is ushered into the presence of the Pope. The Pope looks at him and asks, 'Are you the accredited representative of the Jewish people?' 'Yes', answers Yankel, 'what are the questions?' So the Pope shrugs and raises a single finger. Yankel looks at him quizzically and raises two fingers. The Pope nods. Then the Pope makes a gesture in which he draws his hands apart to each side. Yankel then places one fist upon the other and rotates them. Again the Pope nods. Then the Pope removes a wafer from a dish beside him and holds it up. Yankel searches through his pockets and produces an apple. Again the Pope nods and says: 'You have answered my questions. Your people are able to stay.' Yankel gives a nod, and leaves.

The Cardinals then gather round the Pope and say, 'Father, we have seen this but we do not understand.' So the Pope explains: 'I have been truly put to shame this day. I asked the Jews to send me their wisest man and they sent me this Yankel. Nevertheless he answered my questions. I held up one finger to indicate that there is but one God. He held up two fingers to indicate that there are two ways of worshipping Him. I moved my hands apart to indicate that we are separated from each other. He held his hands together to indicate that we could be united. Then I took out the unleavened wafer, which is the bread of God, and he took out the apple, which is the fruit of God.'

Meanwhile Yankel goes home and tells his uncle to stop packing because he has answered the questions. Everyone is curious and asks him what happened and how he managed to answer. He replies that he is not altogether sure himself. 'I got in to see the Pope and stood before him. Then he raised one finger as if to say: "I'll poke your eye out!" So I raised two fingers and said "I'll poke both your eyes out!" Then he made a gesture to say: "I'll cut your throat!" and I said: "I'll strangle you!" And then we had breakfast!'

Now on the level of humour it works very well. But it does seem to me to contain a number of elements that are worth exploring further. Firstly, it works as humour because of the 'cognitive dissonance' between the two parties. Though in effect they were in 'dialogue' with each other, and came to an agreed conclusion, they both understood what happened in completely different ways.

Secondly, it has to be noted that this is a Jewish joke that arises out of a deadly serious and indeed bitter situation of the mediaeval disputations in which Jews were forced to justify their faith in public debate with representatives of the church. In real life, even if the Jewish participant might win the argument in defence of his tradition, the superior power of the church ensured that the church came out the winners in reality, often with expulsions or book-burnings as the consequence. So this humour has a bitter edge to it and is a kind of revenge, the revenge of the powerless using words alone. It allows Yankel to triumph, so is reassuring to a victimised Jewish audience. But by making Yankel into something of a simpleton, it also undermines further the alleged intellectual and spiritual superiority of the church, represented in this case by the Pope.

Perhaps it is also an inner reminder to a Jewish audience of the need for the sharpening of their intellect as the only defence available to a people with no recourse to other kinds of power.

But what is saddest, and in some ways most relevant to our subject, is that it shows one problem at the heart of interfaith dialogue: the way in which people, despite their encounter with the other, may remain completely within their own set of presuppositions, may interpret the views of the other without testing them out against reality, and may end up with a totally false picture of what was said and of who the other is, leaving the door open for problems in the future. Even though they use the same kind of discourse, in this case a neutral sign language, the two participants in the dialogue never understand each other.

One does not have to go back to mediaeval experiences to see this kind of problem. Rabbi Lionel Blue tells the story of a discussion he had in Germany many years ago with a number of Christian theologians. His German was not very good, but he thought he understood what was being said. The discussion was about the two 'kingdoms', the heavenly and the earthly, in German, the two *Reichs*. Lionel thought that by the two *Reichs* they meant the Federal Republic and the DDR. So when he contributed to the conversation they sort of assumed he was introducing some profound Jewish insight, even if it did not quite make sense.

But having pointed to the lack of comprehension between Yankel and the Pope, it has to be said that Yankel was quite right in interpreting the actions of the Pope in this story as aggressive. However sophisticated the theology, the end of the matter was also clear: as with all these disputations it was effectively an assault on the Jews with the view of converting them or expelling them, or sometimes worse.

How far is this story a reflection of the relationship between the three religions today? Clearly it is not so for those actively engaged in interfaith dialogue, but it certainly accords with the situation in the past in its many complex forms. It may also be true for the majority of today's adherents of our three faiths, who are still conditioned by past attitudes and a host of suspicions and indeed actual conflicts that reinforce fears and negative stereotypes of each other. The kind of interfaith dialogue that we have grown accustomed to in the West is still a rare flower that needs to be nurtured.

TRAINING IN INTERFAITH DIALOGUE

The one institution I know that has made a conscious effort to address the question of how to educate religious leaders in the experience and importance of interfaith dialogue is the Leo Baeck College, the rabbinic seminary in north London that trains rabbis for the Reform and Liberal Jewish movements in the UK and in Europe. Clearly my own experience in the field has been influential in developing this work, but there are other background factors as well. One of them has to be the tradition of open-minded scholarship the college inherited from the Berlin Liberal Jewish seminary, the Hochschule für die Wissenschaft des Judentums, of which it is the European successor. The Hochschule as an academic institution welcomed Christian students in the liberal atmosphere of Berlin in the twenties and thirties. With the advent of the Nazis and the prevention of Jewish students entering universities, the Hochschule expanded its range of courses, finally to be closed by the Nazis in 1941. The last director was

Rabbi Dr Leo Baeck, who was the spiritual leader of German Jewry during that dark period. As a scholar of the early rabbinic period he wrote much on Christianity, in particular demonstrating the Jewish sources to be found in the gospels. Surviving the war in Theresienstadt Concentration Camp, Dr Baeck came to England after the war. As early as 1949, in his presidential address to the World Union for Progressive Judaism, he advocated closer links with Islam.

> And now Islam, too, has again moved into the close neighbourhood, the inescapable proximity of the Jewish spirit; once more, as in a great period of the Middle Ages, the two are regarding each other. Today they are almost compelled to face each other, not only in the sphere of policy, but also in the sphere of religion; there is the great hope, maybe one turning to some remote future – but mankind lives also on remote hopes – that thus they will behold each other and then meet each other on joint roads, in joint tasks, in joint confidence in the future. There is the great hope that Judaism can thus become the builder of a bridge, the 'pontifex' between East and West.

Rabbi Dr Werner van der Zyl, himself a student of Leo Baeck and the founder of the Leo Baeck College, encouraged this kind of openness during his time as director of studies, and welcomed Christians who wished to study at the college on a part-time basis.

But my personal interest goes back to before I became a student there. In the sixties, a few young people in the circles around the college, members of the youth section of the World Union for Progressive Judaism, became particularly aware of the lack of Jewish spiritual resources available to us. We organised a number of conferences looking at the situation of the European Jewish community and trying to find young people who might wish to study to become rabbis. The leading figure in this work was Rabbi Lionel Blue, who introduced us to the importance of the spiritual dimension of our activities and encouraged us to work with any teachers we could find, of whatever religious background. I know that meeting and sharing with certain Christians, Muslims and one particular Vedantist, were very influential in my own journey, which led eventually to the Leo Baeck College. It is one of the paradoxes of interfaith dialogue that it may lead us back into our own religion with renewed commitment. It may also be that the particular point of entry into our religious life remains of special importance. Certainly the pleasure of working with the people I considered my spiritual teachers, and the desire to discover that kind of relationship with others as well, became an essential part of my own religious life.

Since those early days, the interfaith activities at the Leo Baeck College have developed and I would like to focus on three aspects: the formal teaching at the college about Christianity and Islam, the impact of the presence of students of other faiths on the Jewish student body and vice versa, and the annual JCM Student Conference in Germany, discussed in the previous chapter, attended by all our rabbinic students as part of their studies.

When I studied at the Leo Baeck College we were fortunate in having as a guest lecturer for a year a Jewish scholar from America who had specialised in the early history of Christianity. A number of Jewish scholars from the turn of the century entered this area, some, like Claude Montefiore and Rabbi Dr Leo Baeck, writing extensively on the gospels. They were able to bring insights from contemporary Jewish sources to bear on their studies of the New Testament, and tried to present an objective, scholarly analysis of various texts. I attended the course on the gospels taught by our visitor. From what I recall he employed the latest scholarship in as fair and objective a way as he could. However, having already experienced something of interfaith dialogue, particularly with Christians, I found myself having a strong reaction against his teaching. For it seemed to me that by dismantling the texts as he had done, any sense of their religious power had disappeared. And though they were not my scriptures, I became quite defensive on their behalf. If that was all there was to them, it was hard to understand how they could possibly have had so profound a religious impact on so many millions of Christians around the world.

Now this is not the fault of the scholar – not being a Christian he was hardly in the business of promoting Christian belief. Moreover, the tradition of academic scholarship he employed felt equally problematic when applied to our own Jewish studies as well. The pursuit of the historical truth about the origins and development of religions had a freshness, fascination and almost messianic fervour to it for previous generations. But my generation could take its iconoclasm for granted, and wanted instead a different kind of relationship with the tradition. That apart, I could not help but feel that despite his integrity as a scholar and his commitment to pure objectivity in his evaluation of the gospels, his conclusions were nevertheless one-sided. Moreover, something of the essence of Christianity was missing precisely because it was not being taught by a Christian. I would demand the same scholarly integrity of a Christian in an academic context such as ours, but I wanted as a teacher someone committed to the texts, however problematic they may be. In this kind of 'disputation in reverse', Judaism clearly won, but largely because the 'game' was rigged in our favour.

Nevertheless, even if the method of teaching was problematic, the fact that a course on the gospels was being taught at all as a subject in a rabbinic seminary was in itself a major statement about the openness of our progressive Jewish community. I do not know whether it was the scholar himself who introduced this concept to the college. Certainly, coming out of the more self-confident Reform Jewish society in America he felt quite comfortable in doing so, and had no compunction about teaching such a course. That would clearly be unthinkable in an Orthodox seminary, and might even have proved problematic to some associated with the Leo Baeck College had it not had the scholar's personal authority behind the decision. Too many ghosts from past Christian persecutions and the Shoah that took place in an allegedly Christian Europe remain deeply embedded in Jewish consciousness. Moreover, the single greatest fear about Christian intentions remains very much a part of Jewish consciousness — that essentially Christians are still seeking to convert Jews, and thus Jews who explore Christian texts, or engage in dialogue with Christians, are at best naive and at worst simply opening the door to this possibility. But the Leo Baeck College had also inherited the traditions from Germany of people like Franz Rosenzweig, especially through his student Ignaz Maybaum, who taught theology at the college. They belonged to a generation of Jewish thinkers in the twenties and thirties in Germany who had struggled to define Jewish identity precisely in relationship to and in debate with its Christian background. Despite the questioning today in Jewish circles of the reality of the so-called pre-war German-Jewish symbiosis and the questions that it still raises, nevertheless the college belonged in that tradition of openness and still pursued it.

Some 30 years on from my days as a student rabbi, the situation has developed. I am not altogether clear about the stages that led to the current situation at the college. Even when I was a student myself Rabbi Lionel Blue, who taught comparative religion, would invite Buddhist and Hindu teachers for a session to speak out of their own tradition, and he took us off to visit various places of worship and to retreat centres. However I believe it was the impact of the annual JCM student conference that we had been organising since 1972 that was the crucial factor. Fr Gordian Marshall, a Dominican, had been involved in planning these conferences from the earliest period. This led to our inviting him to teach a course in Christianity, something he has come to share with Karen Armstrong in recent years. It is only a one-semester survey, but the principle is now firmly established that it be taught by a Christian, or even by more than one, so that the students encounter a variety of authentic voices. Once the principle was accepted, and as our dialogue work expanded, it was logical that we extend this programme to include Islam as well for another one-semester programme. Now clearly in the time available, very little can be conveyed about the complexities of either faith; nevertheless it allows the students to fill in gaps not otherwise addressed at the student conference itself, and, even more important, helps build a relationship through the particular teacher with a living tradition and a living community.

Perhaps one of the other impulses to this programme has been the policy since the foundation of the college to be open to Christians who wish to study Judaism in a Jewish environment. These have included a number of Sisters of Sion, who have completed either diploma or degree courses with us, and theology students, usually from Holland or Germany, who have studied for one or two semesters during their theology degree programme. Here I think it important to note that this is not simply a neutral academic experience for such students, and perhaps their desire to undertake it already reflects their own questioning about aspects of their Christian tradition. Some of them find the direct experience of Jewish life very attractive, and the directness of Jewish approaches to God in positive contrast to their own theological background. Indeed, this has from time to time led to a crisis of religious identity that has needed considerable personal support, though in the end it has usually resulted in a maturing of the student's personal faith. For this reason we have made available a tutor for them, one of the Sisters of Sion who graduated from our course and who herself had to address a number of such issues during her time of study. Here, perhaps, we are beginning to come closer to the core issues surrounding such a programme of dialogue, where the intimacy of contact moves people far beyond the purely academic approach to their studies. Most complete the programme having resolved their difficulties and strengthened their own religious belief and commitment. Indeed, this is a common result of dialogue when it is approached with integrity by all participants.

Nevertheless, over the years of my own involvement with teaching at the college, I am aware of a few Christian students who have taken the step of formally converting to Judaism. However, in all cases this was a possibility that they had already begun to explore before they joined us, and was merely confirmed by their time at the college. Nevertheless, it is something that must be recognised as a potential outcome of such an engagement with another faith, and each tradition has to decide how it is able to cope with such things.

I referred above to the impact of the presence of Christian students on my own Jewish students, and I can identify an evolution over time that is very healthy. In the earlier years it came as a shock to our students to realise that some of the opinions they held about Christianity could actually prove offensive to students sitting with them in class. We are used to being a minority group in a Christian environment, and had to learn what it was like to be in a majority situation and how hard it was for a Christian to spend time as a minority in our circle. It was a situation that was even more difficult for German students with all the burden of recent history upon them. With time, a greater sensitivity has simply become part of our college culture. But it has also been important for our Jewish students to realise that it is not possible simply to generalise about what Christians are like and what they believe. Each new student who has joined the college has been able to point out that they did not necessarily believe the things that it was assumed or even asserted they believed. They could also point to a wide variety of views available within the church.

It has been an important lesson for our rabbinic students to recognise their own presuppositions, and indeed prejudices, about Christianity. This two-way traffic in de-mythologising the other has been extremely valuable and can only happen through prolonged exposure in a supportive environment.

On the same principle, the course in Islam is taught by a Muslim academic, currently a Palestinian woman, which raises a number of eyebrows in our movement. But it is precisely the result of years of dialogue and trust-building, that we have the privilege to be able to study together despite the delicacy of so much of Jewish–Muslim relations. My only regret is that until now we have had no Muslim students joining us for a semester, though I hope this will happen one day.

The third element I wish to discuss, the JCM Student Conference held annually at the Hedwig Dransfeld Haus, would require an entire chapter to do it justice. It grew out of an intuition on the part of a few rabbis and Christian clergy in the wake of the Six-Day War that it was important for the future spiritual leaders of the three faiths to meet as students and understand one another. The initial idea was to bring together students training for the ministry in their respective traditions. Our hope was to influence them so that they would bring into their later congregational work an awareness of the other two faiths and gradually build a network of contacts. Unfortunately there was no symmetry here when we tried to work on this basis. Whereas Christian theology students and student rabbis from Leo Baeck College were easy to find, there seemed to be no Muslim equivalents in Western Europe. In fact part of the problem of interfaith dialogue in general is this lack of symmetry. There needs to develop in Europe Muslim institutions that offer young local Muslims a training that equips them to lead their communities here in the West.

As a solution to this particular problem, we broadened the range of participants who could attend the conference to include community and social workers and teachers from the three faith communities. This also had the effect of introducing new skills in the techniques of dialogue work. It also led to an interesting range of tensions, especially on the boundary between religious and secular approaches to the community. The mutual suspicions between those who saw themselves as 'believers' and those who were agnostic or avowedly secular, forced us to examine a different dimension to our dialogue from an early stage. As the programme evolved, we realised that what was important was the experiential component of the encounter as much as the intellectual input. Thus formal lectures are restricted to just three on the particular topic of the conference, one from each faith, and most of the work is done in one of two types of group work – discussion groups which are carefully composed to include an equal balance of people from the three faiths, a mix of genders and people with ability to translate between German and English, and a series of less-formal meetings, often based on non-verbal communication which allows for other levels of personal encounter, such as art or meditative dance. Incidentally, by 'students', we mean people of all ages – and the presence of families with young children helps create the feeling of a normal community situation.

Of particular importance is the attendance at each other's services and a shared morning meditation, which offer a sense both of the closeness and the otherness of our respective faiths. It must also be added that any number of spontaneous events and often a sharing of musical traditions add other dimensions. The arrangement of vegetarian food, the absence of alcoholic drinks and the provision of time and space for prayers create a degree of security for many coming for the first time. They recognise that we are sensitive to their needs. One side effect, however, is that having to give up alcohol and meat also provides a shared sense of suffering for the sake of the conference as a whole among some of the participants. (As a result, interesting discussions also take place till the early hours of the morning in a local down the road!) In short it is a powerful week, in what is essentially a 'safe space', where there is room for individual exploration and growth. By making attendance at the conference a required part of our rabbinic training, we are also signalling to our students and communities the importance we place on this particular area of training.

LIVING IN EACH OTHER'S SPACE

What are the consequences of such programmes? The first is both obvious and deeply challenging. The presence of Christian students at the college means that a discourse that has been held totally within a closed group in the past is now being observed by someone from outside. Moreover, that person belongs to a faith community that has often been the other against which we have defined our own selves. Suddenly all the simplistic comparisons are no longer available – in part out of respect for the guest in our midst, but also because our own errors, projections, fantasies and misinformation can be instantly corrected. In many ways this is healthy and invigorating once they have recovered from the shock.

Furthermore, it opens the door to a number of discoveries. The presence of the other and the particular qualities they display encourages us to look for the same qualities in our own tradition, elements that may simply not have been emphasised in recent times. Moreover, we obtain a different perspective on ideas and values within our own tradition that we may have taken for granted. Seen through the eyes of the other they take on new dimensions, and we may learn to value them afresh. It is also sanguine to learn what some of our most valued truths sound like through the ears of someone else – sometimes their narrowness or polemic nature are exposed, which can be most disturbing. Arguments about exclusivity, uniqueness and 'special emphases' that belong to our tradition 'alone' may sound a little hollow when we encounter them elsewhere, even with minor variations. The commonality of many religious ideas can even be quite disconcerting when we have built up our own views in contradistinction to an imagined other. Certainly, such a situation takes the edge off the customary trium- phalism that has all too often been the hallmark of our encounters in the past. This leads to a potential for major upheaval in our own thinking that will not be easy to undertake. For such encounters relativise our own truth claims so that a new approach is needed, including the question of what remains uniquely ours. However painful this may be, it can also offer the opportunity to purify what have often become stale assumptions.

The other side of this is the need to make theological space for the other, which is itself a delicate matter. For we need to create for ourselves an understanding of where we locate the other, but without falling into the old trap of creating simply a new stereotype, even a more positive one, that still does less than justice to their complexity and multifaceted reality. That is to say we have to become engaged in a process of continuing adjustment, reflection and empirical testing rather than settling for a tidy, closed formulation.

I need hardly add that even contemplating such a change is an enormous challenge to our programmes of theological training that are already over-burdened with the materials we have to teach about our own tradition, let alone the skills needed to enable our students to function effectively in their clerical roles. The resistance to even entering such an area, com-pounded of traditional misapprehensions of the other, old prejudices, fears of change and vested interests in existing power structures, not to mention the practical problems that would have to be overcome, make the prospects for such a long-term development very problematic. The question therefore is whether it is something we are prepared to undertake – or, if we are to take seriously the call for a global ethic from Hans Küng, or other similarly expressed ideas, we can afford not to enter into this level of dialogue.

VENTURING ABROAD

One of the consequences of such intimate encounters may be the invitation to address in public the community of the other. Sometimes it is the direct result of the dialogue process itself: a participant feels sufficiently confident to invite a dialogue partner into his or her own space. This can be an occasion for bland, mutual well-wishing, which may be a necessary stage in initial confidence-building. Nevertheless, the concerns present in the private encounter are also present and just as likely to surface. Sometimes it is advisable to air them more directly as an opening stage in what must be a long process of shared debate.

If one is aware, through personal experience of dialogue, of the sensitivities, concerns and potential traps, it may be possible to anticipate some of them and help all present to move through them and beyond – through there will always be surprises and challenges.

In the next section of the book I have included some examples of addresses to Christian and Muslims. Two of them, on Jewish views of Jesus and Muhammad, were delivered in the 'neutral' context of an annual trialogue conference in Cologne. In both cases they are responses to frequently asked questions about Jewish attitudes to central figures in the other two faiths and the source of potential conflict. The other two examples were addressed respectively to Christian and Muslim audiences. In all cases they were well received, even through, in the case of the former two, they trod on very delicate ground.

To conclude this chapter here is another story based on the disputation situation. This time it is a bishop who challenges the local Jewish community. Again it reflects a difficult historical reality. Often the 'Christian' representative in the disputation was a converted Jew, sufficiently know-ledgeable of Jewish sources to use them against his former community with the zeal so often associated with a convert. In this version the Jewish community is invited to formulate a question which their champion will ask the priest, a Jewish convert who represents the church. If the priest can answer the question, the Jews have to leave the area or convert to Christianity. But if he cannot answer the question they can stay. Again the Jews start to pack – except for our friend Yankel. When he stands before the priest, and has to ask the question he says 'What is the meaning of the Hebrew "*lo yadati*"?' (Now the words '*lo yadati*' actually mean 'I do not know'.) So without thinking the priest answered 'I don't know'. And lost the contest. When Yankel goes home and tells the people what happened they are very impressed. But they cannot understand how Yankel, who is not very clever, managed to think up such an intelligent question. Yankel is puzzled. 'It wasn't so difficult,' he says. 'I was sitting in class the other day and someone asked the Rabbi, what does "*lo yadati*" mean, and the Rabbi said "I don't know". So I figured, if the Rabbi doesn't know the Priest certainly won't know!'

All the same issues apply to this story as to the first, except that today the result would have been a bit different. The priest, not a convert, would know Hebrew well, having studied at the Hebrew University in Jerusalem or at Leo Baeck College. He would also know Jewish jokes, so he would not fall into the same trap. Instead of a disputation, the bishop would be hosting an interfaith conference. And Yankel, after years of experience of dialogue, would never do anything to embarrass his friend and colleague the priest. And the story itself would have been told by a Sufi Muslim who had studied in Cairo and London, instead of by a rabbi. For now that is only partly true. I hope that in years to come it will be something we can experience everywhere.

10
Jewish Perceptions of Jesus[1]

Two anecdotes reflect the kinds of concern experienced by Jews in undertaking a dialogue with Christians, let alone discussing the Jewish perception of Jesus. The first begins with a telephone call from a publisher, who was about to publish a major book on the world religions – a popular guide for people interested in interfaith studies. There was a slight problem with the Jewish symbol they were using on the cover, and they would be grateful if I would look at it to make sure it would not offend a Jewish audience. I was happy to do so and waited for the fax to arrive. When it did I was astonished to find that the entire page was dominated by an elaborate Orthodox Christian cross that reached from the top to the bottom of the page and effectively divided it up into quarters. As a result, the symbols of Judaism, Islam, Hinduism, Buddhism and so on were displayed around the cross, but about an eighth as large. The message was obvious. Whatever the title of the book and the actual contents said about understanding world religions, the front cover asserted that Christianity was the central and dominant religion in the world! The other religions were relatively minor and perhaps of some interest to Christians, but nothing more. I was relieved to discover that the editor of the book had the same problem as I had but that it was the publisher who insisted on this form of the cover. The reasoning behind it was that in this way it might appeal to a large audience of American Christian fundamentalists, although it was also pointed out that these were precisely the people who were least likely to be interested in other religions! I registered my reservations about the cover. In the final version that I saw quite by chance, the cross was considerably smaller but still dominated the centre of the page.

The other anecdote goes back a few years to one of the Jewish-Christian Bible Weeks in Germany that I have been co-leading for over 30 years. It was one of the anniversaries, perhaps the twentieth, and I spoke about the importance of the Bible Week and how true interfaith dialogue strengthens our commitment to our own religious tradition. Afterwards, an elderly Christian lady was heard to say how disappointing it was that after 20 years working at this Catholic house I had not been persuaded to become Christian!

Such examples could be multiplied. In neither case could one ascribe to the person concerned any ill feeling about Jews or Judaism, or any other religion for that matter. They simply spoke and acted out of the conviction that they were Christian, that in their experience Christianity was the major world religion and especially the religion of the West, and it was self-evident that everyone should acknowledge this, and eventually come to accept Christianity for themselves.

But though there was no ill intent behind the remarks, they also point to the very basic series of difficulties that Jews have when confronting or thinking about Christianity, and behind Christianity the figure of Jesus. The first example points to the simple fact of the numerical imbalance between Christianity and Judaism. When it comes to dialogue between any two groups they have to find some way of meeting on even ground. When representatives of a majority encounter representatives of a minority this power differential is crucial. The smaller group experiences itself as being at a disadvantage, possibly under threat and certainly in no position to yield any of its hard-won autonomy. The majority group is often quite insensitive to the problems, perspective or concerns of the minority group. It can take for granted its position of power and may understand its willingness to meet with the other as a generous act of magnanimity that it feels the other should appreciate much more.

Unless both sides can recognise the extent to which this power differential affects their encounter it is very hard to go any further. Even setting aside the history of Christian treatment of Jews over the centuries, precisely because of the Jewish experience of being a minority, and a numerically declining one at that, it has been very hard for Jews to think in positive terms about their relationship to Christianity.

That having been said, it is clear that there have been enormous changes in official Christian attitudes to Jews and Judaism since the war, and in particular since Vatican II. Much has been done to allay Jewish fears and suspicions, and indeed to re-educate the church to a new understanding of Judaism and the way in which Jews should be considered and addressed. But it takes time before this kind of change reaches down to the grassroots, and before it has its impact on the average Jew as well.

The second story, however, illustrates precisely the perception that Jews have about Christian intentions in their encounter with Jews. Christianity is perceived by Jews as a missionising faith, with Jews as a prime target in this quest for converts. As I understand it this is a view that is still affirmed by many Christian churches, whereas it may be modified or even set aside by others. Here again we encounter a kind of imbalance. There was a time when Judaism was a missionising religion, and may even have been in competition with Christianity in the race to win the Roman Empire. But this has long since ceased to be the case. To a large extent this was not a matter of choice by Jewish communities. Under both Christianity and Islam at different times, those who wished to convert to Judaism, and those who helped them in the process, did so at the risk of their lives. So we have learnt to make a virtue out of a necessity. In some Jewish circles we have even made it extremely difficult to accept potential converts. There are some voices today, particularly within the Reform movement in America, that see in the vast reduction in Jewish numbers because of the Shoah and the shrinking Jewish population, such a great threat to our survival that they advocate that we should set about missionising on a grand scale. Nevertheless, this remains a fundamental difference between Judaism and Christianity and raises for Jews serious questions about the motives of Christians with whom they interact. In such circumstances, if a Jew says something positive about Jesus, he or she may be regarded with considerable suspicion by other Jews. Have we been betrayed? Is this simply a preliminary step towards conversion? I need hardly add that the cruellest insult that Orthodox Jews throw against Reform Jews is to accuse them of really being a different religion, and of becoming Christian. That this could be such a decisive insult and could wound so much is further proof of the way in which Christianity is perceived in certain Jewish circles.[2]

So there are no comfortable ways to address this subject from a Jewish perspective. Undoubtedly it is possible for Jews and Christians to meet, share many values, collaborate on taking responsibility for aspects of our society and even discuss religious matters in some depth – but at the point where the figure of Jesus is evoked in a serious way, a whole range of delicate problems arise. The fact that Jesus himself was a Jew might theoretically offer a point of unity. And I can imagine how from a Christian perspective, though perhaps a rather naive one, this idea could be put forward. But when we came to test out the implications in any real Jewish community setting, too much history, pain and misunderstanding and, even today, fear, get in the way from the Jewish side.

Curiously, if Jews do have some feeling about Jesus it is to regard him as simply another Jewish martyr, one of many anonymous Jews crucified by the Roman oppressors. In this regard he would stand alongside the roll call of figures in the Talmud who suffered torture and death for their beliefs, foremost among them Rabbi Akiba. Moreover, it is one of the paradoxes of the twentieth century that an artist like Chagall and a writer like Eli Wiesel, when trying to express their horror at the fate of the Jewish people at the hands of the Nazis, use the image of crucifixion. We seem to lack a Jewish iconography of suffering and martyrdom, and turn to this potent figure instead.

The question of who Jesus was or might have been is actually of interest to very few Jews. Or to be even more precise, among most Jews he has no significance whatsoever, but if pressed they will speak of him in negative terms, simply because of the appalling Christian treatment of Jews over the past almost two millennia. In the name of Jesus, Jews have been persecuted, cheated, exploited, tortured, forcibly converted or killed. The debate about the role of the churches during the Nazi period continues but few doubt that 2000 years of Christian anti-Jewish teaching provided a background set of prejudices and attitudes that helped make the Holocaust possible. That having been said, there have always been exceptional Christian individuals with whom a more positive relationship has been established, but the norm, and certainly the perception of that norm, is very negative. I need go back no further than my father telling me that in his native Glace Bay, Nova Scotia, in the early years of the twentieth century, it was not safe to go out in the streets at Easter because they called after the Jews, 'Christ killer!' and threw rocks. The individual, Jesus of Nazareth, is utterly lost behind this history and the perception of crimes committed against the Jewish people in his name.

The roots of this go back to the very origins of Christianity, which are bound up in conflict and anti-Jewish polemic. Whatever the gospels may be as the central documents of Christian self-understanding, and however they developed historically, in their final form they appear to have as their audience the gentile world, and in order to reach that audience they have to reject a central aspect of their origins – their rootedness in the Jewish tradition, culture and life in first-century Palestine.

Suppose we were to set aside for the moment the grassroot Jewish suspicions of Christianity in general, we may distinguish a number of perceptions of Jesus of Nazareth in the Jewish world. Of those who have sought some kind of understanding of Jesus, we should probably separate out those who have approached him, and through him, Christianity, as a part of a religious journey. For many Jews, after the Emancipation (the process of granting civil rights to Jews beginning in the eighteenth century) conversion to Christianity was the only open door through which it was possible to enter fully into the new society. Figures like Heinrich Heine, Benjamin Disraeli or Gustav Mahler immediately spring to mind. But there were others for whom it was a much deeper personal spiritual quest, whether they actually converted, like Edith Stein, or at the last minute withdrew and rediscovered their Judaism, like Franz Rosenzweig, or somehow floated between the two faiths, like Simone Weil. The potency of the appeal of Jesus of Nazareth is clear and it must be said that there are elements in Christian spirituality that are very attractive, precisely because they are not so readily apparent in traditional Judaism. Or, better said, Jewish spirituality is very firmly based on a body of knowledge and experience that is not always available to Jews today and so more direct kinds of spiritual experience have been sought elsewhere. With Christianity being taboo for many young Jews, the Eastern religions have offered instead a satisfaction for this hunger. Nevertheless, since the Emancipation the attraction of certain aspects of Christian life, allied to a negative Jewish self-image, inculcated by their treatment and fate over centuries, has led to a number of Jews converting to Christianity.

In our day there is a variant on this theme, that of those who feel it is possible to make a synthesis between Jewish tradition and the figure of Jesus – groups that bear names like 'Jews for Jesus' or 'Hebrew Christians'. They tend to be quite missionising in their attempt to bring other Jews into their ranks, which reinforces the condemnation they get from Jewish circles that feel they are preying, illegitimately, on our community. Oddly enough, they also seem to have an uncertain place within Christianity, partly, as I understand it, because they may sometimes insist that because they are of Jewish origin they are closer to the beginnings of Christianity itself and are in some way more authentic. Insofar as they are therefore marginalised in the Christian community, they are, ironically, acting out a typical Jewish fate. However, since they have to all intents and purposes left the Jewish world as it defines itself, whatever they may claim for themselves, I will exclude them from this discussion.

For those few who have tried to approach the figure of Jesus in a more scholarly or theological way, a variety of approaches may be observed. Some, particularly in the nineteenth century, felt the need to refute Christian claims to have superseded Judaism, with all the consequences that have flowed from them, and tackle Christianity on its own ground through academic studies of the historical sources. Sometimes they thought they were being purely objective in their analysis but may not have noticed their own bias ('*Tendenz*'). Others sought either to reclaim Jesus as a Jewish teacher or at least to locate him within the broad spectrum of his contemporary Jewish world, which also meant reading the gospels through the eyes of contemporary Jewish documentation.

It has been suggested that, like others engaged in such an exercise, they tend to remake Jesus in their own image. So he emerges as a revolutionary political figure, or a marginal kind of liberal Jew, or as a slightly unconventional but nevertheless recognisable pharisaic teacher.

One notable German Jewish scholar to approach the figure of Jesus is Rabbi Dr Leo Baeck. He wrote a number of essays on early Christianity and its emergence out of the contemporary Jewish world. In one celebrated essay, 'The Gospel as a Document of the History of the Jewish Faith', he analysed the gospel accounts of the life of Jesus, and tried to excavate the various layers of editing that went into the final versions and return to what he considered the original Jewish core. Essentially his method, followed by others in the field, was to assume that anything that might be construed as 'anti-Jewish' must belong to a later hand, as part of the process of translating Jesus for a pagan world. According to a brief biography of him by Dr H. I. Bach, written within a few months of Baeck's death, he kept his equilibrium during the years of 1933–38, when he was the effective leader of German Jewry:

> by translating three times the whole of the Gospel from Greek into Hebrew, in order to sift the oldest parts in it by Hebrew-speaking Jews, including Jesus himself, from later extensions and accretions; and he succeeded against determined resistance of the Nazi censorship in publishing a slim little booklet, 'The Gospel as a Document of the History of the Jewish Faith'.[3]

In this essay, having stripped away all that he felt was extraneous, he came up with the following description and evaluation of Jesus:

> In the old Gospel which is thus opened up before us, we encounter a man with noble features who lived in the land of the Jews in tense and excited times and helped and laboured and suffered and died: a man out of the Jewish people who walked on Jewish paths with Jewish faith and hopes. His spirit was at home in the Holy Scriptures, and his imagination and thought were anchored there; and he proclaimed and taught the word of God because God had given it to him to hear and to preach. We are confronted by a man who won his disciples among his people: men who had been looking for the messiah, the son of David, who had been promised; men who then found him and clung to him and believed in him until he finally began to believe in himself and thus entered into the mission and destiny of his age and indeed into the history of mankind. These disciples he found here, among his people, and they believed in him even after his death, until there was nothing of which they felt more certain than that he had been, according to the words of the prophet, 'on the third day raised from the dead'. In this old tradition we behold a man who is Jewish in every feature and trait of his character, manifesting in every particular what is pure and good in Judaism. This man could have developed as he came to be only on the soil of Judaism; and only on this soil, too, could he find his disciples and followers as they were. Here alone, in this Jewish sphere, in this Jewish atmosphere of trust and longing, could this man live his life and meet his death – a Jew among Jews. Jewish history and Jewish reflection may not pass him by nor ignore him. Since he was, no time has been without him; nor has there been a time which was not challenged by the epoch that would consider him its starting point.

When this old tradition confronts us in this manner, then the Gospel, which was originally something Jewish, becomes a book — and certainly not a minor work — within Jewish literature. This is not because, or not only because, it contains sentences which also appear in the same or a similar form in the Jewish works of that time. Nor is it such — in fact, it is even less so — because the Hebrew or Aramaic breaks again and again through the word forms and sentence formations of the Greek translation. Rather it is a Jewish book because — by all means and entirely because — the pure air of which it is full and which it breathes is that of the Holy Scriptures; because a Jewish spirit, and none other, lives in it; because Jewish faith and Jewish hope, Jewish suffering and Jewish distress, Jewish knowledge and Jewish expectations and these alone, resound through it — a Jewish book in the midst of Jewish books. Judaism may not pass it by, nor mistake it, nor wish to give up all claims here. Here, too, Judaism should comprehend and take note of what is its own.[4]

This is an extraordinary conclusion, especially given the place and circumstances within which it was written. It could only come from someone securely rooted in his Judaism and as liberal in his values as Baeck. But one must also presume that there is another agenda under the surface of any such text published in 1938 in Berlin. This powerful reclaiming of Jesus for the Jewish world, this emphatic repetition of the adjective 'Jewish', is a defiant gesture to a Christian world subverted by Nazi ideology. It comes as no surprise to learn that the volume in which it appeared, *Aus drei Jahrtausenden: Wissenschaftliche Untersuchungen und Abhandlungen zur Geschichte des jüdischen Glaubens*, was printed but never published. The Gestapo destroyed almost the entire edition before publication. The essay on the gospels was also published separately in one of the small volumes of the series, *Bücherei des Schocken Verlags*, also in Berlin in 1938.

Between then and now stands the Shoah. The world of Liberal Judaism that Baeck knew, with its intellectual and cultural wealth was one of the first victims of Naziism. The sense of trust in Western European life and values is called into question. Moreover, it is not a Jewish reconstruction of a Jewish Jesus that we encounter today but any number of different Jesus figures. There is the ecumenical, or better, the interfaith, Jesus of some Protestant and Catholic theologians, and I have a great respect for the revolutionary re-evaluations they have made, sometimes at the cost of the place within the church they might have expected to occupy. But there is also the Jesus of fundamentalist Christian groups and of Orthodox churches that still promote a clearly defined role and destiny for the Jewish people. It is precisely in this diversity that a major problem enters the discussion.

The Jewish position as regards interfaith encounters is to emphasise the need for both partners to seek to understand and respect the faith of the other as the other understands and experiences it. But in practice this is often a one-way street, with the Jewish partner expecting a Christian re-evaluation of its approach to Judaism. In fact, the problem is particularly complex. Christian theology in the past has defined not only the role of Judaism from its own perspective, but somehow assumed that Jews either do conform to this view or, worse still, should do so. 'Judaism' and 'the Jewish people' in this sense become Christian constructs, often with little relationship to what an inner Jewish self-understanding might be. It is dramatised in the kinds of questions asked by Christians in the early days of dialogue: what do Jews think about resurrection, salvation and the messiah, Jesus? These are issues that operate within a Christian frame of reference and, to use modern jargon, simply do not 'compute' within a Jewish context. For us, issues of identity, survival, our relationship to traditional Jewish law, the interpretation of the revelation at Sinai and the nature of the Jewish state are the challenging and divisive questions.

Christians have accepted this request by their Jewish dialogue partners, and this is reflected in much that has been produced by the churches in recent decades. The only problem is that, sometimes, in trying to find a new place for Jews or Judaism within a Christian understanding, there is a risk of creating yet another Christian theology which imposes a Christian definition onto the Jew. We remain thereby a construct of some-one else's religious imagination. Something of this sort is inevitable, given the nature of theological discourse, so the possibility has to be kept in mind and constantly checked against the reality of Jewish existence.

But when we look to the Jewish side of the equation we encounter a failure that must also be noted, a failure to show a real curiosity about the Christian partner and to be prepared to think through a Jewish religious understanding of Christianity for today. The reasons for this failure lie within the kind of issues mentioned above, particularly the sense of being a minority group under threat in a Christian *milieu* and the millennial history of Christian persecution climaxing, in Jewish perceptions, in the

Shoah. But even granted these factors, Jews have been slow to recognise the changes in Christian approaches to Judaism and the Jewish people brought about by Vatican II. Indeed, we are all too often still at the stage of projecting onto Christianity our own worst fears and prejudices and have hardly even begun the task of trying to see the world through the eyes of a Christian self-understanding.

The need for a new Jewish approach has been well expressed by Colette Kessler in a lecture to the 1995 Convention of the World Union for Progressive Judaism in Paris. Incidentally, Mme Kessler is a vice-president of the World Union of which Rabbi Dr Leo Baeck was the President in the immediate postwar period. She criticises a Jewish lack of awareness of the many Christian documents, published by Catholic and Protestant churches, in their reassessment of Judaism. She also argues for a move beyond polemics and apologetic:

> The Jewish-Christian encounter must be accepted as an appeal to deepen our faith, to search for truth, to be coherent in our attitudes. It should lead us to accept a shift in our spiritual quest, in our identity. That does not mean that we should become like the other, but rather that we should become ourselves by listening to the other, by opening our minds to his message. Sometimes we may thus be led to rediscover within our own faith, our Torah, some 'forgotten values', i.e. some of its deepest contents, that we had kept to ourselves in order to better distinguish ourselves from our neighbours. Many times we have heard Jews claiming that 'humility is a Christian value not a Jewish one' or that 'silence and personal prayer are specific elements of Christian spirituality'. Our problem is that we must overcome a fear that remains visceral in the minds of a large number of Jews: the fear that there may be similarities in the expressions of the two different religions.[5]

Kessler concludes with challenging questions to the Jewish world:

> Are the Jews of our time ready to receive the Christian as a brother, both alike and different, as a partner of the Covenant in God's design? As a partner, chosen by God Himself, in the quest of His kingdom? As belonging to a community of faith in spite of all differences? Are we ready to recognise that, while the Christian needs the Jew, it is equally true that the Jew needs the Christian in his confrontation with the world and with God? (ibid.: 132)

But she recognises that there is an essential precondition for these questions even to be addressed:

> In order to be able simply to formulate those questions, one must have intensely participated in many Jewish-Christian encounters, involving common biblical studies, doctrinal exchanges, shared silences and prayer. One must have felt how much these

meetings help us today – in a Jewish world that is more open than in the past, but nonetheless still retired within itself...(ibid.)

There are voices, particularly in America, like those of Mme Kessler. Most recently a document titled '"Dabru Emet" ("Speak the truth")...': A Jewish Statement on Christians and Christianity' has been published by a group of American Jewish scholars offering 'eight brief statements about how Jews and Christians may relate to one another.'[6] Though it has led to both acceptance and debate within Jewish and Christian circles directly engaged in interfaith dialogue, it nevertheless remains a slow and difficult process to encourage a sensitive Jewish approach to Christianity amongst the broader Jewish population.

One of the main reasons that has not been mentioned before is the confusion within the Jewish world about its own nature, purpose and religious basis. The divisions between Orthodox, non-Orthodox and secular Jews that are the consequences of the Emancipation are further confused not only by the horrendous destruction of the Shoah, but also by the equally challenging impact of the creation of the state of Israel. For the first time in 2000 years an entire Jewish society is developing in which the religious assumptions about the nature of Jews and Judaism appear to many to be utterly irrelevant. As a national entity, the Jewish people on their own land must inevitably have a radically different set of concerns and priorities, and their relationship with the Jews of Diaspora history is anything but clear. On the other hand the power given to certain Orthodox groups within the state of Israel has its impact on the Diaspora communities, with a consequent increasing polarisation between Orthodox and Liberal movements. These and other factors lead to a deep-seated insecurity, particularly when it comes to dealing with religious matters. Without a certain security in one's own identity it can be quite threatening to enter dialogue with another faith community, though those of us who have experienced dialogue know that the encounter with the other may actually help us to define our own identity in the process. That is part of the paradox of dialogue.

Given such inner turmoil within the Jewish world, Jewish-Christian dialogue comes very low on the list of priorities. But if the experience of the growing numbers of people who have attempted interfaith dialogue of quality is anything to go by, this is an essential process for both faiths. From the Christian side it has something to do with a necessary repentance for the past; for the Jewish side it is part of a necessary healing and rediscovery of our own universalism. So even if the figure of Jesus today does almost nothing to unite Jews and Christians, we may be entering a time when the figure of Jesus will, at least, do less to divide us.

11
When I See What Christians Make of the 'Hebrew' Bible[1]

Any Jewish attempt to discuss the figure of Jesus is fraught with difficulties, as was indicated in the previous chapter. Far less problematic is the growing amount of shared study by Jews and Christians of the text of the Old Testament. Jews are understandably uncomfortable with the term[2] and may speak of the Hebrew Bible or use the acronym TaNaKH, which stands for its three traditional divisions of Jewish editions, 'Torah' (the Five Books of Moses), 'Nevi'im' ('Prophets', the volumes from Joshua to Malachi) and 'Ketuvim' ('Writings', including the Psalms, Proverbs and Job to the end of the Second Book of Chronicles). Certainly academic scholarship of these books crosses denominational lines, with the joint production of editions of the Bible using both Jewish and Christian scholars. At the level of popular Bible study, much of this scholarship has filtered down, though it is often rejected, or consciously ignored, by fundamentalist groups within both religions. When Jews and Christians do come together to study some surprising things emerge. It was in the context of exploring the difference in approaches that I was invited to discuss with Christian clergy how I viewed the Bible itself and the Christian use of it.

My starting point is an observation about what biblical books are most studied. The librarian of the Leo Baeck College was recently reorganising the biblical section of the library. He drew my attention to what he considered an interesting peculiarity. Here we were, a rabbinic seminary, but the section on the Torah took up relatively little space on the bookshelves compared to other parts of the Hebrew Bible. When I had a closer look I could only confirm his findings – though it must be admitted that the classical rabbinic commentaries on the Torah were stored elsewhere and took up a considerable space. What we were looking at were the works of contemporary biblical scholarship, some by Christians, a few by Jews, some by scholars for whom the Bible is not a matter of particular religious significance but a work of world literature to be studied like any other. But what were the biblical books that took up the greatest amount of shelf space in the 'academic' section? Genesis, Isaiah and Psalms. Compared to these three the other biblical books seemed to attract relatively little interest.

This perception is in part borne out by my experience of the Jewish-Christian Bible Week that I have been co-organising at the Hedwig Dransfeld Haus for over 30 years. We have been working our way system-atically through the Hebrew Bible starting with Genesis, and by now we have almost reached the end of the Minor Prophets. (I have to admit with a certain amount of guilt that we skipped over the Book of Leviticus because I did not feel qualified at the time to deal with it!) Here too, the Genesis stories attracted many people, as did Exodus. The number of participants certainly dropped off once we started working through Joshua, Judges, Samuel and Kings – though they picked up a bit when we dealt with King David. Again it was with Isaiah that the larger numbers returned and since then we have built up a core of people willing to read anything.

Clearly the Genesis stories, the patriarchs and their family struggles, are favourite points of identification for many – Christians and Jews alike. The Psalms have a liturgical significance that inevitably makes them par-ticularly popular. (I was once asked by a Christian in all seriousness, 'Do the Jews have the Psalms as well?' They are, of course, a major element in Jewish private and liturgical worship.) But Isaiah remains a major text for at least some groups of Christians, presumably because of the degree to which it was seen, and is seen, as proclaiming the coming of Christ, as evidenced by citations in the New Testament. Of course, even within Isaiah the passages that are well known are relatively few, and I suspect it comes as something of a shock to people when they begin to realise just how difficult the language and poetry of Isaiah can be. All of this is to say that, apart from Christians who may make it a part of their spiritual life to read the whole of the Bible on a regular basis, much of this treasured Old Testament remains very much a buried treasure.

Let me take this a step further. Perhaps the one biblical passage that belongs to universal currency, despite the decline in biblical literacy in the past few decades, is the phrase 'You shall love your neighbour as yourself'. It is often thought by people who quote it that it is a quintessentially Christian statement, indeed one said by Jesus. The more informed will know that it is actually a quotation from the Hebrew Bible, and of all unlikely books, from Leviticus. Indeed it is part of a fascinating semi-legal discussion about interpersonal behaviour within the covenant community, But, apart from the fact that people often do not know the Bible well enough to recognise the origin of the phrase, to many it appears to be inconceivable that such a significant verse, and indeed one about 'love', could emanate from the Old Testament. After all, is not the Old Testament all about the jealous and violent God of the Hebrews, and indeed the Jews. Surely this religion of legalism has been superseded by the New Testament, with its proclamation of love. Again, those who know their Hebrew Bible are aware of the great diversity of materials it contains, including books that embody the deepest emotions and passions of love – Song of Songs, Ruth. But the Hebrew Bible remains all too often the victim of a negative propaganda that belongs to a Christian ambiguity towards its own origins within Judaism and the apparent need to make the 'new revelation' significantly different, and better than the old one.

There are notable exceptions to this approach, and we all benefit from the changing emphasis brought about over 30 years ago by Vatican II. In Germany in particular, the various church documents attempting to redefine their relationship with Jews are important contributions.[3] I also know from my own experience of lecturing in Germany at different conference centres and communities that there is a small but committed group of people willing to approach the Hebrew Bible in its own terms and study it for its own unique values. The interest in Judaism is reflected in the large attendance at sessions dealing with Judaism and Jewish teachings at both the Kirchentag and Katholikentag, major public conferences of, respectively, the Protestant and Catholic churches, in Germany. Organisations like the International Bible Reading Association now include pieces on the Hebrew Bible written by rabbis in their publications. I am sure there are countless other initiatives and circles where the Hebrew Bible is studied with all seriousness. Nevertheless, such activities remain relatively limited, and old attitudes still prevail in much of the Christian world.

The negative view of the Old Testament is also to be found in unexpected places. With the rise of ecological concerns, theologians attempted to find the source of our abuse of the environment. Numerous writers put the blame firmly on Genesis 1:28, God's command to the first human couple to 'be fruitful and multiply and fill the earth and conquer it and rule over the fish of the sea and the birds of the air and all living beings that creep upon the earth'. This was seen as the source, and indeed the divine sanction, for exploiting the earth and animal kingdom, once again the Old Testament being the cause of our misfortunes. Such a reading totally ignores the many passages that indicate the restrictions placed on our freedom to exploit the earth – from sabbatical years where the land lies fallow, to the law prohibiting destroying trees even in a situation of war, to the law against muzzling different kinds of animals together. The key sentence is again to be found in Leviticus 25:23: 'The land may not be sold in perpetuity for the land is Mine, for you are strangers and settlers with Me.' We are not free to use the earth as we wish, for we are lease-holders answerable to the 'landowner', God. So once again a highly selective and biased reading of the Old Testament bases itself on a pre-existing stereotype and reinforces it.

The most regrettable contemporary manifestation of negative attitudes to the Hebrew Bible is to be found in the writings of some feminist theologians. It is particularly unfortunate because it betrays the tolerance that is supposed to lie at the heart of the feminist approach, and is divisive in circumstances where solidarity is so important.[4] Issues like the alleged Jewish obsession with women's 'uncleanness' during menstruation are addressed. But the writers often show ignorance of the biblical concept (the Hebrew *tamei* and *tahor* refer to ritual purity and impurity that equally affect men, and which do not carry in Hebrew the moral implications of the English 'clean' and 'unclean'). They are no less ignorant of later Jewish tradition in such matters. As Rachel Montagu points out, even positive matters, like the fact that prophetesses such as Deborah and

Huldah say 'Thus says the Lord', are recorded with evidence of amazement (Montagu 1996:29). How can such things be possible in a patriarchal society? Which reminds me of my own argument that people tend to say 'What's a nasty passage like this doing in a nice book like the Bible?' instead of starting with the contents of the Bible and only then trying to understand what kind of a book it is. Though this is outside my immediate topic, the attitude of Jesus to women is likewise selectively read: is he the first feminist who breaks with the unacceptable values of his Jewish environment, or does he actually express the attitudes of his culture? While there has also been a degree of self-criticism and awareness about such attitudes within feminist writings, some still effectively perpetuate negative stereotypes in a new guise to a new generation.

Moreover, there is a further price paid for such insensitivities. If the whole of the Old Testament is dismissed out of hand, it is very difficult for those who are sensitive to its strengths and weaknesses to address issues that do require a critical approach, such as the laws concerning the treatment of the inhabitants of Canaan. One becomes wary about adding more ammunition to those who are so negative in their approach.

Contrary to all this negativity, I would like to underscore the obvious fact that studying the Hebrew Bible actually helps us expand our understanding of concepts such as divine love, and offers far wider dimensions than we conventionally assume. I suppose that as a rabbi with 2000 years of rabbinic interpretation of the Hebrew Bible to call upon, such a view is self-evident. From my own perspective, the study of the Hebrew Bible should be seen as an extraordinary opportunity for personal growth, as indeed would be the case with the deeper study of any sacred literature. In fact it is precisely the open-endedness of the Hebrew Bible that gives it its special authority and power.

Suppose we stay for a moment with the question of divine love and the way it expresses itself. The 'love' shown by the biblical God is rarely explicitly described – it is rather for the reader to glimpse it through the stories about and encounters with God that are to be found throughout. Nevertheless there are passages that are explicit in their depiction of God's concern for humanity, both within and without Israel:

Tender and compassionate is the Eternal
slow to anger and full of love.
Not for all time does God accuse,
not forever keep His anger,
not according to our failings has He dealt with us,
not according to our deceit has He treated us.
As high as the sky over the earth,
so great is God's love over those who fear Him;
as far as east from the west,
so far has He taken our misdeeds from us.
As a father is tender to his children,
so the Eternal is tender to those who fear Him;
for it is He who knows our nature,
remembers that we are dust. (Psalms 103:8–14)

Suppose we stay with that image of God as a father, loving his children, willing to accept their mistakes and forgive them. It is not the only metaphor used to depict the relationship, but let us see how it may work out in practice.

It is in the role of father and teacher that we glimpse God in the posing of questions to biblical characters at key moments in their lives. A good question opens up realms of potential awareness that we ourselves can discover. For a liturgical passage I once began to assemble a variety of such questions that can be found scattered throughout the Hebrew Bible. They have a cumulative power.

When Adam eats of the fruit that has been forbidden and God seeks him out, it is with a question, 'ayekka?' 'Where are you?' (Genesis 3:9). As the mediaeval biblical commentator Rashi points out, this is not a question about Adam's geographical location, rather it is an opening, an invitation to talk and admit what he had done. It is effectively the question, where are you in your life, what has led you to wish to hide from me? What is sometimes read as an angry interrogation can also be seen as a gentle introduction to a necessary conversation.

More dramatic and of enormous significance is the question posed to Cain. The simple phrase 'Where is Abel your brother?' (Genesis 4:9) opens up the whole of our humanity to inspection. Who is our brother or sister? What responsibility do we have to him or her? How far are we prepared to acknowledge the harm we may do to each other, and hence be able to seek reconciliation and healing? Here is no accusation but again an invitation to explore together what is for Cain, and in a sense also for the God of Genesis, a new territory opened up by the horror of the first slaying.

If the hero of the early part of the Book of Genesis is Abraham, we might expect God exclusively to be concerned with him. But the tragic figure of Hagar also receives considerable attention. Elevated in her status to a second wife to Abraham, she anticipates a significant future for herself and her son, only to be cruelly abandoned. When a jealous Sarah oppresses her, Hagar runs away and might have disappeared from the story, since her involvement with Abraham is entirely a human initiative and in fact runs contrary to God's intentions. But she is equally the subject of divine intervention, and there is the angel of God waiting for her with the precise question that she needs to help her assess her situation: 'Hagar, handmaid of Sarah, where have you come from and where are you going?' (Genesis 16:8).

As with Hagar, it is not only Israelites but even the dread enemies of Israel who are addressed by God. Balaam, the magician with the power to bless or curse, has been asked by King Balak to curse Israel. There follows a massive internal struggle within Balaam. On his part there is the desire to offer his services, perhaps for the wealth and prestige promised him by Balak, perhaps because of his own animosity towards Israel. But against that desire is the explicit refusal of God to allow him to do so. How the conflict is finally resolved is another of the fascinating stories of the Hebrew Bible, but at the beginning God's question once again leaves Balaam free to decide which way to turn. 'God came to Balaam and said: "Who are these men with you?"' (Numbers 22:9).

One of the most dramatic figures in the Hebrew Bible is the prophet Elijah. He suddenly appears on stage, proclaiming a famine or challenging the prophets of Baal to a competition. In both cases this seems to be his own initiative, and God is somehow forced to do what is required to back him up. But for all his zeal, or perhaps because of it, Elijah becomes burnt out, believing that he is the only person still loyal to God. His bitter speech about his isolation is answered by God with wind, fire, earthquake and a still, small voice. But despite these revelations of God's power, Elijah simply repeats his litany of despair and God sends him to anoint Elisha as his successor (I Kings 19:9–15). This clearly does not please Elijah either, and he continues to reappear in biblical stories. But at the deepest point of his despair, there is God waiting for him with another question: 'What are you doing here Elijah?' (I Kings 19:9), offering the prophet his first ever opportunity for introspection, and the floodgates open as he expresses what he sees as the hopelessness of his situation.

This does not exhaust the questions asked by God of individuals within the Hebrew Bible. But as we have seen, each question shows respect for the person in their particular situation and, I would argue, with loving sensitivity, invites their responses. These examples and the myriad other examples to be found in the Hebrew Bible offer any number of opportunities for us to deepen our understanding of the workings of God with human beings, let alone the subtle interplay of the various actors in these dramas. So I would only conclude that the reduction of the Hebrew Bible to some kind of ideological precursor of the New Testament, which requires a highly selective reading of its contents, has effectively robbed at least some parts of the Christian world of a wealth of spiritual insight and experience. Any simplistic dismissal of the Hebrew Bible under some such categorisation is, for me, one of the greatest failures in the Christian use of it.

Let us pursue this line a little further, because one of the results of the particular Christian emphasis on certain limited aspects of the Hebrew Bible has actually helped determine the Jewish agenda as well. So much of past Jewish exegesis was spent on defending Judaism against either the attacks or interpretations of Christians that certain areas have taken on an almost distorted prominence and significance.

Most obvious, of course, is the Christian search for proofs of the messiahship of Jesus in the pages of Hebrew prophecy. For every verse that Christians have interpreted as foretelling this event, and every character who has been understood as a type of Jesus, Jews have been forced to seek alternative possibilities. I use the word 'forced' because this was precisely the case in the mediaeval disputations, during which Jewish scholars had to defend in public their refusal to accept Christian interpretations – often at risk to their lives. There is a two-volume set compiled by S. R. Driver and A. D. Neubauer, published in 1877, in which they include well over 60 different Jewish readings from the earliest rabbinic writings to the late Middle Ages, offering views on who is meant by the 'suffering servant' in

Isaiah 53, seen in Christian tradition as Jesus. They range from the messiah yet to come to the prophet Jeremiah, whose suffering is echoed in this passage to the Jewish people as a whole.[5]

I have two reasons for mentioning this particular volume and what it symbolises. The first is that I suspect that, but for the Christian emphasis on the figure of Jesus as the messiah, the concept of a messiah (only one aspect of biblical eschatology) might have had a far more limited role to play in later Jewish thought. Certainly after the defeat of Bar Kochba in the rebellion against Rome, whom the great Rabbi Akiba thought was the messiah, there was enough scepticism around to warrant forgetting the idea altogether because of the dangers that it posed. Later, pretenders to this title within the Jewish community often did considerable damage to the Jewish people. If the idea had simply been allowed to die, Judaism would have been very different. Now I am not saying whether this would have been better or worse for the Jewish people and the world — simply that the constant need to justify our rejection of Jesus as the messiah has made this figure far more prominent in later Jewish thought than it might otherwise have been. Moreover, the figure of Jesus as developed in Christian thought would have imposed limitations on Jewish explorations of the messianic idea.

Secondly, what a narrowing of the range and breadth of texts, materials, ideas, stories, poems and experiences are to be found in the Hebrew Bible, if only those relatively few matters are taken up, and only so as to prove one narrow set of theological contentions. It is an impoverishment of the text, and an impoverishment of Christianity, if its use of the Old Testament is to be limited in such a way.

The same problem applies to other Christian affirmations that seek their justification in the biblical tradition: for example, the understanding that Christians have superseded the Jewish people, as illustrated by passages such as the New Covenant mentioned in Jeremiah 31:31–33. Again, Jews have been forced to seek out apologetic responses. Yet any objective reading of the passage makes it perfectly clear that the prophet is explicitly speaking about the restoration of the two kingdoms of Israel and Judah following their destructions by, respectively, the Assyrians and Babylonians, and it would take a remarkable rereading of the text to draw any other conclusion. Which is a further reminder that Christianity has had to develop an entire hermeneutic strategy, which radically rereads the biblical text, for its own purposes. One can also see how difficult it is to argue against such a reading, that is so remote from the plain meaning and is not based on any shared set of beliefs. But this narrowing of proof texts and unlikely reading of them has a further consequence. It leads to a simplistic understanding of Jews by Christians as being those who have refused to accept what should be blatantly apparent from these passages which they understand in this narrow Christian interpretation. Anyone who has been confronted by a Christian missionary, quoting his few passages with sincere conviction and a total lack of understanding of their innate complexity or subtlety, knows how frustrating such an encounter can be. I think that Christianity is ultimately the poorer because of these strategies.

I could probably find other examples, but I think that these are enough to show a particular Jewish problem with the use of the Hebrew Bible in Christian circles, and indeed the price Jews have had to pay as a result of this use.

There is a further dimension to this that raises problems for Christians today. In the first few years of the Jewish-Christian Bible Week, the Christians were more than content to sit at the feet of the Jews and absorb the various interpretations that emerged from our rich exegetical tradition. The Midrash (early rabbinic commentary on the Bible) and the mediaeval Jewish commentators like Rashi and Ibn Ezra provide materials of enormous breadth and depth. In fact this variety of interpretation was often threatening for the Christian participants to learn that a single text could yield so many meanings. Their particular tradition often included an assumption that only one meaning could be the true meaning, and what was important was to know what that one meaning was. Once they had got over the shock, they came to view Jewish exegesis as offering a great release of creativity and imagination, as well as appreciating that there can be many different strategies for reading a given text.

Nevertheless, in time a kind of reaction set in, with people asking, 'where is our specifically Christian interpretation of these passages?' It was clear that there were very few scholars for whom the mediaeval Christian commentators were alive in the same way that their Jewish counterparts were for us. In part this was precisely because of the limited typological approaches to the material that simply did not speak to a contemporary audience. Moreover, though I do not want to overemphasise the degree to which Jews are familiar with their tradition of biblical commentary, it is certainly alive in the students and graduates of the Leo Baeck College who teach at Bendorf as well as in other more traditional circles. So if the avenue of mediaeval Christian interpretation was blocked, they said, let us hear about the specific Christian interpretation of today. I asked what they had in mind and someone answered – the theology of the Yahwist and Elohist (hypothetical sources uncovered by early modern biblical scholarship from which the text of the Hebrew Bible was assumed to be compiled).

At this point I remembered an article by Hans Walter Wolff on the Kerygma of the Elohist, in which he began by pointing out that despite advances in scholarship that had seemingly killed off the Elohist, he was still alive. Now it is again not for me to question the sincerity of the belief that the Yahwist and Elohist offered theological values for a Christian, but it does seem an extraordinary situation. The hypothetical composers of pre-biblical sources, discovered through much-debated methods which are dependent on questionable historical assumptions, have been elevated into Christian spiritual teachers even though they existed prior to the creation of the Hebrew Bible itself, let alone the advent of Christianity. Since they are themselves the creations of a particular scholarly mindset of the nineteenth century that existed within a largely Christian *milieu*, it is not surprising that a later generation raised with the same mindset should discover in them values that reinforce their own presuppositions. The whole exercise is effectively a circular argument, and again is dependent upon premises that are themselves very much called into question.

Which, to me at least, leaves unanswered the genuine question of where one can find a uniquely Christian Bible exegesis today. But to that issue belongs the question whether indeed this, or for that matter any other recognisably denominational exegesis, including a Jewish one, can be found at all today. Certainly as members of the same cultural environment, products of the same traditions of secular biblical scholarship, including the newer literary studies, it would be hard to identify anything that is not ultimately a minor variant on the same set of assumptions about the nature of the biblical text.

The problem of the Christian understanding of the Old Testament has a long history, going back to the New Testament itself. It begins with the very different nature of the Hebrew Bible and the New Testament that belong to this discussion. Here I would refer to the thoughtful study by Gabriel Josipovici,[6] who comes to biblical studies from his work in European literature. He notes the open-endedness of the Hebrew Bible and the richness of views it contains, many of which are contradictory and so leave the reader to resolve them or simply live with them. In contrast, the New Testament is far more insistent that its truths be accepted, for example through the quotations from the Hebrew Bible to which is added the phrase 'that it might be fulfilled'. We are dealing with a very different mindset and agenda, which start with assumptions about the life and death of Jesus as completing and sealing a particular process, and must therefore convince people of this truth. The openness, the range of religious options and the questioning of the Hebrew Bible are left behind, and without them our spiritual life is the poorer.

I must make it clear that I do not object to a Christian reading of the Hebrew Bible, nor for that matter, the specific ideas that this entails. There are rabbinic interpretations that are no less radical and unexpected, and that even contradict or effectively eradicate the plain sense of a passage. That is the inevitable fate of any revealed text that forms the basis of community over a period of time. But what I do expect, in the light of the Jewish experience this century in the heart of Christian Europe, is that these interpretations be examined with sensitivity to their potential effect on Jews. Anything less than that is to betray the spirit of Vatican II and the opportunity to undo the horrendous injustices done to the Jewish people over almost two millennia in the name of Christianity.

I hope I have not been too harsh. My brief was to look from a Jewish perspective at the Christian use of the Hebrew Bible, and we have 2000 years of conflict between us that must be addressed. To summarise, two issues have emerged. The first is the impact on Jews and Judaism of the Christian understanding of the Old Testament. Much of this impact has been negative, leading to mistreatment of Jewish communities. But Christian emphases have also had a direct result on some aspects of Jewish thought that might otherwise have taken different directions. The second is the effect of a particular kind of Christian exegesis that may have limited Christian access to the diversity, richness and challenges of the Hebrew Bible.

Perhaps the important point to make in conclusion is that the past need not stand in the way of the new opportunities before us today. The Hebrew Bible remains a common meeting-ground between us. Interfaith dialogue offers innumerable opportunities to meet and learn from each other.

12
Jewish Perceptions of Muhammad[1]

A number of difficulties arise in attempting to explore the perception of the Prophet Muhammad amongst Jews. Some of them are inevitably of a political or partly political nature. As a Jew who has attempted for many years to enter into a dialogue with Muslims, I am sensitive to the politics, ultimately related to the conflict in the Middle East, that surround any contemporary Jewish opinion about Islam and the figure of Muhammad. It is possible unwittingly to anger, insult or generally upset Jews and Muslims alike with virtually any position that is taken. Since such a result is probably inevitable, this offers a curious kind of freedom. Nevertheless, it does mean that what someone says on the subject is not likely to be heard as one would wish it to be heard, and that is a sad perception with which to begin.

But even setting this aside, there are issues that would arise even if I were discussing leading spiritual figures within Judaism, let alone the founder of another major religion. These have to do with the degree to which I would approach such a Jewish figure from strictly within the traditional view, and how far I would step outside it to attempt an historical reconstruction of his or her life. Such a difference in approach provides the great dividing line down the centre of Judaism today. The traditionalist feels forced to defend the tradition in what is sometimes a highly selective but nevertheless genuinely held way, as a truth that cannot be called into question. The historian takes the same traditions and sees them as materials with which to work, amongst many others, in an attempt to discover the truth of 'what really happened', or as close an approximation as is possible. Both work within a fairly clearly defined set of assumptions that are sometimes held with the same uncritical conviction. As someone committed to interfaith dialogue I would not wish to upset Muslim religious sensitivities in anything I might say about the Prophet Muhammad, but at the same time the historian in me demands that a degree of detachment be used in examining something of the Jewish–Muslim relationship and the perceptions of Muhammad that this has led to in the past. From the purely historical point of view, it is obvious that in a matter as delicate as the relationship between Jews and Muslims, as evidenced by statements in the Holy Qur'an and later Muslim teachings, both sides will take a different line of interpretation, irrespective of any current political issues that affect our two faith communities. Though historical dates and facts may be to a large extent objectively verifiable, any historical judgments that are derived from them are inevitably partial or flawed, and certainly likely to be biased. This is not an easy field of study.

In order to illustrate a contemporary Jewish historical approach, the following summary comes from Erwin I.J. Rosenthal. His approach is that of someone full of admiration for the achievements of both Islam and Judaism, but even he has a few critical comments about Muhammad from a Jewish perspective:

> It has often been remarked that there is little if anything original in substance in the leading ideas of Islam. They can all be traced to Judaism or Christianity, normative or sectarian. But, viewed as a whole, Islam is not simply the sum total of one or more of its predecessors. The genius of Mohammed, its founder, has mixed the various ingredients in such a way that something new, something fresh, different from its sources, has emerged. A strong personality, full of confidence in his mission, determined, single-minded…created out of well-established ideas and concepts a new world-faith which his dynamic successors imposed in quick succession on one country after another which fell to their advancing armies. Had it been otherwise, Islam would have shared the fate of many a Jewish or Christian sect.
>
> Although much of his preaching ran counter to Arab ways of thought and life, basically it appealed to a contemporary religious longing among the Arabs, winning enough influential support to let Islam prevail in Arabia and spread far and wide abroad. It was, therefore, less the matter borrowed than the manner in which Mohammed presented it to his Arabs that counted. The material was transformed in his hands to suit the temperament of his countrymen and to meet a particular situation in Arabia. The social and economic situation was no less favourable to Mohammed's message

than the spiritual unrest. To underline the latter he relentlessly warned against the impending divine judgment which could be met and possibly averted only by a radical break with the prevailing paganism and by the exclusive worship of and devotion to Allah. (Rosenthal 1961:3–4)

This view of Muhammad as the historical creator of a religious movement takes us into the heart of a second problem that confronts us, particularly when we see him in the light of the 'founders' of the other two mono-theistic religions, Judaism and Christianity. The problem lies in a particular paradox I can see within Islam that is also difficult to address as an outsider. On the one hand the person of Muhammad himself is clearly crucial as the prophet through whom God gave the revelation. Indeed, his personal history, the journeys he undertook, the alliances he made, the conflicts he experienced, are all factors that led to further quite specific revelations. Moreover, it is argued that, unlike the earlier Jewish and Christian scriptures, the historical truth of the Holy Qur'an can be taken for granted because the background events are so well documented. But at the same time Muslims insist that they are 'Muslims' and not 'Mohammedans' – not followers of the man Muhammad but those who have surrendered themselves to Allah. Thus, Muhammad, in the physical reality and details of his personal life, is essential for there to have been a revelation, although at the same time his own person must not be confused with the source of the revelation itself.

Jews have much the same difficulty with the figure of Moses, because of the mythic nature of the traditions surrounding his life. Jewish tradition insists that Moses is only a human being, a mere agent through whom the unmediated word of God comes to us. The problem is dramatised in the Passover Haggadah, the account of the exodus from Egypt that is read during the domestic service on the first two evenings of the festival. In the Haggadah the rabbis strictly excluded any reference to the activity of Moses during the events of the exodus, insisting that it was all achieved by God directly and alone, without human mediation. (That Moses is actually mentioned once in a biblical reference further dramatises his absence from the main events, particularly considering his dominant role in the biblical account itself.) All of this is to indicate further the difficulty for an out-sider who is not a scholar of Islam to know how best to tackle the figure of Muhammad, especially since this issue has doubtless been the subject of much internal debate and interpretation. Should one approach him and his achievements as the historical person whose life and activities should be evaluated and judged, or as the prophet who, so to speak, becomes transparent so that the revelation of God can simply shine through? To all these difficulties must be added the fact that anything I discuss is very much dependent on the work of other scholars in this field.

When it comes to the particular texts of revelation, a further challenge arises. It was dramatised for me at a conference by a young Palestinian, who explained that he had a difficulty with the stories in the Hebrew Bible about Abraham and Ishmael. He asked me how he could identify with the Jewish people if he was a descendant of Ishmael, who was the rejected child of Hagar who had been sent away by Abraham. It comes as a shock to Jews to discover that biblical stories that we see as anchored in the past could have much relevance today, especially to others. We forget that the Hebrew Bible is seen by many as an account of contemporary Jewish life and values. In the Middle Ages the figure of Ishmael was used by Jews to discuss their views of the Arab world and Islam, just as Esau was used to discuss their relationship to Christianity. Today such a practice is continued in some traditional Jewish circles, nevertheless, for most Jews such an association seems of little significance and few would understand the need to justify Abraham's treatment of Hagar and Ishmael as reflecting contemporary Jewish realities. But the converse cannot be said about the way that Jews are referred to and treated in the Holy Qur'an, whose message is much more directly alive today.

Here I come to one of the most delicate and serious issues in the relationship between Judaism and its 'daughter' religions. Jews are used to being attacked and libelled in the Christian New Testament. Of course, being used to something does not make it any more acceptable or comfortable. Nevertheless, the accusation that the Jews killed Christ, and all the horrible consequences that followed on from that, up to and including the Shoah, have been part of our Western consciousness for a very long time. However, those of us who have been involved in dialogue with Christians know what considerable steps have been taken to reinterpret such texts in the wake of Vatican II so as to remove their poison.

Yet when Jews encounter the Holy Qur'an for the first time, or hear the rhetoric of some Muslims who claim to base themselves upon it, we are shocked and understandably scared by what is said about us. I would like to illustrate the problem by quoting from *A Guide to the Contents of the Qur'an* by Faruq Sherif. I cannot evaluate the materials presented here, except that they seem to be a straightforward account for a Muslim readership of the contents of the Holy Qur'an, presented with no value judgment. He writes, for example, about the expulsion of the Bani Nadhir:

> No single event has been commented on in the Qur'an at such length as that of the expulsion of the Jewish tribe of Bani Nadhir from Medina. Shortly after the battle of Uhud, in June 625, Muhammad found it necessary to raise funds to meet some pressing obligation to settle a blood feud. For this purpose he paid a visit to the Jews of Bani Nadhir. During the conference with the council of the tribe he suddenly felt a suspicion that they were hatching a plot to kill him. He abruptly left the meeting, and lost no time in sending an ultimatum to the tribe to leave Medina within ten days. The tribe demurred at first, expecting their allies to come to their help. But as this did not happen, and as the Moslems laid siege to their stronghold and started burning or uprooting their palm trees, they decided to surrender. Within a few days they vacated their dwellings and their lands, loaded their goods and chattels on 600 camels and departed...(Sherif 1995:108)

The writer then goes on to quote some of the verses of Sura LIX which throw light on this episode: 'On divine help in causing the surrender of the Jews: "It was He that drove the unbelievers from among the People of the Book out of their dwellings..."'(ibid.). (I am intrigued and somewhat consoled by the language that speaks of the 'unbelievers from among the People of the Book', and elsewhere of 'some of the People of the Book'. Such differentiation is better than a wholesale condemnation of the Jewish people in its entirety.)

Far worse is the following passage on the extermination of the Jewish tribe of Bani Qoraiza:

> Verses 26 and 27 of Sura XXXIII refer to the extermination of the Jewish tribe of Bani Qoraiza. They appear as a sequel to the verses relating to the battle of the Confederates, because during that battle the Jews of the said tribe behaved in a way that led to their being accused of conspiring with the enemy. Because of this accusation they took fright and on the same day that the siege was lifted shut themselves up in their strongholds some three miles to the east of Medina. The Prophet ordered a siege of the community, which lasted 25 days, after which the Jews surrendered. They asked to be allowed to depart in peace, but the Prophet did not consent, and ruled that their

fate should be determined by an arbitrator. The latter, the chief of the Aus tribe which was in alliance with the Jews, gave his verdict on the basis of the Old Testament law laid down in Deuteronomy XX 13 and 14. This meant the extermination of the tribe. In verses 26 and 27 of Sura XXXIII the Qur'an says: 'God cast terror into their hearts so that you slew some of them and took captive others. He made you masters of their land, their houses and their goods and yet another land on which you had never set foot before.' The reference to 'some' who were killed is a euphemism; all historians agree that all the male members of the tribe, numbering at least 600, were put to the sword, their women and children were sold as slaves and all their property was seized. (Sherif 1995: 111)

In discussing the same event, Karen Armstrong, in her attempt at a sympathetic Western account of the life of Muhammad, points to the inevitable analogy:

It is probably impossible for us to dissociate this story from Nazi atrocities and it will inevitably alienate many people irrevocably from Muhammad. But Western scholars like Maxime Rodinson and W. Montgomery Watt argue that it is not correct to judge the incident by twentieth-century standards. This was a very primitive society - far more primitive than the Jewish society in which Jesus had lived and promulgated his gospel of mercy and love some 600 years earlier. At this stage the Arabs had no concept of a universal natural law, which is difficult - perhaps impossible - for people to attain unless there is a modicum of public order, such as that imposed by a great empire in the ancient world...In the early seventh century, an Arab chief would not be expected to show any mercy to traitors like Quraysah. (Armstrong 1991:208)

Armstrong rightly continues to note the horror of the episode, but points out that it was not the last word in Muhammad's relationship with the Jews.

Even in Muhammad's own time, smaller Jewish groups remained in Medina after 627 and were allowed to live in peace with no further reprisals. It appears that the second part of the Covenant of Medina, which deals with the Jewish population of the settlement, was composed after this date. (ibid.:209)

She goes on to write about the religious freedom enjoyed by Jews under Islam until this century with the creation of the State of Israel, and concludes:

The Jews of Islam never suffered like the Jews of Christendom. The anti-Semitic myths of Europe were introduced into the Middle East at the end of the last century by Christian missionaries and were usually scorned by the populace. But in recent years some Muslims have turned to passages of the Qur'an which refer to the rebellious Jewish tribes of Medina and tend to ignore the far more numerous verses which speak positively of the Jews and their great prophets. This is an entirely new development in a history of 1,200 years of good relations between Jews and Muslims. (ibid.: 209)

Of course, from a Jewish perspective the episode cannot simply be set aside. Rosenthal offers a very different view of Muhammad's behaviour:

> When Mohammed had failed to win the Jewish tribes for his new religion, he made cruel war on them, and they had to pay with death or exile for their refusal to join him…At first he had welcomed the Jews of Medina as allies, and in the 'Statute of Medina' they figure as an *umma* who form, together with the 'believers', the *'umma of Islam'*. All members of this community stood in a relationship of *dhimma*, mutual protection, to one another. (Rosenthal 1961:6–7)

Rosenthal continues: 'This term *dhimma* underwent an interesting narrowing down to protected, second-class members of society, being later restricted to the "People of the Book"' (ibid.:7).

More could be said about the status of the *dhimmi*. But that takes us away from the point I want to make about these particular episodes and the fact that they have a place within a document of divine revelation. They are thus open to use, and indeed abuse, by anyone who is convinced that such actions are actually models for behaviour ordained by God, models that can be applied again today. It is precisely the availability of such passages that allows for, and indeed sanctions, current attitudes and tragic and bloody actions undertaken by some today in the name of Islam. Which is a further reminder that the interpretation of any scripture is not entirely an objective or neutral science. The interpretation and application of scripture is ultimately in the hands of those with the power to enforce their views, and their selection of passages is in turn determined by contemporary political realities as much as by spiritual values. That explains Jewish concerns about the antisemitism being preached today by Islamist groups as far apart as the highlands of Afghanistan and the campuses of universities in Britain. In a study of this tendency, Martin Kramer concludes:

> As the Arab–Israeli peace process evolves, the Islamic world is becoming immersed in an unprecedented debate on the Jews - on whether Muslims can or should ever live in peace with them. The outcome of this debate is impossible to predict. In the course of it we will overhear words which will encourage us, and words which will alarm us; the Islamists in particular will say more and more to alarm us, because their very world view is at stake. (Kramer 1995:8)

So a question arises today for the Jewish world about the extent to which it is possible for Muslims to address the Holy Qur'an with the same critical judgment and sensitivities towards its impact on Jews that Christians have themselves begun to undertake as regards the anti-Jewish sentiments to be found in the New Testament. Is such a line of interpretation of the Holy Qur'an possible irrespective of, or perhaps despite, the situation in the Middle East? Or to put it the other way around, there is no doubt that without a satisfactory resolution of the Israel–Palestinian conflict, any negative understandings of Jews within the Holy Qur'an will be seized upon and used, thus further inflaming the conflict. Could a conscious promotion of the positive verses about the Jews help establish a counter-attitude that might allow room for new approaches and attempts at reconciliation? In short, could religion for once help defuse a political conflict rather than further inflame it? Sadly, even to pose the question suggests the unlikelihood of such a possibility. Such an approach would require a role for the moderate voice of religion that is rare in our times and very difficult to sustain in the wake of the anger, hostility and violence so often perpetrated in the name of 'authentic' belief.

The Middle East apart, there is a deeper level to this problem of the use of scripture. It is something about which Jews are understandably particularly sensitive, having been the object of the pronouncements and value judgments by both Christian and Islamic scriptures. Behind the attitude towards the Jews expressed in the New Testament is a family quarrel within the Jewish world of that time. What began as an argument, both religious and political, became a polemic – particularly at the point when the appeal was made to a wider audience. But at that stage something radically new occurred: the instrumentalisation of the Jews for the sake of promoting the new belief. The 'Jew' becomes a symbolic figure, a representative of evil and, through the inevitable application of the name 'Judas', the one who denied and betrayed God. While this is understandable within the rhetoric of early Christianity, it feels very different from the perspective of the Jews who have not chosen that role and find it forced upon us. Our individuality and our humanity become lost. We become instead a symbol, in this case, of the unacceptable other, trapped in someone else's ideological construction of the governance of the universe. It is a short step to the demonisation of that other, seen as whatever it is that stands in the way of the ultimate victory of good over evil, and from there an even shorter step to victimisation and, as we have seen this past century, genocide.

Of course, it is not necessary to take the issue to such an extreme. Nevertheless, it is evident that the Christian who only knows the Jews and Judaism through the prism of the New Testament does not know anything about the real, flesh and blood Jew. Even a benign presentation is less than honest, and so it diminishes the humanity of the person portrayed and the one who does the portraying. It is ironic that today Christians have to face the same problem at the hands of Muslims that Jews have experienced from Christians: Muslims who only encounter the 'People of the Book' through the prism of the Holy Qur'an and the later traditions have a similarly limited perspective. Presumably, many traditional Muslims would deny this, as have traditional Christians, since what is at stake is not some detached, objective perception of the other but the upholding of the truth about the other as given in a text revealed by God. Nevertheless the effect of modernity and particularly of globalisation and the increasing interconnectedness of peoples is precisely to force a confrontation with such contradictions. Interfaith dialogue requires that we recognise the other in their own terms and not just the projections we place upon them, however sincerely they are held and however much they are endorsed by our respective scriptures. Again, the importance of interpretations of scripture that are appropriate to a changing human situation become of crucial concern, linked to the political will to promote them.

Such issues are not one-sided, and as a Jew I also have to acknowledge the different ways, some of them quite problematic, with which Jews today view Christians and Muslims, based on our historical experience but also our own different ideological positions. I will return to these later, but here I would point out that I must take the same self-critical responsibility for myself and my Jewish community that I would hope to find amongst my Christian and Muslim partners in dialogue.

Jewish scriptures must also come under critical scrutiny, because the process of identifying and ultimately demonising the other is to be found there as well. Some parts of Deuteronomy, calling for the extermination of the local inhabitants of the land of Canaan, may well have been hypothetical constructions at the time of their composition, at least seen historically. Moreover, they were largely argued out of existence by later rabbinic interpretation. Indeed, they could only be seen as abstract concepts during

2000 years of exile. Nevertheless, they create a rhetoric of violence under divine justification that has its echo in the scriptures of the two daughter religions. They are also available today to feed the imagination of Jews who see only violent solutions to contemporary struggles in the Middle East. Jews are in no position to demand changes in the interpretation of the ideas within the scripture of others unless we are equally prepared to acknowledge the problems inherent in our own. Such issues are a challenge to all of our traditions and are present at the very heart of the dialogue enterprise.

In some ways I seem to have leapt to the end of my presentation without directly addressing past Jewish views of Muhammad and Islam. Much of this is self-evident and well-documented. There is no doubt that Judaism and Islam have had enormous mutual influence upon each other. The Holy Qur'an shares with the Hebrew Bible a chain of figures that it views as prophets: Moses, Aaron, Abraham, Lot, Noah, David and Solomon, Job, Ishmael and Idris (Enoch) (Sura 21 The Prophets). The greatest of these is Abraham, and Muhammad's mission is to restore the pure religion of Abraham (Rosenthal 1961:15). The advantage of focusing on Abraham is precisely that he predates Moses, and hence the specific beginning of the Jewish people as a people and Judaism itself, and Jesus, and hence Christianity. Thus, Abraham represents a return to the origins of the human encounter with and surrender to God. Not only are biblical characters and their stories to be found in the Holy Qur'an, but also some of the early rabbinic teachings about them.

Nevertheless, this closeness is itself a source of additional problems. The issue is best illustrated precisely through the figure of Abraham and the question about which of his two sons, Isaac or Ishmael, is to be regarded as Abraham's spiritual successor. Reuven Firestone summarises the issue as follows:

> According to Jewish tradition, Ishmael's history became irrelevant to the sacred history of God's people. Sacred history rests in the line of Isaac. But according to Islam, Ishmael is the progenitor of God's greatest prophet who will one day lead his people to establish God's rule on earth. The sacred history of the redemption of humankind through submission to Islam rests entirely in the line of Ishmael.
>
> The Jewish and Islamic versions of the legend of Abraham and his progeny represent a classic example of two religious traditions narrating different and even competing stories about the same paradigmatic characters. (Firestone 1993:44)

Firestone goes on to draw the results of these differing traditions:

> Each monotheistic religious tradition evolved its own exclusionist defense against the claims of others. Jewish and Christian tradition tended to consider the Islamic claims as mistakes or attempts to distort religious truth in the name of the new temporal power of Islam. Islamic tradition in turn tended to consider Jewish and Christian claims to be the result of tampering with the text of revelation, which originally contained clear prophecies telling of the coming of Muhammad and the rise of Islam. (ibid.:45)

Again, this is a subject that needs to be addressed in the context of today's interfaith dialogue. However, it is important to recognise that even such seemingly irreconcilable differences did not prevent an extraordinary symbiotic relationship between Jews and Muslims, particularly during the centuries of the golden age of Spain. The poetry, religious and secular, of Judah Halevi and countless other Jewish writers, the philosophy of Moses Maimonides and others, the biblical scholarship of Abraham Ibn Ezra, based on the work of earlier and contemporary grammarians of the Hebrew language, the codification and systematisation of Jewish law ethical writings and mystical speculation, not to mention treaties on medicine, astronomy and other sciences – all these and more are the result of the challenges to Judaism presented by Islam, which evoked a necessary Jewish response and new synthesis, becoming part of a rich and highly influential legacy.

Rosenthal sums up this legacy as follows:

> The religious and 'secular' sciences of mediaeval Islam have stimulated Jews within its boundaries to prodigious feats of intellectual endeavour which resulted in the first systematic presentation of Jewish religious and ethical values. Jews cultivated their own religious sciences which they firmly established, or developed and consolidated in the case of law, and handed them on to future generations of Jews including our own. Although their form is timebound, their substance is of permanent value. Mediaeval Jews under Islam also made an important contribution to the natural sciences and to philosophy as independent disciples of the Muslim disciples of the Greek and Hellenistic masters. They transmitted to the West this Greek-Hellenistic legacy in a form sufficiently recognisable to prepare the ground for the Renaissance and to lead Western thinkers and scholars to the clear springs of Greek and Hellenistic thought. Muslims and Jews advanced medicine, science and philosophy appreciably and lastingly. (ibid.:46–47)

But how did Jews in that earlier period view Islam itself as a revealed religion? Rabbi Dr Norman Solomon cites four 'mediaeval Jewish models of interfaith relations', but is quite blunt about the circumstances that evoked them:

For more than a millennium and a half in Christendom, and almost as long in the Islamic world, Judaism was the 'despised religion'; Jews were allowed to survive, allowed in principle if not always in practice to follow the religion of their fathers, but forbidden to raise their heads high and under pain of death or worse should they dare to offer to others what they believed to be the truth of God.

But it was precisely this abject condition which forced the Jews of the Middle Ages to formulate their attitudes to 'other faiths' – Christianity and Islam – without any immediate expectation of becoming the dominant faith themselves. From this necessity a certain virtue was born, that of justifying the status quo, the fact that God must have his reasons for allowing other faiths to flourish. (Solomon 1997:4)

Rabbi Solomon suggests four models within this context. Firstly, the view of other religions as idolatry, though not necessarily as bad as in the biblical period. They are simply the inheritors of a mistaken tradition and not to be held responsible for their beliefs and practices.

The second view is that both Christianity and Islam are in error but are nevertheless preparing the way for the Messiah. This is the view of Judah Halevi (c.1075–1141) in the Kuzari, and is clearly stated by Maimonides:

The teachings of him of Nazareth (Jesus) and of the man of Ishmael (Muhammad) who arose after him help to bring all mankind to perfection, so that they may serve God with one consent. For insofar as the whole world is full of talk of the Messiah, of words of Holy Writ and of the Commandments – these words have spread to the ends of the earth, even if many deny their binding character at the present time. When the Messiah comes all will return from their errors.

The third model is ascribed to the provencal rabbi, Menahem Hameiri (d.c.1315), who did not wish to identify his contemporary Christian neighbours as idolaters, and so coined the term 'nations bound by the ways of religion'. This allowed for greater acceptance of their way of life which had practical consequences in terms of day to day contacts.

The fourth model is the most radical – that of the Yemenite Jewish philosopher Nethanel ibn Fayyumi (d.c.1164). He writes that, just as God sent revelation to prophets before the Torah was given, nothing prevents God from sending revelation to prophets afterwards so that the world would not remain without religion. Thus, revelation came to Muhammad specifically for the Arab peoples. Though the most radical and positive view of other faiths, it has had little impact on Jewish thought.

Is there a Jewish position on Muhammad and Islam today? Of course it is never possible to speak of a single Jewish position on anything, let alone something as sensitive as this. I have to acknowledge that as a British Jew, of the Ashkenazi – East European – tradition, which had little direct historical contact with Islam, I can come to the subject with a degree of neutrality. This is not the case for Sephardi Jews, at least those whose views of Islam are coloured by direct personal experience, much of it negative, this past century. One of the frequent assertions of Sephardi Jews in Israel is that they alone know the Arab world – which nevertheless leads to quite divergent views, from outright mistrust and hostility to an almost sentimental yearning for a kind of relationship of friendship and mutual respect and loyalty that existed in their particular situation during previous generations. Nevertheless, these latter views tend to be set aside given the current political realities in the Middle East, leading to a very negative view of Islam, and clearly they are not helped either by the policies of Israel or the Arab states, or by terrorist actions.

In some ways, with individual exceptions, Israel and the Jewish world of the Diaspora have been slow to seek the kind of dialogue with Islam that is increasingly more common with Christianity. Of course, the initiative for the latter has come largely from the Christian side as part of a critical re-evaluation in the wake of the Holocaust. Clearly no such cause exists in the Muslim world, and indeed the political situation rather militates against any such quest for dialogue. One might have expected a far more concerted effort on the part of the state of Israel to initiate a dialogue with Islam in order to find alternatives to the confrontational political situation. In part this has been hindered by the siege mentality of the state, but there are other reasons as well. They include the fact that the founders and leaders of the state of Israel were predominately of Ashkenazi origin, a background with ingrained attitudes of Western cultural superiority that some still assume, and that also colour their attitude to their own fellow citizens of Sephardi origin. So a radical re-thinking is required, something still only partly underway despite the beginnings of *rapprochement* with the Arab world in the wake of the peace process. Clearly there are crucial issues that can never be properly addressed without a far greater understanding of and dialogue with Islam. For example, no Israeli intentions about the future of Jerusalem can have any hope for success without taking into account its importance to Islam, however difficult it may be for Jews to understand or accept this.

There are important academic departments of Islamic studies in Israel, and the beginnings of exchanges between scholars in various fields. But in the popular Israeli consciousness, as reflected in literature, there is an 'absence of reality', to quote the title of an article by Glenda Abramson, when it comes to describing Arabs or Islam. She concludes her survey of the depiction of the Arab in Israeli fiction since the foundation of the state:

> In summary, the literature which features Arab characters is almost exclusively a response to political events: war and the Israeli occupation. Exceptions are the stories and novels of David Shahar and Samy Michael who offer a realistic portrayal of Arab and Palestinian communities in Israel and the relationship between them and the Jews. However, if we are seeking a view of Islam in Hebrew literature we shall not be successful. As we have seen, the literature as a whole avoids investigating the religious and historical sources of the Arab-Israeli conflict but presents only an introspective response to its present outcome. At best the delineation of the Arabs and their experience is vague and subjective, at worst stridently tendentious.
>
> Radical literature makes little attempt to understand Islam, or to present a global view of it and its imperatives. Through their depiction of Arabs the authors are working through problems specific to themselves and Israeli society…Perhaps the writers leave it to the reader to derive a notion of the nature of Islam from the generalisations they supply: the pastorality of the Arabs, their historical religiosity, their love of the homeland, their pain at its loss. This portrait is unfairly reductionist, and has more to do with the ontological premises of the Jews themselves. (Abramson 1993:16)

In the Western Diaspora, some beginnings have been made to a dialogue process, sometimes in the context of a trialogue involving the three monotheistic faiths. But the amount of ground to be covered is enormous, and the process is only in its infancy. It is always likely to be hostage to events in the Middle East – which more than ever makes it important that channels of communication and exploration be kept open and areas of mutual understanding and trust be built. In this dialogue the figure of Muhammad himself has not really been central. Rather, it is the internal struggles to find contemporary expressions of Islam and Muslim identity in a rapidly changing world that will determine whether his legacy will unite or divide the three monotheistic faiths.

13

The Challenges Facing
the Muslim Community[1]

The risks of projecting the experience of one community onto another have already been noted in chapter 4. Nevertheless, there are many possible parallels between the fate of successive waves of immigrant communities into the same country that make comparisons potentially valuable. In the case of the Muslim community coming to Britain, there are obvious similarities to what happened to Jews a few generations earlier, so I have been invited on a few occasions to address Muslim audiences on this topic. In most cases, simply recounting the Jewish experience has been sufficient to spark off a discussion from which the Muslims themselves drew their own conclusions. However, on one occasion I was invited to go beyond scene-setting and speak about what I saw as the challenges facing the Muslim community in Britain at this stage in their development.

The sheer amount of common ground between the two religions is vast. We have a shared commitment to justice as a central value for society, and a comprehensive legal system as the way of expressing it. We share a vocabulary whereby the similarities between Hebrew and Arabic terms in many cases allow for instant recognition of what the other intends. Certain key statements are common to both traditions, for example the teaching that to kill an individual is as if one had destroyed the entire world. We are both strict in our commitment to monotheism, the belief in one God, and we both recognise that God is greater than all the theologies, philosophies and metaphors that human beings create to define God, and thus limit the divine power. We share the conviction that love, compassion, friendship, mercy and pity for a suffering world are at the heart of everything our two faiths stand for, despite the ways in which both of our traditions have been slandered over the centuries as lacking in such values.

Nevertheless, there are areas of difference, some of which derive from the Jewish experience of living in a Christian environment for centuries in the West. Judaism employs a religious language which both reflects and tries to define itself in contrast with Christian concepts and concerns. The belief in a personal messiah is a constant debating point between us. Judaism, at least today in the West, shares with Western Christianity a greater stress on individual rather than collective forms of spirituality, in addition to well-developed theologies of human suffering and more complex liturgical forms than Islam. Most significantly, we have both gone through the experience of the Enlightenment, with its emphasis on reason and hence its challenge to the sources of our tradition, including our holy scriptures, and the commitment to historical truth as determining the legitimacy of religious values.

There are also unique features of Judaism, in part, as indicated before, because of the complex relationship between peoplehood and faith. We also have a tradition of arguing with God, calling God to account for the evils in the world – which can be shocking to Christians and perhaps even scandalous to Muslims. In short, like family members, we both share with and differ from one another at all levels of belief and practice.

Nevertheless, we share so much with Islam that it must be possible to find ways of living in harmony with each other now as close neighbours in Europe, just as we did once before in the golden age of Spain. Moreover, we have today the possibility of a healthier relationship than we had in the past. In the mediaeval period we did not meet as equals because Islam, like Christianity, had power, and the Jewish people, as a minority, had to accommodate itself to the reality of that power. Today, in our secular world, where religions have lost much of their material power, there are societies, like those in Western Europe and the US, where we can truly meet as equals – and a sharing can take place as never before.

It would be naive to ignore the things that stand in the way of such a meeting. The political realities of the Middle East, the suffering inflicted by all parties on each other and the tragedy that threatens at all times to engulf us, cannot be set aside. Nevertheless, Jews and Muslims need each other today, especially in Europe, and we must draw the consequences from that or we both will be damaged even further.

I can only talk about Islamic societies I know here in the West. Here we share together the experience of being a minority, and at times a barely tolerated minority, in a nominally Christian society. Christian values may have diminished as the power of the church has waned but, as we know only too well, old prejudices persist. Jews have had a long residence in Western Europe. We have had time to adapt, but, as the Holocaust shows, we did not read the reality of this civilisation very well.

Europe today is not the same as it was those 60 years ago – if only because we have seen once what can happen. But those same destructive forces are still present under the surface and we cannot simply hope they will go away or leave it to the good intentions of those in power to address them. I don't think that either of our communities, Jewish or Muslim, can afford to be complacent – we need to ensure that our voices are heard in all matters that affect us, directly and indirectly.

We need effective representative bodies that both reflect and guide the thinking of our communities. In Britain the Jewish community obviously has the advantage of the length of its stay, but less than a century ago the Jewish community was made up of all sorts of tiny immigrant groups from different parts of Eastern Europe and elsewhere – they shared certain religious traditions but in many other ways were suspicious of each other and were competing and struggling to survive in a hostile environment. Such internal squabbles remain today, even though to outsiders the community seems successful. We say with pride in the Jewish community: two Jews, three opinions (I have heard a similar view expressed by Muslims as well). In fact, this indicates a paradox that seems to be equally relevant for the Muslim community to address. The Board of Deputies of British Jews, the umbrella organisation of Anglo-Jewry, regularly debates its own nature and the degree to which it is actually representative of the entire community and how effectively it fulfils this role. Nevertheless, it has a tendency to gloss over our internal differences and present to the outside world a united Jewish point of view – especially on matters such as solidarity with Israel. In some ways this has always been a hopeless task, since Jews are divided on most subjects – but it led to a strange situation where any Jewish group that took an independent line, such as the Jewish Socialists, for example, was seen as a greater threat to the Jewish people than some of our real enemies outside. We were told we had to speak with one voice! But the catch was that at the same time the same leadership would be bitterly complaining that people were stereotyping Jews, putting a label on us and saying that we were all the same.

There is, therefore, on the one hand the need for both communities to have the kind of representative bodies that effectively put their case to the outside world and offer a point of reference for all kinds of political, social, educational, economic and cultural issues. But that should not prevent the recognition and indeed celebration of the enormous diversity that is also present within both communities. This is vital because of the notorious ability, especially of the media, to oversimplify all issues and reduce complexity to headlines and soundbites. Most notoriously, the extremism of some self-styled leaders is taken to be the Muslim position of all, and the moderation of the many is ignored. If either of us is to survive in this troubled European society, we have to be courageous enough to fight for our cause in the public arena and at the same time acknowledge the deep differences in opinions that are to be found within our communities. They should not be seen as a sign of weakness – but rather of the richness and diversity available within our faith and the different possibilities and choices we can offer.

It is clear that there is in Western thinking a demonisation of Islam that has deep roots in European history – presumably going back to the Crusades. In this sense it shares much with the phenomena of racism and antisemitism, in its all-pervasive quality and in the difficulty of confronting it and containing it. There are some things that can and should be done – above all by using the law in appropriate ways: by challenging together any and every manifestation of racism, islamophobia and anti-semitism as they appear – in short, becoming a bloody nuisance, so that whoever is in authority cannot afford to ignore us. But such an approach also requires the lobbying and persuading of many other groups within our society to take up the cudgels on our behalf as well as our offering to do so for them. In such matters we need each other, alongside all other ethnic or other minorities in this country — if for no other reason than to show just how far this society has become pluralistic, how enriching this is for the community as a whole, and how much can be gained by collaboration across the ethnic and religious barriers. What is good for us is good for the public interest as a whole. But pluralism and tolerance do not just happen — they have to be earned. New organisations within the Muslim community such as FAIR (Forum Against Islamophobia and Racism) do represent the taking up of such a challenge by a younger generation of Muslims born in Britain.

But having raised the delicate issue of antisemitism, there are aspects of this too that need to be raised in any Jewish–Muslim dialogue. From what I have learnt about Islam, like any richly diverse tradition, it is possible to find within it a justification for diametrically opposed views on most subjects, including that of the perception of Jews and Judaism. We are either seen as the first bearers of the prophetic tradition who are to be respected and protected as the 'People of the Book' or we are described as dangerous and treacherous enemies who are not to be trusted. When this latter view gets compounded with the issue of Israel and Palestine, it becomes an explosive mixture and an incitement to hatred. One of the most distressing experiences it is possible to have as a Jew seeking to dialogue with Muslims is to find antisemitic literature on sale in mosques. I was deeply saddened on a visit to Jordan to find copies of the *Protocols of the Elders of Zion*, an infamous nineteenth-century forgery claiming that there was a Jewish conspiracy to rule the world, on sale in the lobby of a major hotel. The market in such materials is clearly enormous, tied inevitably to the Middle East conflict, but also furthering the kind of conspiracy theories and fantasies that make any hope of a rational settlement even more remote. Antisemitism, like islamophobia or any other kind of racism, is as destructive to those who use it, teach it, preach it or disseminate it as it is to the victims it produces — because, like all prejudice, it undermines the humanity of those who promote it, and that is a betrayal of the integrity of God. Before we are Jews or Muslims we are human beings, made, as Jewish tradition teaches, in the image of God. If we diminish the humanity of another we diminish it within ourselves — and that is the way to our own self-destruction.

I would like to move on to a more positive suggestion. The religious opinion-makers in this country are relatively few but they can have an important impact. But where do you find them? My own rabbinic seminary, Leo Baeck College, is in a strange position in that two of its graduates, Rabbi Lionel Blue and Rabbi Julia Neuberger, and one of its teachers, Rabbi Hugo Gryn, have had an extraordinary impact on the media – representing both popular spirituality and the public conscience. On one level this should not be a surprise. In a pluralistic society dominated by the media, we need spokespersons for the different religious communities that are here. But where are such people to be found? None of the above-mentioned rabbis were democratically elected for the job, nor did they get such prominence because of some alleged Jewish influence on the media – they just happened to have the right religious credentials at the right time, and a remarkable ability to communicate their faith directly to others. But they are drawn from a pool of British-educated and trained rabbis who have been exploring for some 30 years the new religious reality of Judaism in this complex secular Western society.

Where are the equivalent Muslim figures who can represent the Muslim community so well? Such people are clearly desperately needed, as in their absence the field is open for the most fanatical voices to be heard, precisely those voices that feed on fears of the other and reinforce – even legitimate – such fears. But such religious authorities who can be effective spokespersons for the community will not appear without setting up the framework and institutions in which they can be trained – where they can bring together the greatest traditions of Islam, together with modern scholarship and a whole range of practical, caring, teaching and community skills. In the remarkable people I know within the Muslim community, all the elements are there to create a new generation of religious leaders who know how to function in the European scene. Many of them may already be waiting to be challenged in this way and supported in their studies, people with a track record of service to the community as teachers or community or social workers. This kind of initiative is an essential step and represents a kind of coming of age of any religious community, when it takes responsibility for its future religious leadership. Without spiritual leaders equally at home in the tradition and in Western culture, it will be increasingly difficult to speak to the second and third generation of European Muslims, and help them interpret the message of Islam for this new society.

It may be helpful to conclude by indicating something of the complexity of this religious challenge that we all face in the West today. Some years ago at one of the JCM conferences, we asked the people in the closing session to say something about what they had experienced there. One young Muslim man got up and said that he was rather disappointed. He had come, he said, expecting to find religious people – but instead he had found secular people looking for religion! I understood what he meant, but I felt that though he was right in his analysis, he was wrong to be disappointed. We who live in the West do live in a secular culture which impacts on all aspects of life, including religion. There is therefore a tendency among religious people to increase the split between the tradition and the modern, to try to keep them strictly apart. I think that this is a mistake. I do not believe that traditional religions are beyond criticism – certainly that is the case with Judaism, just as I do not accept whole-heartedly the values of secularism. But being born and living here, we contain both elements within us, and it seems to me that we can use the secular challenge to help purify the tradition, just as we can use the tradition to offer a spiritual dimension to our material life. Not either/or, but both/and. And I suppose I cannot point out too often that, but for secularism, the kinds of interfaith dialogue that have begun to develop over the past century would not have been possible – for secularism has brought with it the tolerance that makes it possible for different religions to meet – and the loss of power that makes it necessary that we meet.

Let me end with a story that somehow addresses for me the essence of the challenge we face in the West and is itself a marvellous example of Jewish/Muslim co-operation. It is a story that I first heard in a Chasidic, Jewish, version, and then was taught the Sufi version. A rabbi was walking in the countryside and saw a Jewish peasant stopping his work and saying a private prayer to God. The rabbi was rather shocked that he did not use the words of the traditional afternoon prayer, went over to tell him off and taught him the correct words to recite. He went home very satisfied with his work, but that night had a nightmare. God appeared to him and said:

'That man used to pray to me with great sincerity. Now he knows that he must not use his own prayer because he thinks it is wrong, but he cannot remember the one you taught him – so I have lost one of my prayers!' According to one version of the story the rabbi dropped dead with shock; according to the other he went back to the peasant the next day, apologised for interfering and told him to go on praying as before. But I was once told a Sufi version of this story, I think by the late Umar von Ehrenfels from Germany, one of the first Muslim partners in the work of dialogue. In his version (let us stay with the rabbi) the rabbi went back to the peasant the next day and told him to continue using his old prayer. But the peasant refused and said. 'Now that I know that there is a traditional prayer for this I cannot go back to my old prayer. What I have to do is to get to know the traditional prayer so well that I can say it with the same sincerity I had before.'

May we always be able to bring together the traditional and the modern, and Jewish and Muslim stories, in such a satisfying way.

14

Towards a
Jewish–Muslim Dialogue[1]

I have stressed two points throughout this book. The first is that we are now in a world of complete transparency. There are no secrets any more. What we say in the 'privacy' of our own community is potentially overheard by anyone who chooses to listen, and how much the more so by those we seek to win as partners in dialogue. Secondly, the hardest task of dialogue may well be the one we have to pursue with our own co-religionists 'back home'. For these two reasons it is necessary to provide a rationale for the Jewish world to address the issue of Jewish–Muslim dialogue, but to offer the arguments in as open and public a way as possible. A couple of personal anecdotes will put this dual task into perspective.

I was in Jerusalem in April 1967 and stayed on through the Six-Day War working in Hadassah Hospital. (My recently acquired medical degree equipped me to spend most of the time in the delivery room doing episiotomy repairs.) I received a telegram jointly signed by three friends, a rabbi, a German pastor and a Sister of Sion who had been meeting at an interfaith conference in Berlin. It read simply: 'Working and praying for all of you!'

I was very moved – but also not sure that I wanted an ecumenical cable to 'all of you' instead of just to me alone – clearly the wording was a committee decision. But at that meeting the seeds were being sown for a series of conferences to try to create an organisation where Jews, Christians and Muslims could have the opportunity to meet each other. The assumption behind this was that beyond the political entities, Israel and the Arab states, were the three great monotheistic religions, and surely their shared faith in the one God could provide enough common ground for dialogue and reconciliation.

This is both true and less than true. The areas of theological agreement and past co-operation offer the possibilities of real meeting. But old rivalries, misunderstandings and mistrust, fed by political problems, can also exacerbate differences. Nevertheless, for over 30 years the Standing Conference of Jews, Christians and Muslims in Europe has sponsored a series of annual conferences, including one for students and one for women, which have kept the idea and reality of such co-operation alive, and have created a network of people with commitment to this goal.

One of the first shocks in my own exploration of dialogue with Muslims came at a conference in Berlin. A young man stood up and introduced himself as a Palestinian. He said that he had a question for the rabbi, though it was not political. He had read the Hebrew Bible and seen the stories about Ishmael the son of Abraham. 'But', he asked, 'how can I identify with the Jewish people when Ishmael is described as the rejected son of the unwanted wife Hagar?'

It comes as a shock to Jews to find the Bible still alive in the minds of others in ways that are almost entirely foreign to us. Historically, it seems absurd to read a text that predates Islam by two millennia as a statement about our contemporary views on Ishmael, the ancestor of the Muslims. Though it has to be remembered that some Jews today turn to the biblical boundaries of the land of Israel out of their particular set of beliefs. Revealed scriptures continue to have a political and spiritual life in unexpected ways.

Of the biblical passages concerning Ishmael, two references are particularly significant. Firstly that Ishmael was also born to Abraham after the promise that his seed would multiply and that great nations would descend from him. It can be no accident therefore that the Bible records in full that Ishmael had 12 sons, all of whom are explicitly named, each of them princes of nations (Genesis 25:12–16). That is to say an exact equivalent to the 12 sons of Jacob. God's promise is equally distributed between the descendants of Ishmael and the descendants of Isaac. In this respect, from a biblical perspective, Jews and Muslims meet as equal inheritors of the promise to Abraham even though their respective tasks will be different.

Secondly, Isaac and Ishmael came together to bury Abraham their father (Genesis 25:9), which symbolises our shared veneration for the patriarch, the father of our respective peoples and the monotheistic faith.

But knowing this does not directly respond to the question of the young Palestinian. Scriptures are fixed texts whose words bear authority and power across time and space. But their very fixed nature in turn demands that they be interpreted to respond coherently to different circumstances. The story of the birth of Isaac and the sending away of Hagar and Ishmael (Genesis 21) is a key text on one of the most important occasions of the Jewish religious year, Rosh Hashanah, new year's day, when it is read alongside the better-known story of the 'binding' of Isaac (Genesis 22) – when God invites Abraham to offer up his son, a story which appears in a different form in the Holy Qur'an. (In the book [Sura 37:102–7] the son is unnamed, though commentators identify him as Ishmael, and his willingness to be sacrificed is stressed.) There are parallels between the two stories, most notably that both are saved on the point of death by an angel and both are promised a large posterity. In the prayerbook published by the Reform Synagogues of Great Britain for the Jewish High Holydays there is a commentary that accompanies these biblical passages. It highlights the significance accorded to Ishmael and concludes with a poem calling for reconciliation between the descendants of both sons of Abraham. Scripture may have the first word but the community has the right to give the last word for its own time.

Given the importance of a Jewish dialogue with the Muslim world on all levels and in all possible ways, it is important to look at some of the motivations for this dialogue, particularly as they may help us define some of the actions that need to be taken. The starting point has to be a general principle about the way Jewish tradition defines how we should conduct our relations with other groups in our society.

> In a city where there are both Jews and gentiles, the collectors of alms collect both from Jews and from gentiles; they feed the poor of both, visit the sick of both, bury both, comfort the mourners whether Jews or gentiles, and they restore the lost goods of both – in the interests of peace. (Jerusalem Talmud Demai 4:6)

The great mediaeval Jewish philosopher Moses Maimonides codified this legal requirement as follows: 'The non-Jewish poor should be maintained and clothed along with the Jewish poor for the sake of peace' (Maimonides, Mishneh Torah, Hilkhot Matnot Ani'im 7:7).

'For the sake of peace' could also be translated as 'for such are the ways of peace [*shalom*]'. It is both a matter of enlightened self-interest and a traditional Jewish ideal and goal to seek peace with all members of society. In this very specific sense the Hebrew *shalom* and Arabic *salaam*, are essential and shared elements of our two traditions.

As well as having the model available to us of a past symbiosis between Jews and Muslims that was very fruitful for both in the golden age in Spain (even if not always as rosy as it is sometimes depicted), Judaism and Islam have a great deal in common – in many ways more than either of them have with Christianity. Again on a personal note, my encounters with religious Muslims have been spiritually enriching. There is a simplicity and directness of expression in Muslim prayer that is highly evocative and moving. Paradoxically, it has been my experience as a Reform Jew to have to learn how to dialogue with Orthodox Muslims and it has been challenging to stretch my own faith language and religious understanding to find common ground. In general, we in the West approach religion from a very different perspective to more traditional Muslim ways so many centuries after the Enlightenment. Religion for us has come to belong far more to the private sphere. It is more individualistic and less collective. We are particularly conscious that Judaism has developed over time and been affected and changed by different historical events and cultural environments. Moreover, the different assaults on religion in the modern world make us question the apparent certainties of traditional beliefs – unless we wholeheartedly and uncritically embrace them in a 'fundamentalist' reaction that all religions are subject to.

Thus, there are many different modes of religious expression living alongside each other today, particularly here in the West, and the challenge is precisely how to meet across the rigid boundaries they seem to impose between 'traditionalists' and 'modernists', whatever terminology we use. Nevertheless, a dialogue between them is possible across the religious barriers within an interfaith situation, even when such a dialogue may be considerably more difficult, if not impossible, within our own faith community itself. The broader purpose of the dialogue itself and the quest to understand the other open channels that are often blocked 'back home' – indeed, the lessons of understanding, respect and tolerance gained from such a dialogue, may have a positive impact on the attempts at meeting and reconciliation amongst our own co-religionists. In general, dialogue, once it moves beyond formalities, is a profoundly important spiritual activity which enriches us on many levels.

But there is a further dimension to dialogue that is important for the religious integrity of the Jewish community itself. It is morally wrong for Jews to participate in the conventional demonising of Islam that takes place in the West. Apart from our experience of the dangers that this entails for the victim, such attitudes diminish us and should be challenged for our own spiritual health. Moreover, when it comes to dealing with the Middle East, a simplistic and largely negative approach to Islam reduces our abilities to differentiate and discriminate, to distinguish enemies from bystanders from possible allies and from real friends. We need the kind of detachment and clarity that only comes when we move beyond prejudice to personal experience and knowledge.

With Israel existing within the 'Muslim world', it is important to know how this world functions and understand its motivations and imperatives, as well as building positive bridges wherever possible. For example, internal Jewish debates about the future of Jerusalem, as symbol and political reality, can only be self-deluding without the recognition of its significance to Islam and the impact this must have on any eventual settlement. In the Middle East the political and religious issues are deeply intertwined. Dialogue can help build a climate of opinion whereby attitudes may ultimately change in political terms as well, but one cannot be naive about the extent of the contribution it can make.

Before the peace process was underway there were scores of different groups attempting Jewish–Arab understanding. Many of them foundered on the same issue: the Israelis sincerely wanted peace, but the Palestinians sincerely wanted justice. That ultimate difference in need and expectation can only be overcome by a political solution. Dialogue can only work when people meet as equals with their self-respect intact.

For our respective communities within Europe we need appropriate channels of communication and relationships to avoid the Middle East conflict spilling over into our respective diasporas. More positively, Jews share with Muslims the situation of being a minority in Western Europe, and thus are also vulnerable. But we are also somewhat more experienced in 'surviving' and indeed flourishing in these circumstances. On political, cultural, social and religious levels there is much to be gained for Muslims and Jews alike from closer ties, occasional shared initiatives and mutual support. This is particularly true of things such as *kashrut* (the dietary laws which include the methods of ritual slaughter that are often under attack), family legislation such as marriage and divorce, education, and defence – given particularly the rise in racism, antisemitism and islamophobia.

Given the need and the desire for such a dialogue, how does one start? There is nothing mysterious about what needs to be done – it is the same as for any other attempt at getting to know a particular individual or group. Firstly, you start to meet with as few presuppositions as possible. Then you take the time to get to know each other as individuals (sometimes using a formal programme of regular meetings as a framework while the personal relationships begin to develop). After that, you begin to define areas of common interest or concern and acknowledge the areas that need to be kept on the back-burner until sufficient trust has been established to explore them. A working principle someone suggested recently was that within the dialogue situation (in time) you may explore the areas in which you differ – for the outside world, you attempt to show the areas that you have in common. You need to establish certain very clear guidelines about confidentiality; about avoiding public declarations (depending on the nature of the dialogue framework), at least until you are very sure of each other; about preventing the long-term process being hijacked by people with private motives or by sudden, burning current events; about giving equal space to both dialogue partners, hearing each other out and trying to listen honestly to the other, even when the other is critical about your own side, without either switching off or becoming immediately defensive; and about not giving public presentations of the other faith based on your own knowledge, assumptions and, inevitably, biases, unless a very clear agreement is first obtained from the dialogue partner.

To follow the old Chasidic story: a Chasidic Jew overheard two peasants discussing. One says, 'Ivan, do you love me?' 'Of course I do!' 'So you know what causes me pain.' 'How could I know what causes you pain?' 'Then you do not truly love me.' One result of dialogue is to empathise that you come to know what gives the other pain.

My own experience has suggested a number of stages in the dialogue process in which people or groups come unstuck, some of which I have noted in the chapter on risk-taking. They are not inevitable, but are worth noting again.

In the first stage, the participants may still be talking to 'the folks back home' rather than to their dialogue partner. They fear they may be seen as 'betraying' their own community, so have to present all the issues that have divided them in the past. If the 'partner' reacts similarly things may end up worse than before the dialogue began! This phase must be well facilitated, or at least recognised for what it is.

Once past this stage, the dialogue partners may begin to meet as 'people', and there begins the forging of mutual trust, respect, friendship and love that allow the religious differences to be enjoyed rather than seen as a threat. It is therefore useful in the early stages to pick a subject of common concern and see how the faiths approach it from their own perspectives, rather than confronting each other directly.

A third phase, often the most difficult, is persuading the 'folks back home', who still retain their suspicions and prejudices, that what has been achieved is legitimate and of value. This 'education', and the broadening of the participation in the dialogue, is essential.

One issue that needs to be addressed from the beginning is the establishing of a 'level ground' for the encounter. Problems include the 'power' differential between the participants: for example, if one of the partners belongs to the majority society and the other to a minority within it. Similarly, in encounters between 'conservatives' and 'liberals' of their respective communities – what may seem a small step by one side may actually be a major one for the other, and due recognition must be given to this. Some majorities do not even see the problems of their minority partner, and great sensitivity must be used in bringing this awareness out. In general, it is the responsibility of the more powerful partner to ensure that appropriate conditions are created.

A key factor, though never an easy one to address, is a degree of self-criticism on the part of both partners. A willingness to acknowledge one's own past failures helps move the encounter from apologetics and self-justifications to a more balanced view of past and present disagreements. Again, it is usually the responsibility of the partner with the greatest degree of 'security' to take the first step in this direction. Every encounter must be treated as a new start, for nothing can be taken for granted. At the end of the day, taking risks in such essential work is not as dangerous as the failure to take any risk at all.

Having addressed the motivations and the operating principles for interfaith encounters, we turn to the agenda, the substance of the dialogue. What are the 'Jewish–Muslim issues' in particular in the UK today? Firstly, how do we, as Jews and Muslims, perceive the other, and how do we challenge and correct misconceptions and prejudices between us? Secondly, how do we work together as minority communities in safeguarding our rights? As I mentioned earlier, this would include such issues as the right to maintain our dietary practices, the right to provision for denominational education, and the right to observe religious festivals in the workplace. It would also include the need to unite in the defence arena, to combat the threat of far-right extremism, antisemitism and islamophobia. Thirdly, how do we contribute as Jews and Muslims to issues facing society at large, as distinctive members of that society? Certainly, both Judaism and Islam have much to say on such matters as the family, education, poverty and charity, crime and punishment, business ethics etc. These too are Jewish–Muslim issues. Perhaps in the long term, this is the most important of the three areas.

In a nutshell, it is about jointly promoting the moral and ethical codes that underpin our two traditions. It is about demonstrating that Judaism and Islam continue to offer a relevant and significant set of moral guidelines for the modern world. It is about engaging, for example, in the national struggle against racism in general, as Jews and Muslims together, to ensure that we may preserve our cultural distinctiveness as equal and active members of the community. And it is about ensuring that the wider society in which we live accepts our 'otherness' and celebrates our diversity.

The methods to be employed are many and varied. Special interest groups can be established – doctors, lawyers, community and social workers, teachers, journalists, academics, university student societies, clergy, members of the business community etc. Exchange visits between synagogues and mosques and between Jewish and Muslim schools can be arranged. Meetings between appropriate partners can be co-ordinated for shared social or political activities – for example, race relations or the seeking of provision of educational and cultural facilities from the state or local government. Existing dialogue opportunities or organisations can be supported and new people encouraged to participate. Help is available from the Interfaith Network, with its excellent directory. Collaboration with Muslim organisations and centres that have been willing to participate in dialogue in the past or present can be encouraged, as can the creation of local interfaith groups and activities.

All such steps imply at the same time an internal re-education of the Jewish world and a re-examination of our own priorities. Our first priority is self-monitoring: we need to watch our own degree of compliance with Western and media stereotypes of Islam – the equation of 'fundamentalism' with violence, the loose usage of terms like 'Jihad' and 'holy war' (which are on a par with the misuse of terms from our own tradition like 'an eye for an eye' – the vengeful Jew). We need therefore to watch our own public pronouncements, for example, from the pulpit, in our own educational material and literature and in the Jewish press. Secondly, we should encourage the publication of documents showing shared values – for example, the order of the shared Jewish–Muslim prayers following the massacre at the Mosque in Hebron (contained in Appendix II) and the pamphlet on shared business ethics published by the Interfaith Foundation. We should encourage Muslim contributions to the *Jewish Chronicle* and other journals, and Jewish contributions to Muslim publications. Thirdly, concerning public events, wherever we have a formal Christian presence, such as inductions of rabbis and civic services, there should be a Muslim one by special invitation. This means cultivating many more Muslims who are able to do so (at the moment, the few Muslims who are available are as overworked as were the few rabbis who took part in the earlier years of interfaith work). Concerning defence, we should support the work of bodies like the Institute for Jewish Policy Research (JPR), which monitors anti-Islamic and racist materials as well as antisemitic ones, and encourage the sharing of information and joint actions with Muslim institutions and academics. Finally, diplomatic links should be pursued wherever possible.

This represents an ambitious programme, yet we cannot afford not to be proactive in this important area. There are no short cuts to dialogue, to the building of trust and friendship. We cannot use dialogue for short-term gains, nor is it sensible to make demands of our dialogue partners that they cannot meet. Until we recognise and accept the constraints under which our dialogue partners operate, our expectations are likely to be unrealistic and lead to disappointments, and possibly further alienation. We often start from quite different premises, with different levels of experience, different degrees of security, and at different degrees of assimilation to Western culture, modes of thought and religious expression. We have to learn to listen to our partners first and try to understand where they come from if we are to expect them to listen to us.

We need to work from the domestic level up and the diplomatic level down. I do not know what the end–result will be, but in the UK and the rest of Europe we have a unique opportunity to find a mutually helpful and supportive relationship. At long last the attempt has begun – it needs all our support.

15

Haman's New Victims

This chapter deserves a special introduction. Its opening is self-explanatory. It was written for the London-based *Jewish Chronicle*. Purim is a Jewish festival when we commemorate the rescue of the Jewish people from the threat of genocide, as recorded in the biblical Book of Esther (Megillat Esther). The villain is a man called Haman, the Jewish heroes are Mordechai and Queen Esther. All three are subjects of the Persian King Ahasuerus. The festival is celebrated in a carnival atmosphere, the scroll containing the biblical story being read in synagogue accompanied by hecklers whenever the name of Haman is mentioned. Beneath the frenzied jollity is an awareness of the seriousness of the threat to Jewish existence at so many stages in our history, and an almost-conscious attempt to deny its truth or drown out its reality for at least one day in the year.

The article appeared on the morning of Friday 25 February 1994. Later that day we learnt with horror about a fanatic, right-wing Orthodox Jewish man, Baruch Goldstein, who had entered the Ibrahim Mosque in Hebron and murdered over 40 Muslims at prayer with an automatic gun. It renders the closing sentence of this chapter chillingly prophetic. One consequence was the calling together of Muslim and Palestinian friends to a joint service of mourning at the West London Synagogue on 6 March. The introduction to that event and the order of service follow this chapter.

*   *   *   *

The invitation to write a piece for Purim reached me in Germany. I had just finished co-organising the JCM student conference that Leo Baeck College rabbinic students attend each year, and was still full of our explorations of the theme of 'Prejudice and Power in the "New Europe"'. Now in Berlin, to lecture at the Jüdische Volkshochschule, I called London from a telephone box on the Kurfürstendam. Just outside, sitting on the pavement, was a woman holding a baby. The handwritten notice beside her explained that she was a refugee from Bosnia and that her house had been destroyed and asked for help to support her child. It confirmed my decision about the subject for this piece – Haman's newest victims.

Two features of the Esther story and of Purim always grab my attention. Haman tells King Ahasuerus that there is a people scattered throughout the countries of his domain whose laws are different and who do not obey the laws of the king (Esther 3:8). This slander, repeated by antisemites since biblical times, seems to point inevitably to Jewish life. But then one realises that Haman, as an Agagite, is also an outsider at the Persian court; his accusation is also a projection of his own situation. Soon it becomes clear that the struggle between Haman and Mordechai belongs to the jockeying for power at court common to all despotic regimes. Similarly, Mordechai's refusal to acknowledge Haman's authority takes on a different colour. But for the difference in their value system, Haman and Mordechai are mirror images of each other. Perhaps that is why we are instructed to drink so much on Purim that we cannot distinguish between 'blessed be Mordechai' and 'cursed be Haman'.

Secondly, the way we read Megillat Esther at Purim is an acting out of the deep Jewish anxiety that the story itself reflects. It is about the frightening dangers of Diaspora life: Jews at the mercy of the whim of an unreliable king, subject to violence generated by inner-court intrigues, and only surviving by even better political manoeuvring and a lot of luck. Worse still, in the Book of Esther, God seems nowhere to be found. No wonder we shout and stamp and drown out Haman's name and reduce the whole event of reading the *Megillah* (the Scroll of Esther) to a shambles. It is too disturbing a book to take straight, so we blot out and deny the dangers around us this one time in the year.

As Emil Fackenheim has pointed out in his book *The Jewish Bible After The Holocaust*, the Book of Esther deserves far more theological prominence today. It is the one book that most faithfully reflects Jewish reality for so many during the Shoah, when no Esther or Mordechai turned up to save us, nor did help come 'from another place' (Esther 4:14). And God, if present, was terrifyingly silent.

This brings me back to the JCM conference, looking at the seeds of prejudice in us all and the disturbing new developments in Europe. As Jews, when we read about the reappearance of overt fascist movements, the rise in antisemitic acts of vandalism against synagogues and cemeteries or attacks on Jewish individuals, we get worried for ourselves. But talk to Muslims about the European scene today and they will tell you of their even greater fears. Because today it is Muslims who are being killed in their thousands in Bosnia, and it is Muslims who have been murdered in Germany and physically attacked in Britain and France. Some Muslims even describe themselves as today's Jews. Like Jews, they remember 1492, when an even larger Muslim population was expelled from Spain – something hardly ever recalled in popular, let alone Jewish, memory. The conventional media reporting of Muslims forever pictures them as violent fundamentalists (a badly misused term), thus feeding back to us our own prejudices and fears. Is this a process of softening up public opinion before some European-wide ethnic cleansing takes place? A piece of graffiti I saw recently in Spain read simply: '1492 Granada; 1992 Sarajevo'.

We cannot read Haman's slanderous words about the Jewish people this Purim without recognising in that description the current popular Western perception of Islam. So where does our Jewish community stand in this disturbing and deteriorating situation?

Some Jewish individuals and groups were among the first to speak out against ethnic cleansing and the dismemberment of Bosnia. That task must be pursued and help provided wherever we can, however frustrating it seems to be. But there is another task closer to home, as close as our nearest Muslim community and neighbours. Some small steps have already been taken towards a Jewish–Muslim dialogue, but nothing like enough. We need to establish even more such contacts, sensitise ourselves to Muslim fears, show solidarity with them in their struggle to get state-funded

Muslim schools like our Jewish ones, and fight against the stereotyping of Islam wherever we come across it. All of this can only come about by learning more ourselves and through personal contact. Our approaches may be met at first with distrust, because Muslim loyalty to the Palestinian cause places great strains on such collaboration. But this should not be the decisive factor. In Europe today we share with Muslims too many of the same beliefs and problems not to find a common language and task, trust and friendship.

The lesson of Purim is still the need for Jewish watchfulness and action for our own self-protection. But as members of a society that seems intent on demonising Islam and misreading it at every turn, with potentially disastrous consequences, we have to recognise our own responsibility to fight against this kind of prejudice – as we experience it in ourselves and as we see it around us. To put in in the same black and white way as the Book of Esther itself: are we on the side of Mordechai or Haman?

16

An Evening of Mourning for the Victims of the Massacre at the Hebron Mosque

SUNDAY 6 MARCH 1994, WEST LONDON SYNAGOGUE

In the wake of the massacre of more than 40 Muslims at prayer in the Ibrahim Mosque in Hebron at the hands of a fanatic right-wing Orthodox Israeli Jew, Jewish communities around the world were in a state of shock. In discussing the matter with rabbinic colleagues and Palestinian and Muslim friends, we decided to hold a small service of memorial, commemoration and solidarity. The late Rabbi Hugo Gryn generously offered the use of a hall at the West London Synagogue as a central venue. In the event, though there was little time to inform people, it became clear that the hall would not be large enough, and the synagogue allowed us to use their beautiful building, despite considerable anxiety about a possible terrorist attack. With Muslim colleagues we assembled texts and invited a few people to speak. The synagogue was packed and the event succeeded in conveying our shared horror and distress at what had happened.

The following is the text of my opening address and the readings from Jewish and Muslim sources.

*   *   *   *

I would like to welcome people from all parts of the Jewish community, from the Muslim community of the UK, from Israel and from the Palestinian community. Judge Finestein, President of the Board of Deputies sends his apologies. I am pleased to welcome other representatives of the Board, the local Member of Parliament. As well as those named participants on your order of events, I am grateful for the participation of Saba Risaluddin of the Calamus Foundation, Tazeer from Hebron and Mehri Niknam, an Iranian Jewish woman.

This event began as a small private initiative by people who have long been engaged in Jewish–Muslim dialogue and in Israeli–Palestinian dialogue. We wanted to express together our horror at what happened in Hebron, our grief for the families who suffered, our shame that such a thing could be committed in the name of Judaism, our prayer that this disgraceful event not succeed in preventing the difficult process towards peace. I think, too, that we wanted a time to mourn together the tragedy and conflict in which we have been so long engaged and trapped.

This event is not a conventional Jewish service – nor a Muslim one. There is no precedent for it that I know of, no guidelines for organising it, nor any familiar landmarks from our Jewish liturgy. We are all finding our way to express our feelings, but also to share some of the values and teachings that we have in common. So we have consulted throughout with Jews, Muslims and Palestinians – Muslim and Christian – in compiling it. If there are mistakes, if somewhere we have shown insensitivity – it is not intended and we apologise in advance.

We will conclude with silence and 'amen'. Those who have taken part will then leave and I would ask that we leave the sanctuary in silence. In the hall outside there will be the opportunity to meet again and refreshments will be available.

Finally I would like to thank all those who have helped to organise this event, who have agreed to participate and you for joining us. In particular we owe a great debt of gratitude to Rabbi Hugo Gryn and the Executive and Council of the West London Synagogue for their courage and sensitivity in making their beautiful synagogue available for this event – especially as it outgrew the dimensions we had originally assumed.

You will find an order of service and the texts that will be read on the sheets. We will begin with a 'niggun', a song without words, as it seemed to us that some feelings cannot be adequately expressed by words alone.

ORDER OF EVENTS

Breaking of the fast — 5.52 pm
Introduction — Rabbi Dr Jonathan Magonet
Niggun — a song without words — Rabbi Mark Solomon
Contributions — Rabbi Hugo Gryn, His Honour Judge Eugene Cotran,
    Rami Heilbron
Readings from Jewish and Islamic tradition
Music — Wissam Boustany
Al Fatihah, in memory of the dead — Saeda Nusseibeh
Concluding silence.

READINGS FROM JEWISH AND ISLAMIC TRADITION

Only one single human being was created in the world, to teach that if anyone causes a single soul to perish, Scripture regards him as though he had caused a whole world to perish, and if anyone saves alive a single soul, Scripture regards him as though he had saved a whole world.
Mishnah Sanhedrin 4:5

That was why we laid it down for the Israelites that whoever kills a human being, except as a punishment for murder or other villainy in the land, shall be looked upon as though he had killed all mankind, and that whoever saved a human life shall be regarded as though he had saved all mankind.
The Holy Qur'an, Sura 5:32 The Table

      *   *   *   *

The first step towards repentance, which is the most essential and at the same time the most difficult, is confession, or rather 'the admission to oneself' that one has sinned. It is not God who needs an avowal or confession from us, for He knows us through and through; in fact, much better than we know ourselves. But we ourselves stand very much in need of honest and unreserved confession; it is to our own selves that we must admit that we have done wrong.
Samson Raphael Hirsch (1808–88), Orthodox rabbi

Those who believe, and who have forsaken the domain of evil, and have striven hard in God's cause with their possessions and their lives have the highest rank in the sight of God; it is they who shall achieve salvation.
The Holy Qur'an Sura 9:20

Here is a good description of Jihad. It may require fighting in God's cause, as a form of self-sacrifice. But its essence consists in a true and sincere faith, which so fixes its

gaze on God, that all selfish or worldly motives seem paltry and fade away; and in an earnest and ceaseless activity, involving the sacrifice (if need be) of life, person or property, in the service of God. Mere brutal fighting is opposed to the whole spirit of Jihad, while the sincere scholar's pen or preacher's voice or wealthy man's contributions may be the most valuable forms of Jihad.
Commentary by Yusuf Ali

A man should concern himself more that he not injure others than that he not be injured. For when a man tries to keep a watch that his fist not injure others, by that very act he enthrones in the world the God of truth and righteousness and adds power to the kingdom of justice; and it is precisely this power which will defend him against injury by others…When a man constantly portrays to himself scenes of terror, when he asserts that everyone wants to obliterate him and that he can rely only on the power of his own fist, by this he denies the kingdom of truth and justice and enthrones the power of the fist. And since the fist is by nature poor at making distinctions, in the end defence and attack become reversed: instead of defending himself by means of the fist, such a man becomes himself the assailant and destroyer of others. Hence, like begetting like, others repay him in kind, and so the earth is filled with violence and oppression.
Aaron Samuel Tamaret (1869–1931), rabbi and pacifist

The good deed and the evil deed are not alike. Repel the evil deed with one that is better. Then lo! he between whom and thee there was enmity will become as though he was a bosom friend.
The Holy Qur'an Sura 41:34

Ben Zoma asks: *eizehu gibbor* – Who is a hero? And answers: *ha-kovesh et-yitzro* – One who controls his passions. (Pirqe Avot 4:1) The Talmud adds: *eizehu gibbor shebba-gibborim* – Who is the greatest of heroes? And answers: *mi sheoseh sonei ohavo* – The one who controls his passions and makes his enemy into his friend.
Avot d'Rabbi Nathan 23

It may be that Allah will ordain love between you and those of them with whom you are at enmity. Allah is mighty, and Allah is forgiving, merciful.
The Holy Qur'an Sura 60:7

The essence of peace is to join together two opposites. And do not be alarmed if you see one man who is in complete contrast to your mind (or way of thinking) and you may imagine that it is absolutely impossible to be at peace with him. And also when you see two people who are indeed two opposites (the one to the other); do not say that it may not be possible to make peace between them. On the contrary! That is the essence of the wholeness of peace; to attempt at having peace between two opposites, just as the Lord, blessed be He, makes peace above between fire and water, which are two opposites.
Nachman of Bratzlav (1772–1811) Chasidic master

If they incline to peace, incline thou to it as well, and place thy trust in God; verily, He alone is all-hearing, all-knowing.
The Holy Qur'an Sura 8:61

* * * *

These are the days of the years of Abraham's life, a hundred and seventy-five years. Abraham breathed his last and died in a good old age, an old man and full of years, and was gathered to his people. Isaac and Ishmael his sons buried him in the cave of Machpelah, in the field of Ephron the son of Zohar the Hittite, east of Mamre, the field which Abraham purchased from the Hittites. There Abraham was buried, with Sarah his wife.
Genesis 25:7–10

O Allah, bless our master Muhammad and the people of our master Muhammad, as thou didst bless our master Abraham and the people of our master Abraham, and bestow thy blessings upon our master Muhammad and the people of our master Muhammad, as thou didst bestow thy blessings upon our master Abraham and the people of our master Abraham. Verily thou art praiseworthy and glorified.
From the Tashahud Prayer

Ishmael, my brother,
How long shall we fight each other?

My brother from times bygone,
My brother - Hagar's son,
My brother, the wandering one.

One angel was sent to us both,
One angel watched over our growth -
There in the wilderness, death threatening through thirst,
I a sacrifice on the altar, Sarah's first...

Ishmael, my brother, hear my plea:
It was the angel who tied thee to me...
Time is running out, put hatred to sleep.
Shoulder to shoulder, let's water our sheep.

Shin Shalom (Shalom Joseph Shapira) b. 1904, Hebrew poet

17

Prayers for Peace in the Middle East

THURSDAY 19 OCTOBER 2000, WEST LONDON SYNAGOGUE

Six years after the massacre in Hebron, when hopes had been high that the peace process was finally underway, violence again broke out, but this time on a massive scale. Again those of us who had been engaged in interfaith dialogue came together for a special service, prayers for peace in the Middle East. This time it was considerably harder for Palestinian partners to join us, nevertheless they were prepared to do so. I tried to reflect their courage in the opening address and in the opening prayer I composed which is appended at the end. It was already clear to me at the time that an automatic loyalty to the state of Israel and the Jewish people should not preclude a stronger criticism of policies of the current Israeli government and a growing concern about the situation of the Palestinians.

*   *   *   *

It is my privilege to welcome you here this evening to join us in prayers for peace in the Middle East.

I want especially to welcome the Muslims and Palestinians who have been willing to join us this evening. For us as Jews living here to attend such a service is a relatively easy step. For them to join us here requires a far harder decision and carries a far higher price. They honour us by their presence and participation. We must do what is necessary to honour them.

Over 30 years ago in Berlin, at an early attempt at a Jewish-Christian-Muslim conference, we were faced with a problem. An Israeli woman, a

188

left-wing film-maker, wished to show a film she had made about Israel. We knew that it was highly critical of the way Israelis treated Palestinians. The Jewish participants were very concerned at giving such a propaganda weapon to the 'other side', and did not wish the film to be shown. Nevertheless, it was shown and it was very painful to watch. Remember, this was still a time when we could believe that in all of history never had there been such a benign occupation! But in the discussion that followed, something extraordinary happened. The Palestinians who were present said that had this been a film made by a Palestinian they would have been pleased with it as propaganda but nothing more. The fact that it had been made by an Israeli, taking such a self-critical stance, forced them to reassess their understanding of Israel, of the different strands of opinion within it, and indeed the importance of self-criticism.

I recalled this moment when we prepared this service. For we found some materials that we wished to include and debated long and hard as to whether to do so and risk upsetting members of our own community. The passage in question is a form of public confession published by Israeli rabbis from across the religious spectrum from Reform to Orthodox. Nothing of what they say is particularly new, but the seriousness with which they are prepared to say it is courageous and especially significant at this time. They speak of the responsibility of those who do have power towards those who do not. Their views would have been almost unthinkable for such a range of Jewish religious leaders even a short time ago. But then it was once unthinkable to talk to the PLO [Palestine Liberation Organisation], or to give back territory, or to accept the possibility of a Palestinian state or to discuss the status of Jerusalem. All these taboos have been broken. Others must inevitably follow.

We have seen in the last few weeks how words can move people to the brink of violence and destruction and beyond. What are the words and gestures that can move us back from that brink, that can create a space for new attitudes and for meeting? What are the words and actions that might make possible a matching response?

The following are passages from a vidui, a solemn confession of sin for Yom Kippur published on behalf of these 80 Israeli rabbis. They belong to an association called Rabbis for Human Rights. For 15 years they have worked to protect the civil and human rights of Arabs and Jews alike within Israel, basing themselves on Jewish values and teachings. What they say addresses the human problem to be faced if something is to change for the better. Their confession tries to affect the attitudes and actions that have fuelled the anger and hatred which have exploded onto the streets and led to so many deaths. It is absolutely one-sided for it is addressed to an inner Jewish world within Israel – but such honesty, and not only on Yom Kippur, is one essential starting point.

I would ask us to hear them out and to respect the commitment of those who composed it to changing the present reality and to building a better future for Israel. For the first step in changing anything is to acknowledge that there is a problem. Their *vidui*, their confession for Yom Kippur this year, reads in part as follows:

> 'For the sin which we have sinned against You by hardening our hearts –
> To the grinding poverty and despair of Palestinians and Israeli Arabs.

> 'For the sin which we have sinned against You consciously or unconsciously –
> Preventing Israeli Palestinians from fully and equally participating in Israeli society,
> and leaving them under-represented in government, academia and business.
> 'And for the sin which we have sinned against You knowingly or unknowingly –
> Allowing the Israeli government to continue to expropriate land, demolish homes,
> build roads, uproot trees and deny water in our name, even while publicly speaking
> words of peace...

> 'For the sin which we have sinned against You by silence –
> When we knew that human beings were being mistreated and said nothing.

> 'For the sin which we have sinned against You by the abuse of power –
> Using excessive lethal force to kill and maim.
> And for the sin which we have sinned against You by justifying –
> The use of excessive lethal force.'

The final confession is something that probably most of us have been guilty of at some time because of the nature of our loyalties;

> 'And for the sin which we have sinned against You by narrow-mindedness –
> Feeling only our own pain,
> Closing our minds to the agony
> of bereaved Arab mothers and fathers.'
> (Rabbi Arik Ascherman)

When I showed this evening's draft programme including this passage to an Israeli friend, a man very much committed to the peace process, he expressed his concern that the programme did not show enough solidarity with Israel at this dreadful time of fear and hatred and anger. When I showed it to a Palestinian friend, she expressed her concern that polite prayers for peace without addressing issues of justice are of no use at all at this dreadful time of fear and hatred and anger. Both are right from their perspective. But such radically different concerns and agendas, now being pushed to extremes of violence and bloodshed, are the terrible reality that makes this kind of service so important. It is possible that our prayers this evening will truly move the heavens. Certainly our prayers this evening must move us, move us onward along the difficult road to justice and peace.

OPENING PRAYER

God of Abraham, God of Sarah and God of Hagar, God of Isaac and God of Ishmael, God of the twelve sons of Jacob and God of the twelve sons of Ishmael, God of Jesus, God of Muhammad, God of the spirits of all human beings, we turn to You for guidance. We are all Your children, descendants of Abraham, entrusted with Your blessing: 'through you shall all the peoples of the earth be blessed.'

We have failed You and each other. We face each other across barriers of misunderstanding and mistrust, of hatred and fear. Where there is injustice, let there be justice. Where there are wounds let there be healing. Where there is pain, let there be relief. Where there is violence, let there be negotiation. Where there is single-mindedness, let there be compromise. Where there is bitterness, let there be forgiveness. Where there is humiliation, let there be honour. Where there is guilt, let there be repentance. Where there is death, let there be life. Where there is hatred, let there be love. Where there is war, let there be peace.

18

From a Narrow Place:
A New Year Sermon

The terrorist action of 11 September 2001 came just days before the Jewish New Year, a time for Jewish self-searching. I had intended to review events in Israel during the past year but inevitably, as for all rabbis, the atrocity in New York overshadowed everything. Nevertheless, I felt it important to bring to the attention of my own Jewish community a human face and a human reality that is all too easily overlooked in the labels we place upon people. I sent this sermon to Dr Raheb, who posted it on his website. A week later an Israeli friend e-mailed it back to me, having found it on another website. In the bitter struggle that continues between Israelis and Palestinians such small gestures have little impact. The only consolation comes from a rabbinic statement: it is not for you to complete the task, but neither may you desist from it.

       *   *   *   *

ROSH HASHANAH, 18 SEPTEMBER 2001

The events of the past week overshadow everything else at this time. But as we look back on the year that has passed, we cannot help but focus on what has been happening in Israel. The Middle East conflict that seemed at this time last year to be near to resolution has moved into an unpredictable, destructive and frightening phase. We listen daily to the radio waiting to hear the latest bad news: whether it be a suicide bomber in an Israeli city or an Israeli counter-attack that has left civilians dead. We are onlookers, but also to some extent participants, in a bitter tragedy, one seemingly bound to escalate to something even worse.

We are looking back on a year of so much pain and suffering for Israelis and Palestinians alike, a year of shattered hopes and bitter, personal tragedies. When it seemed that a peaceful settlement was within our grasp, everything suddenly fell apart. People on both sides of the conflict have equally strong opinions about why this happened. They allot the responsibility and blame, perhaps inevitably, to the other side. Not surprisingly, any such one-sided convictions, accusations, actions and retaliations do not stop the bloodshed, change attitudes or offer hope.

Whatever our feelings about the policies of the Israeli government, this is a time to show solidarity with the people of Israel and everyone who has family and friends there keeps in touch and offers support in any way we can. As you know there is a rally for that purpose on Sunday the 23rd September. But at the same time that we mourn with those who have been the victims of terrorism in Israel and offer comfort and encouragement to them, we have also our own additional responsibilities. For precisely because we in the Diaspora have a certain distance from the political conflict, we need to consider what we can offer to help change the situation. We are in the position to keep open channels of communication with Palestinians and the wider Muslim world. Such a challenging idea may not be easy to accept. But the High Holydays demand of us a larger view and the taking of our own responsibility on behalf of the Jewish people as a whole. For this reason I want to introduce you to someone who belongs to the 'other side'. For just a few moments I would like us to see the world through his eyes. For this is the season for confronting our prejudices and challenging our stereotypes.

Every two years the Protestant church in Germany holds a major four-day conference called the Kirchentag, 'Church Day'. Up to 100,000 Christians descend on a particular town for a programme of lectures, seminars, services, concerts and other events. It is not unlike the atmosphere and variety that we know at Limmud [an annual Jewish gathering to study], though enormously larger. For several years there has been a strong Jewish contribution to the Kirchentag — both in terms of Jewish-Christian and more recently Jewish-Christian-Muslim dialogue, and what is called the 'Lehrhaus', an opportunity for Christians to attend lectures and study programmes conducted by Jews. I have taught there on a number of occasions over the past few years.

This June it took place in Frankfurt and I gave a number of sessions on biblical texts and took part in a couple of interfaith meditations. As you can imagine, in such an enormous organisational task, the occasional thing can go wrong or communication break down, and when I received the programme I found that I had been put down for an extra session that I had not known about. It was to take part in a shared biblical study on Psalm 118 with a Christian clergyman, something I've often done before. But my partner was to be Dr Mitri Raheb from the International Centre of Bethlehem. This session was to be held at the start of what was to be a Middle East Forum including sessions on life, religion and politics in Jerusalem. In all the sessions Israelis and Palestinians were taking part so it was appropriately balanced. But I felt for a moment that I had been hijacked into a session that could be very difficult.

I had met Dr Raheb at a conference on religious education some years before in Nuremberg and remembered him as a highly intelligent man, a scholar and serious and responsible Lutheran leader. I even owned a photo taken at the time of us shaking hands. So I agreed to take part.

Up until the last moment we did not know whether Dr Raheb would be able to attend. Israel had placed severe restrictions on the movement of Palestinians in the wake of some terrorist activity. The Palestinian youth delegation only just managed to catch their plane after strenuous efforts by the Kirchentag authorities and sympathetic Israelis. Dr Raheb was also able to get out, literally at the last possible moment, after considerable difficulties and delays.

The Psalm we were to study together is one that we know from the Hallel [a series of psalms read on Jewish festivals], though, as is so often the case, when we read or sing it in services there is little opportunity to try to grasp what it is about. So I welcomed the opportunity to analyse it and found that there are really two distinctive parts that have been blended together. In one of them a lone person describes his experience of being in a dangerous, life-threatening situation. He had prayed to God and been delivered, so he had come to the temple to express his gratitude.

But surrounding this individual voice was a chorus sung by the temple choir, changing this individual prayer into a large triumphal choral hymn of thanksgiving and praise. I arranged the text as a kind of dialogue for different voices and sent it to the organisers so that it could be read aloud in this way. During the session itself I went through the text highlighting the different voices and showing how it was constructed, adding some rabbinic ideas about it.

The psalm begins:

> *hodu ladonai ki tov – ki l'olam hasdo*
> Give thanks to the Eternal who is good
> for God's love is everlasting.

But the first individual voice reads:

> *min ha-meitzar karati yah*
> *anani b'merhav yah*
> Closed in by troubles I called on God
> God answered me and set me free.

The word *meitzar* literally means narrowness, straits, confined. Out of this situation of being hemmed in by enemies the psalmist calls out to God. In answer God gives him merhav, which means breadth, room, space.

When it was Dr Raheb's turn to speak I took quite detailed notes of his remarks. He thanked me for freeing him from having to deal with the exegetical details. He explained that he read the Psalm as a Palestinian Christian, pointed out that the Psalm comes from Israel and asked: 'What can I do with this as a Palestinian? Should I put it aside? It is read on festivals – at Easter, for the Psalm says: "This is the day God has made". Is it too pious and naive to use it? I have problems with this Psalm. Is it only the people of Israel's experience? The "narrow" situation – no-one knows this better than Palestinians. It is too narrow for us. For example in Bethlehem we are surrounded by eighteen Jewish settlements. Two new ones will be built to close the last gap. There is no room to build a house. Tanks go through all the streets and destroy the roads. I can only drive two kilometres from my house. It is too narrow. God will you bring me out of this narrowness?'

He described the struggle to get travel documents, which only came the day before from the military. He added: 'Only on the plane did we understand what it means that God puts our feet on a broad place. In Germany we are free to travel. We pray that all our people can stand on a broader place.'

He went on to point out that he had another problem with this psalm – not with the words of the individual but with the choir. 'It is military language - the enemy will be cut off in the name of God. How much violence is conducted in the name of God, not only in the Middle East. How many use the name of God. Verses 15-16 speak of the right hand of God acting mightily. The hebrew word is *hayil*, a term used for the Israeli army! In other parts of the psalm, where the enemy surrounds us, it is clear where God stands - God is mine.' He added: 'The individual voice cries to God - this speaks to us. But when placed as a national religious ideology it becomes a problem - worse still it is anchored in liturgy. Man is also narrow in this Psalm.'

He went on to take a wider view. 'The greatest challenge to us: can we as Jews, Christians and Muslims give God space to take us out of our nationalistic ideologies. It is not only the enemy that makes us narrow. Let us let God work on us and through us, to free us from these narrow nationalistic ideologies so that we can leap over these mountains. God's friendship can never be limited. I hope we can make this step with the help of God. We make the world narrower today.'

I was very moved by his words. They were critical and understandably so, but were said with great restraint. I cannot read the psalm any more without thinking of his reading.

I was reminded of this occasion because of an e-mail I received at the end of last week. It is one of a number from different sources reacting to the atrocity in America. Amongst them were statements from the Muslim community in Germany, from friends who have attended the annual Jewish-Christian-Muslim Student Conference that I organise each year in Bendorf. All condemned the terrorist attack as being totally unacceptable to Islam. Amongst them was an open letter from Dr Raheb. I can only imagine the kind of tightrope he has to walk on behalf of his Christian community, given their particular embattled situation amongst a Muslim majority. But as a Palestinian he is caught up in the complex web of nationalism, and their deep-seated feeling of an injustice done to them, let alone the experience of being under constant siege in the territories. Ironically, as his piece suggests, the only people who feel as paranoid as Jews about adverse media coverage are Muslims and here Palestinians. It is also clear from his message both the sincerity of his feelings and the need to assert the humanity and rights of his own people. I quote:

> With deep sorrow and profound grief we write this message to offer our heartfelt condolences to the mothers, fathers, children, friends and families of the thousands of innocent people who have been the victims of the terrorist attacks yesterday morning on the USA. We would like to reach out to all of our American friends to assure them that we stand by them at this difficult and tragic time. Constantly, for the past eleven months, we have received many messages from our friends from America expressing their solidarity and sharing with us our grief. Never in our worst nightmares did we imagine that we would be witnessing such a horrendous event and human tragedy inflicted on our American friends. We care for every life and we pray for all those who are mourning the loss of loved ones taken away by this indiscriminate act of organized terror. Our thoughts and prayers are with you all.
>
> We are aware that the media has shown President Arafat's shocked reaction to this act and his strong condemnation of it. Unfortunately, the media has also shown scenes of a few Palestinians celebrating this tragedy. We want you to know that these few do not speak for or represent the entire Palestinian people. What the media failed to acknowledge was the majority of Palestinians who were shocked, saddened and mournful. We believe that this media campaign is biased and aims at dehumanizing the Palestinian people. Such a campaign follows the same logic of the terrorists, since it deliberately attempts to punish innocent people indiscriminately. In our grief we are asking ourselves why did the people immediately associate us Palestinians with the perpetrators rather than the victims.
>
> As Palestinians we can very well understand the pain of our American friends. We know what it means when political leaders are targeted and are not safe in their own offices. We understand what it means when planes attack security headquarters. We know how it feels when the backbone of the economy is assaulted. We do not want to compare suffering, since every suffering is unique and this particular tragedy has such hideous dimensions. Yet, never before have Americans and Palestinians shared so much.

He makes some proposals, including prayer vigils, consciousness raising about the role of the media and the dangers of stereotyping. He concludes with a prayer that is striking because despite all that he and his people have experienced, he is able, and courageous enough, to include Israelis within it:

> [Let us] commit to prophet Micah's vision that 'they shall sit every person under his vine and his fig tree and none shall make them afraid.' So that no American, Palestinian, Iraqi, Israeli, Japanese etc will be afraid to be in his or her office, home, or airplane, no matter what nationality they hold.

At a time when extremism seems to be on the increase, when stereotyping blunts any hope of recognising the humanity of 'the other', I wanted to remind us of another voice. His words also address our own feelings about the tragedy that struck America last week. Somewhere in these shared feelings there has to be a way for us to meet beyond the conflict that diminishes and corrupts us all, Jew, Christian, Muslim, Israeli, Palestinian alike. There are no simple answers to the political conflict. But there are possibilities of meeting each other at the level of religious understanding. Whenever we read the Hallel, that Psalm can also be a call to us to escape the narrowness of vision that lumps all people together, that denies their uniqueness and humanity, and reduces them to a label or a slogan, the other, the enemy.

> *min ha-meitzar karati yah*
> to get out of this narrowness I called on God.
> *anani b'merhav yah*
> God answered me with a broader vision.
> *hodu ladonai ki tov*
> Give thanks to the Eternal who is good
> *ki l'olam hasdo*
> for God's love is *l'olam*, for the whole world,
> and God's love is *l'olam*, it lasts forever.

19
The Journey to Dialogue

JCM CONFERENCE 4–11 MARCH 2002 SHABBAT MORNING SERMON

The annual JCM Student Conference has managed to continue, even in years when events like the first Intifada and the Gulf War overshadowed it and caused other interfaith encounters to fall apart. The conferences in 2001 and 2002 were deeply affected by the Second Intifada and the conflicting loyalties of participants. In response to the painful emotions expressed throughout the week, I felt it necessary to address the issue during the Shabbat morning sermon.

*   *   *   *

I know with absolute certainty the subject about which I do not want to preach this Shabbat. In fact, I have spent much of this week trying to think of ways of avoiding it. I looked at our Torah reading for today and started working on one of the texts. But it felt increasingly dishonest to play clever word games or score elegant theological points.

The subject that I do not want to preach about, of course, is Israel and the Palestinians. Conversations over dinner, hot debates in public spaces – these are one thing. But a sermon provides a privileged platform that should not be abused. For me, at least, the sermon is not the place for party politics, however much others may use it for such ends. But the moment such a subject is chosen, the sermon does become a political event. You will have to judge whether this turns out to be a legitimate use of this pulpit or not.

I grew up in a middle–class Jewish family in Britain. My father was a Zionist at a time when this was not a popular cause in our Jewish community. I do not think he was an ideological Zionist in any way. For him the establishing of a homeland for the Jews was a very basic gut feeling. He had come to England from Canada at the beginning of the Second World War to work as a doctor and do his bit against the Nazis. As far as he was concerned, Israel was a refuge for his people and that was the beginning and the end of the matter. He would have happily settled there as he never felt at home in the formality of Britain, but my mother was completely unwilling and could never have coped. That may have been the greatest disappointment of his life.

My own Zionist education was more marginal and frustrating. For some reason as a young man I found propaganda of any kind distasteful and dishonest. The idealised picture of young men and women sitting on tractors and dancing the Hora seemed one-dimensional. I visited Israel as a student, had a great time, but hated the simplistic messages with which we were bombarded, the repeated call to settle there and the negation of our life in the Diaspora. There was too much ideology and too little reality.

I qualified as a doctor, worked for a year in hospitals to become registered and prepared to enter Leo Baeck College to study to become a rabbi. In spring 1967 I went to Israel to study Hebrew. When it became clear at the end of May that war was inevitable, I made the decision to stay with my people, and I volunteered to work in Hadassah hospital. They looked at my medical credentials and put me in the delivery room doing episiotomy repairs. I spent days wandering around the underground wards and corridors, overflowing with wounded, doing practical things where I could. One night I played my guitar and sang songs for some doctors.

The period in Jerusalem before the war had been an astonishing few months. I fell in love with the city, met extraordinary people who became friends and teachers until today, and wrote dozens of songs. I breathed the heady air of that city, with an ugly wall running through the middle. A few days after the Six-Day War, alongside thousands of others going both ways, I crossed over the suddenly open border to the Old City. I experienced the extraordinary hope and joy of that period. I say hope and I must make it clear what it felt like in Israel for so many. The walls had fallen, two populations long since separated, met each other. Like the fall of the Berlin wall it seemed that a new opportunity for unity, mutual understanding and peace was possible. From my contacts with people in East Jerusalem at the time it seemed that they too shared these hopes.

Of course the euphoria did not last. I never shared the inflationary ideas that came to grip both Israelis and Jews worldwide. Surely the talk of 'greater Israel' was just a temporary fantasy. Rather this seemed like the moment to give territory back, to make some kind of gesture that would seal a new and enduring relationship.

I do not feel guilty about my emotions at the time. I do feel guilty that I had not the imagination to understand what the war meant for the Arab world and more specifically for the Palestinian population. There was little room for such considerations because we were completely caught up in an extraordinary re-interpretation of our recent Jewish history. The equation was shockingly simple, and all the more potent for that. God had taken six million Jews in the Shoah, and given us back Jerusalem! It was, and remains, a potent myth, however much one argues against its appalling implications. After all that horror, God was somehow now back on our side and directing our history. That is part of the irrational power behind the settler movement and any number of fundamentalist, messianic tendencies till today. For those of us whose Judaism is deeply affected by our sense of history, by liberal values and a healthy dose of secularism, such simplistic equations are totally unacceptable. But as my colleague Rabbi Lionel Blue has often pointed out, he has never met anyone crazed with liberalism. We on the liberal wing of Judaism have to a large extent abdicated our responsibility and left the ideological initiative to our fundamentalists.

My own comfortable reading of the Six-Day War was quickly shattered. Back home, some of my colleagues had begun the painful and deeply challenging work of meeting with Palestinians and Muslims. They had recognised that there were two parties to the conflict and that nothing had been resolved by the war and that a very different kind of initiative was needed if we were to have a shared future. That was the beginning of the activities that led to the founding of this conference. I will only mention one moment that was for me a turning point. At a meeting in Berlin we were asked to explain why we had come to this encounter. A young Egyptian man began by saying that his brother had been killed in the Sinai. There was a moment of silence when we all waited to hear what he would say, expecting the worst. He went on: If no peace results, then my brother died for nothing. So I have come here to meet Jews to try to build that peace. This was such a reversal of all my assumptions, prejudices and fears that I resolved at that moment to do what I could to meet his vision and generosity. Whenever things have been hard in the dialogue process over the years I remember him and that moment and try to carry on.

Thirty years later we are still in search of that peace as we meet here. And it seems to be as elusive and impossible to achieve as ever. The physical and psychological trauma experienced by both peoples, the failures of leadership and the self-destructive impulses, the abuse of their power by Israel, the desperate actions by Palestinians, all these are chronically in place and offer little hope. Someone said that wars only stop when people get too tired to fight. In the bitter words of Bob Dylan, how many deaths does it take till they know that too many people have died?

Is there anything at all that we can offer? A British sociologist once pointed out that every time there was a right-wing extremist action in Britain it shifted the entire political spectrum to the right. Because those on the conservative wing could simply argue, of course we are not as bad as those people and justify their own more extremist policies. So how do you move back from such extreme positions towards the middle ground? What counterforce can be exerted against the repeated triumph of extremism? One answer has to be the kind of interreligious, intercultural dialogue that we are engaged in, with its assertion that it is possible to meet across barriers and boundaries. When things become pushed to the extremes, it is precisely then that we need dialogue; not less of it but more, more often, more intense, for more people. Regaining the middle ground, regaining the possibility of encounter, and of negotiation, that is the task that desperately needs to be undertaken. When we take the risk of meeting the other, we have to accept the consequences of the relationships we have built. We may not be able to put out the flames, but we must do what we can to avoid feeding them. Perhaps our only choice is to be crazed with liberalism, to become fanatical moderates, to join the radical middle!

That means to listen and recognise the truth in what we hear. It means to acknowledge the pain of others, even despite our own pain. It means allowing ourselves to be challenged and to act on that challenge wherever we have influence or power.

Every bit of hatred that is tossed into the world breeds more hate. The only thing that can change it is when someone says enough, it stops with me. I do not think this is naive, romantic or sentimental. That kind of personal commitment is at the heart of the dialogue we try to develop here. Friendship, mutual respect, trust, love – these are very fragile weapons especially when the conversation is being conducted with tanks and bombs and rockets. But they are real, and they grow in strength the more we use them. And when the guns finally stop firing, they are the currency we will need to repair the human damage that has been done and build some kind of future together.

Afterword

by Karen Armstrong

The day of 11 September 2001 was an apocalypse and revelation in the original sense of these words: it laid bare a reality that had been there all the time, but which we had not seen before.

For decades, a militant brand of piety, often somewhat misleadingly called 'fundamentalism', had been developing in all the major world religions, and had latterly become more extreme. Fundamentalism is rooted in fear; every single fundamentalist movement that I have studied in Judaism, Christianity and Islam is convinced that secular, liberal society wants in some way to wipe out religion. As a result, fundamentalists, who believe that they are fighting for survival and that 'their backs are to the wall', have often neglected those elements of the faith that speak of compassion and respect for the sacred rights of others, and have developed a pernicious view of the other. When this defensive religiosity gets sucked in to a long-established secular conflict – as has happened in the Middle East – the result, as we have seen, is lethal. Jonathan Magonet has long been aware of this danger, and for three decades has worked to build bridges between the three religions of Abraham. It would be difficult to imagine a religious task that is more urgent. Almost every day in our newspapers we see the perils of hatred and bigotry, when they are given divine sanction by people who distort the very tradition they are trying to defend.

Nobody has experienced the fearful impact of prejudice more acutely than the Jewish people, and that is why this book is so valuable. It shows that it is possible to use our own experience of pain and alienation to understand the sufferings of others who also feel the power of misrepresentation. This is of the essence of religion in all the great world faiths. When asked to sum up the whole of Judaism while he stood on one leg, Hillel, an older contemporary of Jesus, replied: 'Do not do unto others what you would not have done unto you. That is the Torah, the rest is commentary, go and learn it.' Jesus taught a version of this Golden Rule, and so, some five centuries earlier, did Confucius, who spoke tirelessly of the importance of *shu*: 'likening to oneself'.[1] The spirituality of empathy demands that we search our inner selves, acknowledge our own pain, but then reach out in an act of understanding that liberates us from the prism of our own limited, fearful viewpoint.

What is particularly inspiring about these pages is that we see, as it were, the nuts and bolts of the process. When Jews, Christians and Muslims come together, how do you deal with problems of diet? How do you cope with the ignorance revealed in a chance word? And how on a day-to-day basis do you find forms of prayer and discussion that do not merely avoid giving offence but which can also inspire? We are divided by centuries of hatred and persecution. A distorted view of the other is often part of our own religious identity, so that a more accurate perception can threaten our sense of our very selves. All this can only be surmounted by long and patient work, of the kind that Jonathan Magonet describes.

But the book also shows that far from being a mere exercise in damage limitation, interfaith dialogue can become a spirituality that leads us directly into the divine presence. This has certainly been my own experience. I limped away from my seven years in a religious order, determined to have nothing further to do with religion. This was largely my own fault: I had been far too young to manage the problems of entering a convent in the years before the reforms of Vatican II had been implemented, and I came away feeling a complete spiritual failure. But years later, after a series of career disasters, I found myself in religious broadcasting, making television programmes about Judaism, Christianity and Islam. My approach in these early years was sceptical, but gradually the material in which I was immersed all day long began to speak to me at a deeper level, and I found that my study of Judaism and Islam gave me back a sense of what faith could be, and what my own Roman Catholic tradition had been trying to achieve.

At quite an early stage in this process, Jonathan Magonet invited me to teach Christianity to the fourth-year students at the Leo Baeck College, under the direction of Rabbi Lionel Blue, and this became an important part of my journey. I found it fascinating to explain the trinity and the incarnation to future rabbis and, as is so often the way with teaching, I learned a great deal myself. The difficulties encountered by the students, and their surprise and occasional delight in observing similarities with their own tradition or in having to revise their own perceptions, showed me that religious discussion did not have to be grim and solemn. It could be warm, energetic and fun. I was having similar encounters with the Muslim community both here and in the US. All this helped me to arrive at my current position, which I often – not altogether flippantly – describe as 'freelance monotheist'. I now draw nourishment from all three traditions, cannot see any one as superior, and am conscious that my discovery of the 'other' two Abrahamic traditions has brought me back to religion.

Rabbi Abraham Joshua Heschel once said that if we put ourselves at the opposite pole from ego, we are in the place where God is. That, I think, is what interfaith dialogue can help us to achieve. It enables us to experience ex-stasis, an ecstasy that is not an exotic state of consciousness, but a true 'going beyond the self', which dethrones ourselves and our opinions from the centre of the universe and puts the other there instead. I see Abraham's meeting with his three visitors at Mamre in Genesis 18 as one of the first interfaith dialogues. Very few of us would take a complete stranger off the streets and bring him into our own home, as Abraham does, but he gives all the refreshment that he can to three people who are potentially threatening, because they do not belong to his ethnic, religious or ideological group. In the course of the ensuing conversation, it transpires quite naturally that one of these strangers is Abraham's god. This brave and generous outreach led to a divine encounter. The Hebrew word for 'holy' is *qaddosh* ('separate', 'other'). Our initial feeling of alienation or even repulsion can give us intimations of the holiness that is God.

In Jonathan Magonet's story, we see how this can work out in practice over the years. But since 11 September 2001 and the escalation of the Arab–Israeli conflict, the desire to build good relations with the other has become an urgent necessity. It not only invigorates our own spirituality, it can become an act of *tikkun olam* ('healing the world') that will contribute to the rebuilding of a devastated world. We are living on the brink of catastrophe. Every act or word of bigotry makes the world a worse place and brings us closer to the edge. But conversely, every attempt to reach out to the other can make the world a better place. Religion was also hijacked on 11 September. If we are to save our world, religion must be reclaimed. What we saw on 11 September was that we share one world, that we cannot cut ourselves off from those who feel dispossessed, that what happens in Gaza today may have repercussions in New York or London tomorrow, and that if we turn our back on the world, the repercussion will come to us in a terrible guise. Initiatives like those described in this book must become more widespread, because in our new global world, we can no longer support the old parochial view of religion, but must learn that we are all members of this global world.

Karen Armstrong
London, October 2002

Appendix I:
What is JCM?

Throughout this book I have referred to the annual JCM Student Conference held at Hedwig Dransfeld Haus, Bendorf, Germany. The conference has evolved over 30 years and developed a mixture of elements that together provide a 'safe space' for interfaith encounter. The following materials give an overview of the aims and methods of the conference.

WHAT IS JCM?

The Standing Conference of Jews, Christians and Muslims in Europe (JCM) was created to provide a forum in Europe for meetings among members of the three religious communities that share a belief in the One God and that find their roots in the figure of Abraham.

JCM organises two annual conferences in Germany at the Hedwig Dransfeld Haus, Bendorf/Rhein: a spring student conference for theology students, community and social workers, teachers and others in the caring professions, and an autumn women's conference. JCM conferences also take place in Berlin at the Evangelische Akademie and in other locations.

In general JCM conferences restrict themselves to issues affecting the daily lives of members of the three faiths living in Europe. These include: the challenges and possibilities of living in a pluralistic society; the secular/religious divide; difficulties faced by immigrant communities and minority groups; education. We also explore the ways in which global issues that affect our three faiths have an impact upon our communities in Europe and upon their interrelationship.

AIMS OF THE JCM STUDENT CONFERENCE

The JCM Student Conference exists to promote dialogue, understanding and solidarity amongst members of the three Abrahamic faiths – Judaism, Christianity and Islam.

We strive to ensure that dialogue can occur in all elements of the conference, both structured and unstructured.

We work on the assumption that this dialogue is best achieved through personal encounter between individuals in a safe and respectful environment. In such an environment all participants agree to take responsibility for maintaining the norms of behaviour which have made up the 'culture' of the conference over the years: moderation in expressing opinions and in interpersonal behaviour, openness in discussing political issues in a contained and structured environment, respect for the integrity of each religious tradition.

Participants of the conference speak for themselves alone. They are not representatives of their faith, their community, nation or ethnic group.

THE JCM APPROACH

JCM examines problems that are faced by all three faith communities. In exploring our approaches to them we help define the things we have in common, and can accept in a positive manner the ways in which we differ.

Because JCM works on a basis of mutual trust and respect we do not make collective public statements or resolutions. All are free to take what they have learnt back to their home community.

We work through lectures, discussion groups and other forms of communication, including creative group work, art or drama.

Because of our common religious commitment, we invite each other to attend the services of all three faiths and to join the worship whenever each person feels able to do so. We share periods of silence and meditation. We study together the major texts of our traditions.

JCM conferences are planned by representative of the three faiths and every effort is made to ensure that the particular needs and sensitivities of each community are recognised. During conferences particular attention is paid to dietary requirements and prayer times. Mistakes inevitably happen and participants are invited to bring them to the attention of the conference organisers as soon as possible.

JCM has no professional staff or support, but a number of individuals give their time to arrange conferences and a variety of organisations encourage their members to participate.

JCM conferences are open to all members of the three faiths who are willing to accept the mutual respect, openness and responsibilities that go with intra- and interfaith dialogue.

JCM GLOSSARY

Over the years of the JCM conferences we have evolved a number of ways of working together:

Speakers' Corner

Participants often bring information, experiences or opinions that they would like to share with others. Speakers' Corner provides a space for people to present their materials to anyone who wishes to attend. The team arranges the time and place but the speaker must arrange for translation. Any views expressed are the responsibility of the speaker alone.

Discussion Groups

The organising team distributes participants in discussion groups on the basis of information from the application forms and previous partici- pation. We try to ensure that all three faiths are present and that the group has people who can facilitate the discussions and help translate. No-one should feel that they are meant to 'represent' their faith but rather speak out of personal experience. Some guidelines for the discussion are provided by the facilitator. It is helpful to the group process to remain in the same group throughout the week, however it is possible to change once after the first session, but please consult with the team.

Project Groups

In addition to discussion groups the JCM Conference explores the topic through a variety of alternative ways of communication – art, drama, movement, text study, etc. Participants are invited to choose one of these groups that will meet during the week led by people with experience in their field. It is helpful to remain in the same group throughout the week, however it is possible to change once after the first session, but please consult with the team.

Morning Meditation

Each morning we offer the opportunity for a few moments together to prepare for the day. Each faith takes it in turn to offer an opening thought for the particular day, following which there is a shared silence. Please be punctual for the start of the meditation and do not enter once the door is closed as the latecomers disturb the silence.

Faith Groups

As well as the many opportunities to meet people form the other faiths during the week, one session at the beginning is devoted to an 'intrafaith' group meeting. Here we can learn the background of others from our own faith community who are here as well as dealing with any technical matters, such as the organising of religious services.

Religious Services

The programme contains the opportunity for all three faith communities to celebrate the religious services that mark their 'special' day in the week. All participants are invited to attend each other's services and to take part as far as they feel able.

DISCUSSION GROUP GUIDELINES

Please make sure that everyone has the opportunity to speak.

Please make sure that everything is translated.

Please make sure that all sessions start and end on time.

All participants are encouraged to take responsibility for the running of the group.

Avoid talking about what 'others' or 'they' think or do.

Please speak out of personal experience.

Be prepared to express when you are hurt or disturbed.

What is said in a group should be treated confidentially.

PREVIOUS JCM STUDENT CONFERENCE TITLES

1972: Founding Seminar (November–December).

1974: 'Election' in the Self-Understanding of Jews, Christians and Muslims.

1975: The Experience of God Today.

1976: Dialogue – Mission – Ecumenism.

1977: Great Teachers in Judaism, Christianity and Islam.

1978: Theology and the Reality of Daily Life: Agreement – Contrast.

1979: Prejudice in the Encounter between Different Religions.

1980: The Pluralistic Society – Hope for the Future? Problems and Possibilities.

1981: The Influence of Religious Education on the Use and Abuse of Power.

1982: The Mutual Influence on Each Other of Social and Religious Values.

1983: The Interaction of Religion and the Caring Professions.

1984: Between Two Worlds I. Living with the Difficulties of Different Cultures, Languages, Religions and Social Situations.

1985: Between Two Worlds II.

1986: Between Two Worlds III.

1987: The Challenges of a Pluralistic Society: Religious and Social Perspectives.

1988: Individual and Families: Relationships of Choice?

1989: The Challenges in Dialogue I.

1990: The Challenges in Dialogue II.

1991: The Challenges in Dialogue III: Interaction between Religious Communities and European Secular Societies.

1992: The Challenges in Dialogue IV: Social, Religious and Political Dimensions of Prejudice.

1993: Are We Prisoners of Our History?

1994: Are We Prisoners of Our History? II. Prejudice, Power and the New Europe.

1995: Are We Prisoners of Our History? III. Women and Men in the Three Religions.

1996: Are We Prisoners of Our History? IV. War as a Challenge to our Religious Traditions.

1997: Tradition and Change. Identity and Visions of the Future.

1998: Tradition and Change II. The Challenge of Human Freedom.

1999: Tradition and Change III. Encountering the Other – Challenging Ourselves.

2000: Tradition and Change IV. Questions to the Millennium – 5760, 2000, 1420.

2001: Education Within Our Faith Communities I. What Do We Learn and What Do We Teach About Ourselves and the Other?

2002: Education Within Our Faith Communities II. The Religious Challenge of Living Between Cultures.

Appendix II:
A Prayer for Interfaith Meetings

Rabbi Lionel Blue and I worked together for several years co-editing the prayerbooks of the Reform synagogues of Great Britain. As well as traditional texts we recognised the need for new prayers that reflected changing situations and attitudes. I composed one to be recited at interfaith meetings. Since appearing in the 1977 edition of *Forms of Prayer for Jewish Worship* the prayer has taken on a life of its own. Versions of it have appeared in anthologies, even labelled as 'traditional Jewish prayer', sections of it have turned up in liturgies composed for similar occasions without any acknowledgement of the source. The original version was a child of its time referring to God as 'Lord of all creation' and to human beings under the rubric 'man'. The language of our own prayerbooks has become more sensitive to issues of gender so this version has a couple of minor changes. But it remains a synthesis of experience and intuition in this delicate area of encounter, and an expression of hope.

> God of all creation, we stand in awe before You, impelled by visions of human harmony. We are children of many traditions – inheritors of shared wisdom and tragic misunderstandings, of proud hopes and humble successes. Now it is time for us to meet – in memory and truth, in courage and trust, in love and promise.
>
> In that which we share, let us see the common prayer of humanity; in that in which we differ, let us wonder at human freedom; in our unity and our differences, let us know the uniqueness that is God.
>
> May our courage match our convictions, and our integrity match our hope.
>
> May our faith in You bring us closer to each other.
>
> May our meeting with past and present bring blessing for the future. Amen.

Notes on the Text

Notes on Foreword

1   A. J. Heschel, *No Religion is an Island: A. J. Heschel and Interreligious Dialogue*, H. Kasimov and B.L. Sherwin (eds) (New York, 1991), p. 15.

2   From the Twenty-first Sacks Lecture, 'Acceptance of the Other: Contemporary Liberal Interpretations of Religion in Judaism and Islam', delivered by Professor Shimon Shamir at the Oxford Centre for Hebrew and Jewish Studies, 12 February 2002; forthcoming, with introduction by El Hassan bin Tallal, in the *Journal of Jewish Studies*.

3   From Rabbi Tony Bayfield, 'September 11: The Case Against Us All', lecture delivered at the Sternberg Centre for Jewish Studies, May 2002.

4   Shimon Shamir, op. cit.

5   From a meditation in 1999 by Albert Friedlander, Rabbi of the Westminster Synagogue, London.

6   Title given to the collected essays of Abraham Heschel (1907–72).

7   *The Muslim Jesus: Sayings and Stories in Islamic Literature*, T. Khalidi (ed. and tr.) (Cambridge MA and London, 2001), no. 92, pp. 102–3.

Notes on Chapter 1

1   Lionel Blue, *My Affair with Christianity* (London, Hodder and Stoughton, 1998).

Notes on Chapter 2

1   *The Code of Maimonides, The Book of Judges*, trans. Abraham M. Hershman (New Haven CT, Yale University Press, 1949), p. xxiii; quoted by Michael Wyschogrod in 'Islam and Christianity in the Perspective of Judaism', in *Trialogue of the Abrahamic Faiths: Papers presented to the Islamic Studies Group of the American Academy of Religion*, ed. Ismai'il Raji al Faruqu (Washington DC, International Institute of Islamic Thought, 1982).

2   Mekhilta, Ba-hodesh I, Lauterbach Edition, vol. 2 p. 198 (Philadelphia PA, Jewish Publication Society of America, 1933) – on Exodus 19:1–2.

3   The Israelite name for God is made up of four Hebrew letters, 'yod', 'hey', 'vav', 'hey'. Traditionally this holy name was not pronounced and instead it was substituted with the word 'Adonay', meaning 'Lord' – hence the word commonly used in many

older English translations. Some modern scholars have transliterated it and use the word 'Yahweh' in translations. The name appears to derive from the Hebrew verb meaning 'to be', which led to a preferred translation from the eighteenth century of the name as 'the Eternal'.

Notes on Chapter 3

1   Of the seven other occasions where *shema* is translated as 'understand', all are explicitly about not 'hearing/understanding' someone speaking in a foreign tongue: Genesis 42:23; Deuteronomy 28:49; 2 Kings 18:20; Isaiah 36:17; Isaiah 33:19; Jeremiah 5:15; Ezekiel 3:6.

2   There has been a build-up of these terms over the previous verses which are organised in pairs, every second verse ending with the phrase 'I am the Eternal':
11–12 fellow citizen
13–14 neighbour
15–16 fellow citizen, people, neighbour
17–18 brother, fellow citizen, people, neighbour
See C. J. Wenham, *The Book of Leviticus* (London, NICOT, 1979), p. 267.

3   The phrase is to be found in all three bodies of legislative materials, the Book of the Covenant, the Holiness Code and in Deuteronomy (Exodus 22:20, 23:9; Leviticus 19:34; Deuteronomy 10:19).

4   See D. Kellerman in '*Gur*', *Theological Dictionary of the Old Testament*, eds G. Johannes Botterweck and Helmer Ringgren, (Michigan IN, William B. Eerdmans Publishing Company, Grand Rapids, 1978) vol. 2, pp. 439–49, 445.

5   The term seems to refer to different groups at different times or in different documents. Thus the Levites, who owned no land in the Israelite society, could settle anywhere in the land as a *ger* and do their work as teachers and organisers of the cult.

6   I have examined this theme in greater detail in my article 'Guests and Hosts: A Contribution to the Festschrift for Fr. Robert Murray', *The Heythrop Journal* 36, 4 (October 1995), pp. 409–21.

7   Following this same direction, later rabbinic teaching would use the term *ger*, in the form '*ger tsedek*', 'righteous stranger', for someone who actually converted to Judaism – and this act also has two essential components: a religious entry into the faith of Israel, but also a process of naturalisation into the community or family.

8   David Biale, *Power and Powerlessness in Jewish History* (New York, Schocken Books, 1986).

9   See, for example, Max van der Stoel 'The OSCE [Office for Democratic Institutions and Human Rights] High Commissioner on National Minorities' in *OSCE Bulletin* 3, 3 (Autumn 1995, Warsaw).

Notes on Chapter 4

1   The core of this chapter is based on a lecture given to the Newton Community Centre in Birmingham (12 November 1998) at the invitation of the then programme director Mohammed Gulbar. It incorporates materials previously used when I spoke to the Sussex Muslim Society at their 15th annual conference (14 July 1991).

2   Michael Billig 'The Return of Fascism: Some Psychological Aspects' *European Judaism* 27, 2 (Autumn 1994), pp. 7–16, 13.

3   For a personal account of the difficulties of mobilising Jewish public opinion against racism, see Edie Friedman, 'Mobilizing Jews Against Racism: A Personal Reflection', *The Jewish Quarterly* 42, 2 (158) (Summer 1995), pp. 26–29.

Notes on Chapter 5

1.   'Indeed, Rabbinic folklore embroiders the story of their fate. A celebrated Rabbinic traveller, Rabbah Bar Bar Chana, a Rabbinic precursor of Münchausen, was shown some holes in the ground from which smoke arose. He was told to listen, and he heard voices, those of the sons of Korach, saying that Moses and his Torah were true and that they were liars! According to his informant, every three days, Gehinnom returns them to this spot as meat is turned in a pot.' (Babylonian Talmud Sanhedrin 110b)

Notes on Chapter 6

1   I have given some of the theoretical aspects of dialogue from a Jewish point of view in two articles: 'The Challenges of Dialogue: A Jewish View', *Christian Jewish Relations* 22, 1, pp. 18–26 and 'This is the Book of the Generations of Humanity: A Jewish Theology of Atonement and Reconciliation', a paper given to the Bradford University School of Peace Studies 1989 seminar on 'The Theology of Peace', pp. 30–31, August 1989 (unpublished).

2   'Active Nonviolence: Liberating Power and Healing Force of World Religions (Acceptance Speech for Niwano Peace Prize '91)', Background Paper for Sub-Theme 1: Learning to Trust, Conflict Resolution, World Council of Religions for Peace International Council Meeting Rovereto, Italy, 27 June–1 July 1991.

3   Something of this questioning of 'nonviolence' as an absolute ideal can be found in the debate between Gandhi and Martin Buber following Gandhi's suggestion that Jews should offer passive nonviolent resistance to Hitler. Gandhi's article appeared in *Harijan*, 26 November 1938, and Buber's reply appears in *Two Letters to Gandhi* (Rubin Mass, Jerusalem, 1939), and also in *Israel and the World* (New York, Schocken Books, 1948) and *Pointing the Way* (New York, Harper and Brothers, 1957). The debate between them is described in Aubrey Hodes, *Encounter with Martin Buber* (London, Penguin Books, 1973).

4   The different views on nonviolence in rabbinic thought of a particular period are described in a valuable article by Reuven Kimelman, 'Non-Violence In The Talmud' *Judaism* 17, 3 (Summer 1968), pp. 316–34. The inner Jewish debate on the subject and its contemporary military significance is discussed in Sheldon Zimmerman, 'Confronting the Halakhah on Military Service', *Judaism* 20, 2 (Spring 1971), pp. 204–12.

5   For an examination of the problem of conflict resolution in situations where there is in imbalance of power, with specific reference to the Israeli–Palestinian conflict, and indeed the whole question of how one develops peace studies, there are a number of important papers by Prof. Benyamin Chetkow-Yanoov of Bar Ilan University, Israel, including 'Conflict as the Dynamics of Power in the Local Community', *Social Work Today*, 7, 8 (8 July 1976), pp. 238–40; 'Teaching Peace to Adults: Dare We Practice What We Preach', in *Toward a Renaissance of Humanity* ed. T. R. Carson (Edmonton, University of Alberta Press, 1988); 'Three Patterns of Establishment/Minority-Group Relations: Implications for Conflict Resolution', presented at the North American Conference on Peacemaking and Conflict Resolution, Montreal, Canada, March 1989; 'Teaching Conflict Resolution at Schools of Social Work: A Proposal', a presentation at the Annual Program Meeting of the Council of Social Work Education, Chicago IL, March 1989; 'The Role of Volunteers in Conflict Resolution', in press.

Notes on Chapter 8

1   This chapter is based on the St. Paul's Lecture delivered in London on 19 November 1992.

Notes on Chapter 10

1   This chapter is a revised version of a lecture at a conference in Cologne (8–10 December 1996) under the title: 'Jesus Unites - Jesus Divides'. It is one of a remarkable series of 'trialogues' between Jews, Christians and Muslims initiated by Gunther Berndt Ginzel under the auspices of the Kölnische Gesellschaft für Christlich-Jüdisch Zusammenarbeit (Council for Christians and Jews). The chapter on Muhammad in this book comes from a later conference in this series.

2   There is a bizarre twist to this 'name-calling'. Following the death of the Lubavitcher Rebbe, a venerated leader of an ultra-orthodox chasidic group, some of his followers, who believed he was the messiah, are still awaiting his resurrection and return, a distinctly Christian understanding of the fate of the messiah.

3   H. I. Bach, 'Leo Baeck', *The Synagogue Review* (January 1957), pp. 137–41, 140.

4   'The Gospel as a Document of History', in *Judaism and Christianity: Essays by Leo Baeck,* translated and introduced by Walter Kaufmann (Philadelphia PA, Meridian Books and The Jewish Publication Society, 1961), pp. 100–102. Original appeared

in *Aus drei Jahrtausenden: Wissenschaftliche Untersuchungen und Abhandlungen zur Geschichte des jüdischen Glaubens* – which was destroyed by the Nazis on printing so it was never published in this form, though it appeared as a booklet in the Schocken Verlag series of monographs on Jewish subjects. Leo Baeck's collected writings are currently being republished, with significant introductory essays, by Albert H. Friedlander and Bertold Klappert (Gütersloher Verlagshaus).

5   Colette Kessler, 'The Urgency of Jewish Response in the Interreligious Dialogue', *European Judaism* 29, 1 (Spring 1996), pp.125–32, 128.

6   These come under the headings: Jews and Christians worship the same God; Jews and Christians seek authority from the same book – the Bible (what Jews call 'Tanakh' and Christians call the 'Old Testament'); Christians can respect the claim of the Jewish people upon the land of Israel; Jews and Christians accept the moral principles of Torah; Nazism was not a Christian phenomenon; The humanly irreconcilable difference between Jews and Christians will not be settled until God redeems the entire world as promised in Scripture; A new relationship between Jews and Christians will not weaken Jewish practice; Jews and Christians must work together for justice and peace. Published by The Institute for Christian and Jewish Studies, 1316 Park Avenue, Baltimore, MD 21217, USA.

Notes on Chapter 11

1   I was invited to speak on this subject in Göttingen (23–25 October 1998) at the invitation of Arnulf H. Baumann. It is not a subject I would have chosen myself, and it is a mark of the openness of much contemporary Christian dialogue with Jews that they are open to a friendly but critical approach.

2   In Germany, following the pioneering work of Erich Zenger, Christians are becoming more accustomed to using the term 'Das Erste Testament', 'The First Testament', reflecting a growing interest amongst Christians in its contents independently of the New Testament and a sensitivity to Jewish concerns. In this regard his work exemplifies the sensitivities of someone committed to the work of interfaith dialogue.

3   An important survey of the issues in Jewish-Christian dialogue, with a particular emphasis on Christian attitudes towards the Hebrew Bible today, is Professor Rolf Rendtorff, *Christen und Juden Heute: Neue Einsichten und neue Aufgaben* (Neukirchen, Neukirchner Verlag, 1998).

4   Katherina von Kellenbach studies the phenomenon in her book *Anti-Judaism in Christian Theology* (Atlanta GA, Scholars Press, 1995). See also the helpful study and literature in the chapter with the same title by Rachel Montagu in *Renewing the Vision: Rabbis Speak Out on Modern Jewish Issues,* ed. Jonathan A. Romain (London, SCM Press, 1996).

5   Samuel R. Driver and Adolf Neubauer, *The 'Suffering Servant' of Isaiah According to the Jewish Interpreters* (Oxford and London, James Parker and Co; Leipzig, T.O. Weigel, 1877, reprinted New York, Hermon Press, 1969).

6   Gabriel Josipovici, *The Book of God: A Response to the Bible* (New Haven CT and London, Yale University Press, 1988).

Notes on Chapter 12

1   Like the earlier chapter on Jesus, this chapter is a revised version of a lecture delivered in Cologne (15–16 September 1998) to a mixed Jewish, Christian and Muslim audience in the series of trialogue conferences organised by Gunther Berndt Ginzel.

Notes on Chapter 13

1   This chapter is based on a talk given at the Jang Symposium at the Commonwealth Institute, on 25 January 1994.

Notes on Chapter 14

1   This chapter is a reworking of a pamphlet under this name issued by the Maimonides Foundation. A second version of the pamphlet included a parallel Muslim essay.

Notes on Afterword

1   Shabbat 31a; Matthew 7:12; Analects 12:2; 4:15.

References

General

Abramson, Glenda, 'The Absence of Reality: Islam and the Arabs in Contemporary Hebrew Literature' in *Studies in Muslim-Jewish Relations* vol. 1 ed. Ronald L. Nettler (Harwood Academic Publishers in co-operation with the Oxford Centre for Postgraduate Hebrew Studies, 1993).

Armstrong, Karen Muhammad, *A Western Attempt to Understand Islam* (London, Victor Gollancz Ltd, 1991).

Boyarin, Daniel, *Intertextuality and the Reading of Midrash* (Bloomington IN, Indiana University Press, 1990).

— *Carnal Israel: Reading Sex in Talmudic Literature* (Berkeley CA, University of California Press, 1993).

Buber, Martin, *Moses: The Revelation and the Covenant* (New York, Harper and Row, 1958).

Canetti, Elias, *The Voices of Marrakesh* (London, Marion Boyars, 1978).

Erwin, I. J. Rosenthal, *Judaism and Islam* (New York, Popular Jewish Library, Thomas Yoseloff, 1961).

Firestone, Reuven, 'Abraham: The First Jew or the First Muslim? Text, Tradition, and "Truth" in Interreligious Dialogue' in *Shalom/Salaam: A Resource for Jewish–Muslim Dialogue* ed. Gary M. Bretton-Granatoor, Andrea L. Weiss (New York, UAHC Press, 1993) pp. 37–51.

Fromm, Erich, *You Shall Be As Gods* (Greenwich CT, A Fawcett Premier Book, Fawcett Publications Inc., 1966).

Greenberg, Moshe, 'The Tradition Critically Examined' in *The Ten Commandments in History and Tradition* ed. Ben-Zion Segal, English Version ed. Gershon Levi (Jerusalem, The Magnes Press of the Hebrew University, 1985).

Kramer, Martin, 'The Salience of Islamic Fundamentalism' *Institute of Jewish Affairs Reports* No. 2, October 1995.

Miller, Arther, *Timebends: A Life* (London, Methuen Paperback, 1987).

Montagu, Rachel, 'Anti-Judaism in Christian Feminist Theology' *Renewing the Vision: Rabbis Speak Out on Modern Jewish Issues* ed. Jonathan A. Romain (London, SCM Press Ltd, 1996) pp. 26–37.

Sherif, Faruq, *A Guide to the Contents of the Qur'an* (Reading, Ithaca Press, 1995).

Solomon, Norman, 'Jewish Sources for Religious Pluralism' a paper delivered at the Amman Dialogue 7–9 November 1997.

Soloveitchik, Joseph B, *Reflections of the Rav: Lessons in Jewish Thought* adapted from the *Lectures of Rabbi Joseph B. Soloveitchik by Abraham R. Besdin* (Jerusalem, The Department for Torah Education and Culture in the Diaspora of the World Zionist Organisation, 1979).

Chapter 5

Boyarin, Daniel, *Intertextuality and the Reading of Midrash* (Bloomington IN, Indiana University Press, 1990).
— *Carnal Israel: Reading Sex in Talmudic Literature* (Berkeley CA, University of California Press, 1993).
Canetti, Elias, *The Voices of Marrakesh* (London, Marion Boyars, 1978).
Soloveitchik, Joseph B, *Reflections of the Rav: Lessons in Jewish Thought* adapted from the *Lectures of Rabbi Joseph B. Soloveitchik by Abraham R. Besdin* (Jerusalem, The Department for Torah Education and Culture in the Diaspora of the World Zionist Organisation, 1979).

Chapter 7

Buber, Martin, *Moses: The Revelation and the Covenant* (New York, Harper and Row, 1958).
Fromm, Erich, *You Shall Be As Gods* (Greenwich CT, Fawcett Publications Inc., 1966).
Greenberg, Moshe, 'The Tradition Critically Examined' in *The Ten Commandments in History and Tradition* ed. Ben-Zion Segal, English Version ed. Gershon Levi (Jerusalem, The Magnes Press of the Hebrew University, 1985).
Miller, Arther, *Timebends: A Life* (London, Methuen Paperback, 1987).

Chapter 11

Montagu, Rachel, 'Anti-Judaism in Christian Feminist Theology' *Renewing the Vision: Rabbis Speak Out on Modern Jewish Issues* ed. Jonathan A. Romain (London, SCM Press Ltd, 1996) pp. 26–37.

Chapter 12

Abramson, Glenda, 'The Absence of Reality: Islam and the Arabs in Contemporary Hebrew Literature' in *Studies in Muslim-Jewish Relations* vol. 1 ed. Ronald L. Nettler (Harwood Academic Publishers in co-operation with the Oxford Centre for Postgraduate Hebrew Studies, 1993).
Armstrong, Karen Muhammad, *A Western Attempt to Understand Islam* (London, Victor Gollancz Ltd, 1991).
Firestone, Reuven, 'Abraham: The First Jew or the First Muslim? Text, Tradition, and "Truth" in Interreligious Dialogue' in *Shalom/Salaam: A Resource for Jewish–Muslim Dialogue* ed. Gary M. Bretton-Granatoor, Andrea L. Weiss (New York, UAHC Press, 1993) pp. 37–51.
Kramer, Martin, 'The Salience of Islamic Fundamentalism' *Institute of Jewish Affairs Reports* No. 2, October 1995.
Erwin, I. J. Rosenthal, *Judaism and Islam* (New York, Popular Jewish Library, Thomas Yoseloff, 1961).
Sherif, Faruq, *A Guide to the Contents of the Qur'an* (Reading, Ithaca Press, 1995).
Solomon, Norman, 'Jewish Sources for Religious Pluralism' a paper delivered at the Amman Dialogue 7–9 November 1997.

Index